'One of the finest writers of our time'   Andrew Neil

'A. A. Gill was one of the last great stylists of modern journalism and one of the very few who could write a column so full of gags and original similes that it was actually worth reading twice'
                                                           Boris Johnson

'A shining intellectual with a remarkable wit. There will never be anyone like him'   Joan Collins

'A giant among journalists … His writing was dazzling and fearless, his intelligence was matched by compassion'
                                        Sunday Times editor Martin Ivens

'He trashed me for 20 years but always with magnificently eloquent savagery and an irritating kernel of truth'   Piers Morgan

'Waspish and ruthless in his print persona, kind and genial in person … [a] golden writer'   Andrew Marr

'Reading a Gill review was a 3D experience with stereophonic sound'
                                                            Ed Victor

'A perception of him was that of the wit, the intellectual, but he was more than that. He was a deeply emotional man drawn to movement and imbalance, the cracks in the pavement where cultural shifts happen. His writing about refugees remains some of his best.'   Stephen Daldry

'The Londoner everyone wanted at their table'   Rosamond Urwin

LINES IN
THE SAND

Sarah.

love

Adrian

Also by A.A. Gill

A.A. Gill is Away
The Angry Island
Previous Convictions
Table Talk
Paper View
A.A. Gill is Further Away
The Golden Door
Pour Me

LINES IN
THE SAND

Collected Journalism

A.A. GILL

WEIDENFELD & NICOLSON

First published in Great Britain in 2017
by Weidenfeld & Nicolson

1 3 5 7 9 10 8 6 4 2

A CIP catalogue record for this book
is available from the British Library.

ISBN HB   978 1 4760515 1
TPB   978 1 47460516 8

Typeset by Input Data Services Ltd, Bridgwater, Somerset

Printed and bound by CPI Group (UK) Ltd, Croydon, CR0 4YY

Weidenfeld & Nicolson

The Orion Publishing Group Ltd
Carmelite House
50 Victoria Embankment
London
EC4Y 0DZ
An Hachette UK Company

www.orionbooks.co.uk

To Flora and Alasdair,
Edith and Isaac

Acknowledgements

Thanks to Alan Samson, Celia Hayley, Lucinda McNeile, Simon Wright, Linden Lawson, Ed Victor, Charlie Brotherstone and Michelle Klepper. Thanks also to all my editors on the publications where these articles first appeared – *The Sunday Times* and *Australian Gourmet Traveller*. And, as always, to Nicola.

Contents

Introduction – Colorado

I'm breaking the first rule of writing. I'm sitting at a small desk in front of a window – never try to compose looking at a view that competes with the one in your head. The only thing you should see when you look up are thoughts and memories . . . and this is a particularly siren vista, very little on the to-do list can compare with this scatter of nineteenth-century wooden cabins from a reborn mining town. The rusting tin roofs of the saloon, the bathhouse and the general store squat on the banks of a trout stream in the bowl of a high wildflower meadow that is quilted into the pine and aspen hills, under the great grey snow-streaked mountains of the Colorado Rockies. The sky is deep blue, the grass embossed in ox-eyed daisies, and I'm sitting in the little mezzanine floor of a log library with bear-skin rugs and a collection of books that lean against each other with a casual eclectic curiosity. How unfussy books are about the company they keep. They don't care where their neighbour came from.

On the path below my window Nicola is teaching our twins to ride bikes. Isaac gets it almost immediately; after a few skiddy wobbles he pedals away from his mother's protective hand and zigzags towards the horizon, shoulders hunched, legs swimming in air, discovering as we all must that riding a bike, like so much else, isn't really about the journey, it's about stopping with decorum and prescience where you actually want to be. Edith, his sister, makes heavier weather of it. Exasperated shrieks and histrionic grasping of shins as the gimpy machine refuses to fulfil its calling. She is competitive . . . as long as she's obviously best.

So I'm watching a circled date in family history. This is where the twins learnt to ride bicycles. This place, with its golden eagles and hummingbirds, coyotes and chipmunks, will always have a bicycle running through it.

I'm supposed to be writing about refugees. This collection starts with refugees. You'll find them camped out in the first section. The *Lines in the Sand* are their stories. I don't want to write about their stoical, desperate treks to some safer place, carrying their bags of tiny comforts and remembrances. They inevitably start with a lot of blankets and food, photo albums, school books, precious objects – as much of their lives as they can carry. Men stagger under suitcases, sacks and bags and then pick up children as a self-imposed Sisyphean punishment for not being able to protect their families. They stagger with tense, bleak faces, wanting heroic proof that they can still support them physically, lift their kids out of harm's way. But as they go on, they leave the stuff. The inanimate once unput-downable is now dead weight. Along the way, refugees slough great winding skins, their past lives that lie in the dirt at the side of long roads. By the time they get somewhere, they're just holding the kids' hands, a mobile phone and a secret warm and grubby fold of money that's never enough, and represents the last value of their lost lives: the bakery, the surgery, the vegetable stall, the car. Why would you want to write about any of that? Why would you ever want to look up and see the lines of refugees in your mind's eye, when you could be looking at your children riding bikes in the Rockies?

I don't really understand what has drawn me over and over to this story, except that my trade as a journalist is to tell tales, and this collective, staggering, saga is the most compelling in the world. Refugees are the biggest tragedy of our moment. As we sit here, there are 60 million displaced people in the world, carrying all they own on their backs, in their pockets, knowing that their children will never get the education they need or deserve. That they will never again practise as a pharmacist, a cobbler or an olive farmer. Maybe in a generation or two their line will be fluent in some new language, but they themselves will only speak with clumsy mouths. That the infant and the unborn will, perchance, prosper – become dextrous in new professions, learn new customs and breakfasts, dance to new music, sing new songs, support new teams. Will strive to join in, to belong to new people, and the skein of cultural identity that was twisted and spooled over generations will be cut and all that will be left will be its frayed end, the tint of a skin, the angle of a nose, a creased photograph, a few rote-learnt stories and a cluster of apocryphal anecdotes. This journey, which for everyone on it is the most epically momentous thing ever undertaken, will shrink to being 'my grandparents came from Syria', from Burma, from Congo, from Eritrea, from somewhere else.

All refugee journeys have the same prayed-for and fervently hoped destination. Not the capitals of the First World, not middle-class cul-de-sacs with WiFi and zoned parking, not the Burgs of full employment, agriculture, manufacturing – not next to you in the West. The dreamt-of, yearned-for, final stop would be back . . . back there . . . back where they started. Back home. To perhaps pick up the thread again, *inshallah*.

Once I started writing the refugee stories, I understood that I would never be able to put them down, because it's a truth so many refused to pick up. The story of the Good Samaritan in Luke told by Jesus – you don't need to be religious to understand this, it's a per- fectly secular parable – of a man beaten, robbed, lying at the side of the road. Worthy religious men, good men, pass by on the other side . . . but a foreigner . . . a Samaritan, who has no friendship for the Jews, stops and offers succour.

Only if you don't stop and help can you continue to have a

level-headed, disinterested, balanced and measured opinion on the 60 million who lie at the side of the road. If you pause, just for a moment, and look at a single face, see the worn, cut and calloused hands, you can't turn away. There is no dispassionate option. No 'sorry for your trouble' shrug.

I'm not a Samaritan, never have been, worked hard not to be. Nine times out of ten, I'm on the other side of the street with the clever, reasonable, purposeful folk with sanitised hands. But my job, my trade, took me to the refugees. And I can't put their testament down. Jesus told the parable of the Good Samaritan in answer to the question 'Who is my neighbour?' Incidentally, there are now only 800 Samaritans left in the world – they are good, bad and indifferent – they have been purged and pushed and displaced for 2,000 years.

Through the window I can see Edith, who's come back on her own to the bike. With a look of fearsome concentration, she's picked it up and forced it, demanded, that it do its impossible balancing act at her command. She doesn't know I'm watching. When she's better at it than her brother, she drops the bike and goes back to her book. There is no allegory here, no parable, no slyly telling juxtaposition, no irony . . . only a determined little girl, blissfully with nowhere to go.

July 2016

Syrian Refugees

Brigadier-General Hussein Zyoud settles himself into a chair. Fretting and plaiting his fingers, he needs a smoke. The lugubrious face sags around a drooping military moustache, the go-get-'em camouflage stands out incongruously in his large office with new multiple flat screens for PowerPoint presentations and CCTV. There are a lot of chairs: for his photographer who records his every handshake, for my photographer, for his translator and my translator and various aides and minders and staff officers.

The General is the custodian of Jordan's borders, and the responsibility of standing on the edge of chaos without a cigarette weighs on his broad epaulettes. He does this a lot – meeting people. He's a popular man with factfinders and international committees. There are hotel-reception flower arrangements and bright flags of the sort young men are supposed to die for. One boasts a large peregrine's head with a map of Jordan in its eye. The kingdom's awkward outline is the reason we all come here: this semi-detached nation is surrounded by the neighbours from half a dozen heretical hells: Israel, Syria, Iraq, Saudi Arabia and a watery sliver of Egypt. A waiter serves cups of coffee; the General capitulates, and fires up a ciggie.

Jordan's borders leak refugees. Throughout the nation's short history after its duplicitous colonial creation in 1946, it has taken in next door's unwanted cast-offs: millions of Palestinians in the 1950s, '60s and '70s, then Iraqis, and now Syrians, who are, even by this 'hood's high standards, fleeing a peerlessly vicious and indiscriminately vile war. As I write, more than a million of them have left the country to claim thin and desperate sanctuary.

I ask the General why he has kept the border open. He shrugs. 'It is our history, we take in refugees. It's what we do. I will show you. I will show you everything. You can go wherever you like, to understand.'

Not only has Jordan kept its border open, but its army actively helps refugees. No other state's armed forces do what the Jordanians are now doing for their neighbours – and nobody dares calculate how much they might be risking by being the Middle East's Good Samaritan. As we leave the office for his 4×4 with a flag on the front, the General pauses: 'We had your Prime Minister Cameron here, you know? I have a photograph.' And there's the PM sporting his best jut-jawed Dave of Arabia face.

Jordan is an arid country, but as we drive north it turns into beautiful rolling green farmland, olive groves and grazing. In the late-afternoon light it looks like a Victorian academy painting of an idyllic Holy Land, with the addition of countless black plastic bags. An oily pall of smoke smudges the horizon. We stop to admire a tourist's view of the border, and the General points out that we can see three countries from here: Syria, Israel and Lebanon; over there is the Golan Heights. It's tranquil, but the hot air carries low thuds, like heads hitting carpet. Mortars. 'They are coming. They are beginning to cross,' says the General. 'Do you want to see? Perhaps it's more dangerous.'

The United Nations High Commission for Refugees has warned us that the official danger level for the border has risen to five. Tom, the photographer, points out that this doesn't mean much unless you know what it can go up to: is it like Spinal Tap and goes up to 11? 'No, it's five out of five,' says the UN official, with a tightly thin smile, and: 'Could you please sign these waivers?' It is, just for this moment, the most hazardous border in the world.

As the light dies we turn onto a rocky track through olive trees and halt in a narrow valley: on one side, a sloping hill; on the other, broken land. The car lights are extinguished and we stand in the blue shadows and cooling dust. 'That is the border,' says the General. I stare at the distance. 'No, no, here. Here in front of you.' The track peters out and half a dozen steps away is Syria: dirt, rock and shrubs that crumple into night.

And then, as I watch, figures appear out of the darkness. It's a shock, I hadn't believed we'd see anything but, bent double under sacks and stumbling across the uneven ground, men and women clutching small children and the flotsam of their lives heave with the scuff and grunt and sighs of folk who are trying to hurry silently in fear. Families hold hands, they move past us like heavy ghosts, not looking to the left or right. Among them now are Jordanian soldiers in full combat gear, helmets and body armour strapped tight, with automatic weapons. In front of them is a long, steep hill; on the far side, in its protective lee, is a makeshift reception centre. This is the last leg of one of the most dangerous journeys on earth. The bare slope faces Syria: it has no cover, just pale scree. At the summit there are already silhouettes on the skyline, moving like a drunken conga, a dance of death against the star-bright sky. I watch for an astonished minute as the flow of refugees rising out of the night increases from a trickle to a migration – they'll have waited for the veil of darkness to make for this invisible line in the sand.

The sound of not-so-distant artillery goads them forward. A woman struggles past me tugging a child – a girl in sandals, little more than a toddler. The mother wrestles a suitcase that swings like a pendulum, and in her other hand she has a large bag. I take the bag from her; she lets go without a murmur or a glance. The soldiers all carry luggage or a child, everybody shares the weight – the General, the translators, Tom, the fixers, the minders and the staff officers, we all grab something and together we struggle up the moonlit hill. This bag is heavier than any case I've packed since my school trunk.

The handles cut my hand, the weight wrenches my shoulder. The summit recedes, the ground is uneven and rolls underfoot. I can't possibly put the bag down or hand it back. This woman has carried it for so long, along with the weight of her responsibility and circumstances. So I crab behind her, arms numb. The skyline remains stubbornly distant, the back of my neck prickles as the ordnance rumbles, and then finally, finally, we're there.

I look back down at Syria, malevolent in the moonlight. On the other side, below us, is a hurried and huddled collection of Portakabins and tents, and the hum of a generator. I drop the bag beside the exhausted mother and her hollow-eyed child and attempt an insouciant smile. She nods. Hala, my interpreter passes, hugging a suitcase. 'Can you ask this lady what she's got in the bag?' There's a short exchange. 'Oil, cooking oil.' She's lugged a gallon of olive oil from Syria to Jordan, the world's thirteenth-biggest olive-producer. I don't say that aloud, I just wish her and her daughter luck: 'Inshallah.'

We have all wondered what we would rescue from the burning house. Photo albums, the jewellery box, a Damien Hirst drawing. What people whose houses really are on fire or blown up take are blankets and shoes and cooking pots and radios and the tools of their trade and their papers – deeds, licences, the proof of who they are or were – and mobile phones. Nobody trains you to be a refugee, there are no helpful government pamphlets.

These newborn refugees are learning as they go; as they sit in family groups there is no sense of joy or even relief, just an exhausted, subdued misery. Tolstoy pointed out that all happy families are alike, but every unhappy family is unhappy in its own way. He was wrong. There is a terrible, bland sameness in despair. Their stories are told in a repetitive monotone, almost banal in their sadness. 'My grocery shop was crushed by a tank. We have nowhere to live. Our house was blown up with a bomb. My family's in prison. My husband is dead. I don't know where my brothers are. We were forced to leave.

We have nothing. Everything is lost. There is no water. There is no food. There is no help. There is no hope.'

There are a few tears, no histrionics, precious little anger, and there's no 'making the best of it', no community singing – this is way, way beyond any Blitz spirit – just a blinking, passive capitulation as the tireless Jordanian soldiers move among them handing out clean water, cartons of juice for children, and biscuits, and their own rations – the officers have trouble getting their men to eat. And there's no gratitude. This isn't a salvation, it's not a new start, it's not a lucky escape when a man, a widow, a family, a village are forced to make the choice to be refugees. It is an unconditional surrender, not just of the house you live in or your profession, but of your security, community, your web of friendships, your dignity, your respect, your history and your future – not just yours, your children's future. The middle-aged man is never going to get his grocery shop back; the mechanic is never going to return to servicing Mercedes.

A bowed gent stands exhausted with three daughters in the queue to register. How old are they? 'This one is four, this one 12 and this one six.' In a whisper, he adds the school years they were in. Earlier, a Palestinian told me that the refugees may think they'll go back in six months, or a year or two. They all bring their house keys. He added: 'I still have the keys my parents brought from Palestine. There are no more doors left to open.' An ancient woman bent almost in half and shrouded in black is helped by two boys, her grandchildren. They forced her to leave their house. She fought them, she wanted to die where she'd lived, but she was the last person left in the village. They say she is 100 years old, older than the country she's been forced to flee.

At the edge of the little reception camp is a hut on stilts, the size of a potting shed, decorated incongruously with peeling wallpaper patterned with butterflies. A soldier in helmet and flak jacket looks at a black-and-white television screen plugged into a geeky box. He has a little joystick and a series of buttons. Behind him is a rough, hand-drawn map of the border. This is the night-sight camera post, panning over Syria. As clear as day we can see an army camp, men walking about, a road with cars, a tank emplacement – and here are refugees dodging down the last track. We look.

'Look,' says the soldier as he zooms in on a small hill. At its crest there are two dark dots.

'Ambush.' A pair of snipers.

'How far away?' I ask.

'Close,' he replies matter-of-factly.

This night there are a handful who have made it across with bullet wounds; they are taken away by ambulance. The rest of the refugees are put on buses that glow magically in the desert like mystery tours. They should be used by the army to take soldiers on leave, but every day the military gives up 450 vehicles to the refugees. On board, the passengers sit in an exhausted stupor, children flop across adults, nobody asks if we're nearly there yet. It's getting late and cold as the dusty luggage is stuffed on board. Something is pushed into my hand. A child has given me a wilting posy of white wildflowers; her mother beside her is the woman whose oil I carried. She says, 'For you, a piece of Syria,' and they get on the bus that bumps its way down the track back into the night.

The refugees don't think the Zaatari camp is in Jordan at all, they talk about Jordan as out there somewhere. This is a limbo, an un-place, as detailed an image of purgatory as you are likely to find on this earth. It has about it an ethereal whiteness: the UN tents and prefab huts are white, the sky is white and the ground it all sits on is white. The Jordanian government offered a lump of de-sert to keep the refugees, but it was so dusty that it posed a serious respiratory-health risk, so the UNHCR imported tonnes and tonnes of white gravel to lay on the sand. People are reduced to ants on this vast, pale sheet, a dystopian science-fiction set holding more than 100,000 souls – the population of Blackburn or Exeter – 70 per cent of them women and children. The logistics of building it in a number of weeks are numbing, and there is no water – Jordan is chronically parched. Imagine the sanitary needs of 100,000 people. Try to imagine the condition of the Portaloos – they make Glastonbury look like The Ritz. The Jordanian police won't patrol the camps, it's too dangerous. Military gendarmes lounge at the perimeter in armoured cars in case of serious trouble – there are sporadic riots. People can't come and go; there is a perimeter fence and security supplied, worryingly, by G4S. It isn't a prison as such, but desperation, utter poverty and powerlessness make de facto prisoners of the refugees, particularly the women.

The cost so far for Jordan is over £465m; contributions from other countries amount to £140m. The UN Refugee Agency, UNHCR, calculates that it needs half a billion dollars to run the camp and look after the Syrian refugees, and that will have to come from donations. But the half-billion will only keep the camp going until June. This is a Herculean undertaking, like a space programme in the desert, and there are 14,000 new arrivals every week. The UNHCR offices are a series of Portakabins cordoned off at the edge of the camp, surrounded by an angry clamour of supplicants. A woman presses against the wire gate. Two small children cling to her chador, and she is alternately begging and demanding from the G4S guard. Finally, someone pulls her inside, the children like limpets. She's taken to an office where veiled women interview her. She arrived three days ago with four children under 12, she has no husband, she has no extended family, and here she begins to weep. They are alone; the children press against her like bookends, and she says she is also six months pregnant and doesn't want to have her baby here, in the white desert. She draws a deep breath, angrily wipes her eyes and whispers: 'I am humiliated.'

Anger blooms in the camp, domestic violence rages as men bereft of respect take it out on their wives and children. A man came into the UNHCR demanding that they do something for his wife – make-up, hair, better clothes – because she was becoming unattractive and he didn't want to have to divorce her. The staff gave him short shrift. Others have asked for another tent so they can have a sex life away from their children. The staff say there are more important things to be concerned with, but privately they agree that, if it is your sex life, there probably isn't. There are also reports of daughters being married off to men who have money or access to outside, who might be guides for the family to a new life. If they're married, they're somebody else's responsibility, and it is also protection against the stigma of rape. There are short-term marriage contracts, a sort of Madam Butterfly prostitution, usually involving older women or desperate widows. The camp is prey to gangs, to politics and vendetta. It feeds liverishly on boredom. Children go feral: there is nothing for them to do, no trees to climb.

A refugee camp is a community with everything good and hopeful and comforting about community taken out. There is precious little peace, no belonging, no civic pride. There is, though, still the gossamer web of human kindness. Villagers who left Syria together collect together to form protective huddles; in one kitchen block, a group of women who have known each other all their lives cook rice, aubergine and a little fried chicken. The smell is wonderful after the camp. They tease me, confident in their togetherness.

Outside, a man beckons me to his tent. He has a generator and is charging mobile phones; it is a little business. He asks me in. He's a big man in a cloth cap and he pushes me hard. I fall through the door and his wife laughs. He says he's a communist and 'in our village we buried the last illiterate person in 1974. Now, look,' his voice rises. 'These children. Will they ever read and write? We are going backwards.' He offers me coffee, insists with anger, insists. To him, hospitality is more than a politeness, it is a hold on the last threads of dignity and self-respect. It is important to accept it from people who have nothing. People give us things all the time, sweets, advice, good wishes, smiles, lectures. There are street stalls where you can buy expensive smuggled goods, from underpants to microwaves

– Syrians are famous entrepreneurs – and even somebody making vivid-pink candyfloss in this desperate desert.

We watch a boy shimmy up an electricity pylon and gingerly attach wires to steal power. Men gather and wave their arms and look at the white sky. They want Scuds to come and kill Assad. 'Where is NATO?' someone shouts in my face. 'Where is your NATO? It is because we are Muslim they don't come. In Europe you treat animals better than we are treated here.'

Refugees are the collateral damage of wars, they are the pieces that have been taken off the board. The hot news story is the conflict itself; this intransigent, complex headache of unwanted, awkward, lumpen people doesn't have the dynamic interest of global politics or the screen-grab of smoke and bodies and Kalashnikovs. Whatever the outcome in Syria, these people have already lost, lost everything but despair and a gut-churning sense of injustice that will fester. Lacking power or influence, swept aside by events that were not of their making, they will slowly turn to dust, go from unconsidered to unremembered, their grief evaporating in a region where every handful of dirt is someone else's calamity.

In Amman, Jordan's capital, old Iraqi men smoke hubble-bubbles and play cards. They were much younger men, with futures and hopes and aspirations, when they dealt the first hands here. They are served by Palestinian waiters who have never seen their homeland. In the camp, a small boy in a red tracksuit is trying to find medical help; he needs a shot for his asthma. His father comes over and says he saw us last night on the border. He starts to tell the story of his village, Deir Ba'alba. 'It was surrounded, burnt and shelled for months. The people couldn't escape and it was destroyed and everyone was killed. The whole village.'

He comes to a ragged stop as he tries not to weep in front of foreigners and his surviving child and his dignity. 'Remember Deir Ba'alba. Please, it's important. Remember Deir Ba'alba.'

A refugee camp reminds you, if you need reminding, that you

are your brother's keeper, but he is heavy. So perhaps you might remember Deir Ba'alba. I only wrote it down phonetically, so say it out loud to someone else.

March 2013

The Congo

The broad, brown, bloated Dungu River slips with a clotted lethargy through the silent bush, as if it were too hot and humid to do anything more than roll over and float past the mango trees, where squadrons of bright ibis squabble over nothing. The still air begins to collate clouds for the afternoon deluge; the temperature trudges up with a practised ennui. It is the end of the rainy season. The river rolls on to meet the equally stupefied khaki Kibali, and here is the small town of Dungu. This is close to being the very heart of Africa, the dark heart of the dark, dark continent. The Democratic Republic of the Congo is the byword for everything that is irreparably, congenitally wrong with Africa. All the bleak white fears, the nose-tapping, knowing racism, the comfortable schadenfreude about the ancestor continent, are all comfortingly wrapped in the dark horror of Congo.

Of all the places I've travelled, I have never had such dire and unanimous warnings against setting foot in a country.

Six-thirty in the crepuscular morning and the Catholic church fills up for communion. Three priests in Roman finery offer the mass in the fluting local tongue. In place of an organ, there are drums. African voices hymning over their rhythm is one of the great spine-tingling, ear-pricking sounds of this continent. A fresco of the Crucifixion shows a white Christ on the cross; his mother is black, a parable of Africa: the white boy rises again and leaves to take over his father's business. The black woman is left to mourn and make the best of it. There are a lot of bereft mothers in the pews.

This is officially the most dangerous country in the world to be a woman. Up here, in the north-east, there is a war being fought by such a world-winning array of militias, rebel groups, renegade deserters, carpetbaggers and mercenaries that the list reads like the combatants in some slasher computer game: the M23, the Interahamwe, the Mai-Mai and the Congolese army. This constantly simmering conflict is taken out on the civilian population. No military group is strong enough to hold ground for long, so they rule through projecting terror and inflicting an inflation of creative humiliation.

There is a pandemic of rape, often the most diabolically and physically debilitating type, and proxy-forced rape, where captured boys are made to abuse or murder their neighbours to crush any sense of community and give them nowhere to escape. There are constant kidnappings of children to be taken as slaves and recruits and, therefore, a concomitant increase in despairing domestic violence. In communities that are traumatised and permanently terrified, the true figures can only be guessed at, but they are without parallel. This is effortfully the worst place in the world.

Angélique, a middle-aged woman, says her departing prayers, crosses herself and rises, beaming. She has a smile that belies all other emotions, all anxiety, and transfigures not just her face, but everyone's it bathes. Angélique is a nun, an Augustinian. She doesn't wear the wimple or robes of her order, but the elegant home-tailored costume of local cloth, a turban and DayGlo, acid-green, Apple-logoed flip-flops. Her skirt is printed with the face of another nun, a local woman who was martyred in a previous war by the Simba for refusing to marry a colonel, who stabbed her to death for pointing out that she was already betrothed to Christ. Angélique is a singular and powerful force for good in Dungu, which has grown to be the terminus at the end of the line for hundreds of displaced people driven from their homes, not by the ruling factions of power, money and mining, but by that darker embodiment of collective psychopathy, the Lord's Resistance Army (LRA): the oldest and most conceivably sadistic terrorist group in Africa.

When I first came across them a decade ago in northern Uganda, they were known as the Rebels Without a Cause because no one who had met them had lived long enough to discover what it was they wanted. Driven out of their native Uganda, they have bled into the ungoverned badlands where Congo, South Sudan and the Central African Republic meet: these are three remedially dysfunctional nations. The LRA wages a campaign of calculated terror, not with governments or other armies, not for diamonds or gold or political gain, but specifically and systematically for survival. They loot and rape and mutilate and murder and kidnap without aim or motive, just a nihilistic imperative to keep going.

The town is poor, a collection of mud huts that hide themselves in the jungle, a few modest municipal buildings, a street of colonial market shops. Beside the single-lane bridge is a derelict hydro-electric plant. There is no electricity. There was once going to be a railway to take abundant farmed produce to Sudan, now there is barely a road. This is a town, a state, a nation, that isn't just slipping, it's been shoved back into the dark. I'll tell you how poor this is: it's so poor there is no advertising, no painted signs for Coca-Cola or mobile phones; so poor there is no rubbish, no blown plastic bags that litter the rest of Africa; too poor even for beggars: no child or destitute widow or cripple ever asks me for so much as a mouthful of porridge or a biro.

This place was besieged and preyed on by the LRA until the UN set up a small, protective force, a detachment of Moroccan soldiers with their armoured Humvees and blue-bereted boredom. It was enough to offer a cordon of stability, a candle of hope, and refugees ebbed in. The UN Refugee Agency, UNHCR, responsible for the displaced, came to help them. Angélique hadn't meant to become involved;

she was a reluctant lifeguard. One day she was in a hospital, and a young woman who had just given birth told her that she knew she was going to die and that someone must look after her infant. Angélique said she would find someone, but there was no one. She saw the dying woman in the street and asked why she wasn't in the hospital. The mother said it was because she was desperate to find someone to save her child.

Angélique, who was preparing to join the refugees herself, said she would go to church and she prayed and agreed to take the baby, and the woman died. Angélique, a middle-aged nun without a family, now had a baby, and for eight months she held it and tended it and then it too died, and people started to bring her babies. She said she couldn't do it again, not after the death of the first, but she did and she found foster parents. She would cajole family members with promises of help and milk and sugar. She got the hospital to give her medicine. Now she lives in her modest hut by the river with six toddlers who clap and gurgle when they see her and climb and hug her legs with beatific expressions like glossy putti, and Angélique's smiles fall on them like a beneficence.

Goodness has a habit of growing in the deficit of its need. Like greatness, some are born to it and achieve it, but the best, like Angélique, have it thrust upon them and reluctantly step up to it. And so, after the orphans came the teenage girls with the children of rape and forced liaisons with soldiers.

Lois is a quiet child with her hair cropped. She's lost two teeth. She was taken from the fields by the LRA when she was just 14 and given to a soldier as his second wife. She speaks of it in a quiet monotone. His other wife hated her, living in the bush was terrible, the constant marches to the Central African Republic and South Sudan, the attacks from the Ugandan army, the brutality of the guerrillas, the executions, the beatings. She bore her rapist husband two children and then, in Sudan, he was scouting for a new camp when he met the Janjaweed, a Muslim militia quite as ruthlessly terrifying as the LRA. They killed him. Lois says she was sad when he died because, she says, 'I would eat sadness.' There was no one to protect her or her infants. The LRA threw her out and she walked through the bush with two tiny children, not much more than a child herself. She doesn't know if her family are alive. She lives in a little camp of refugee women that Angélique has set up. The children play in the hot earth, she constantly watches them, and though she would be accepted back into town life, it won't be so easy for them. I ask what she felt about this man who was their father. She looks up with an expression that is too deep to read and says with a pure, stern finality: 'They are my children and the children of a wild animal from the bush.'

Angélique has formed the women into a collective. They fry doughnuts to sell in the morning, cook catfish lunches for the NGOs, she has charmed and begged and demanded sewing machines so they can start a business, she's opened a school so these young women can take back some of the rudimentary education that was stolen from them along with everything else. They have been given some land to grow food on. Angélique has bought some soya and they plant maize and manioc, pondu – a spinach-like leaf – and peanuts, as a basic protein. The fields around Dungu blend into the jungle with their plantain and palms and mango trees, full of birds and butterflies. They look like Victorian paintings of a savage Eden. This is a miraculously fertile country: they get three harvests a year without fertiliser by rotating crops; no one starves. Children suck on maize cobs contentedly, and why Congo isn't feeding Africa, feeding Europe, isn't so much a mystery as a terrible, sinful shame. But these fields are also the places of most danger. This is where the LRA came to steal women and boys and kill their men.

Here is Pascaline, whose two boys were taken from the fields two years ago. One was killed for being too weak and too young, the other has, against all prayers and odds and hope, returned. He surrendered to the Congolese army, but has been shot and lost a hand.

Pascaline is racked with conflicting emotions: ecstatic to have him home, desperately sad for his loss. 'He is 18,' she says. 'I have to dress him. It's not right to be crippled.' Here, where all life is physical and dextrous, it is a sentence to charity and uselessness. She says he has changed – he's dark, it's difficult. But these girls, these women, are not broken reeds. They don't behave like victims, they work together with mutually gleaned strength and energy; they laugh and there is not just a single person bent over a job, there is always company, there is always another hand. The children are looked after by each other and by all. There is one young woman who is obviously severely subnormal. She lives with her sister's family and sits on a small stool while the village works, grinning and counting her fingers, but every other girl takes a moment from their work to wink or to wave, to joke and include her. They fold into each other, like the dough they knead, all rising together. The collective resilience and power of women in this continent is a constant source of speechless admiration.

The UN keeps track of LRA attacks on a map, collated by a friendly and excitable Indian tracker. The red pins cluster in what they call, with a bureaucratic understatement, the Triangle of Death. The village of Ngilima is at the apex of this triangle. Its population has already decamped to Dungu and filled again with ever more desperate refugees from more remote communities in the bush. The UN says the hour-long drive is too dangerous without an escort, so the Moroccans have agreed to accompany me with an armoured car, but I'm woken in the morning to be told there had been a little hiccup. The Moroccans say they can't come after all because it's Ramadan – but never mind, a contingent of Congolese police have agreed to ride shotgun. They are a fabulous force of desperados straight from some Hollywood central casting: dark glasses, berets and bits of uniform, Kalashnikovs and ancient Belgian FN rifles. They all carry looks of obsidian menace and malevolence. We're not entirely sure that they've got actual bullets and I rather hope that they don't, because they keep pointing their guns through our windscreen. You can get a phone signal almost everywhere in Congo, you just can't physically get anywhere. The lack of access makes everything else – government, security, health, news, trade – virtually impossible, so the UN is building roads, which will do more for the country than a squadron of Hercules full of fact-finders and politicians' conferences. Already a little business is being driven in from Uganda on a new safe route and here, on the red-earth road, we pass occasional diggers and crews of navvies protected by Nepalese soldiers opening up the interior. But we leave them behind, and the road that began broad gently narrows until the jungle crowds in, tapping the windows, dousing the light. We drive along a cratered, waterlogged path that looks like tikka masala. The police hunch their shoulders and stare manically into the wall of green, the engines howl and wheels spin, the tension ratchets up, the turned LRA boy soldiers say they watch the trucks from the side of the road. Finally we run into a clearing that is the little village of Ngilima: a row of shops, churches, a smatter of mud huts.

I'm taken to talk to Jean. She bends through the low door shyly, sidling into the room that smells of smoke and damp. She's nervous, weary, she's barefoot in a faded dress, with a headscarf and eyes that reflect a terrible, resigned pain. The bottom half of her face is a coarse lump of wrapped tissue, as if sculpted by a child, with a cloacal hole poked in it. It is the primeval disfigurement of rage. She sits and talks quietly, her mouth opening and closing like a sea creature out of water. She was in the fields with her husband, the LRA came out of the bush and beat him to death in front of her; she knelt on the ground cradling him and they came for her with a machete. But the officer said no, not the machete, not the gun. 'He asked, did I want to live or die? I was crying, holding my husband. "Kill me," I said. He was angry and said, "You're mocking us," so they took a razor and cut off my mouth.' She draws her finger around the lump of scar. 'It fell in my lap like a doughnut.' What? 'It fell in my lap like a doughnut. I went to pick it up. They cut my mouth then each side, cheek to ear. "Go and tell the soldiers," they said. "Tell them to come and get your husband."'

Nobody knows how many LRA soldiers there are: they split and they split and they split into smaller and smaller groups. They have 25 years' practice in inflicting the most atrocious and fearful horror. Terror is a force multiplier: it moves thousands; it paralyses a land the size of Britain. Nothing that the sated imagination of Hollywood or what the trolls on the internet have constructed is as powerful or prehistorically, shriekingly effective as the living nightmares that stalk the hot darkness of Congo. The women come and tell me their stories one after the other. I don't interview them, I just ask them to talk as they see fit, and they speak with a disconnected matter-of-factness as if to distance themselves from the words; they look away from the images they conjure of themselves. Amenisia: her brothers were killed, she escaped into the bush with five children, one died. Marie is 34; her husband, father and uncle were killed in the fields. She is now the second wife of a man who doesn't support her; she misses her father. 'If I say more, I will cry.' She stops. Her 14-year-old daughter is pregnant.

Clementine: Clementine lost her mother and father, fled with six siblings and her four children. Another Marie had a disabled sister and a blind brother; both were murdered. Her husband abandoned her with four children. Florentine doesn't know her age but she was born within the time of the Simba. Her brother was killed on his bicycle; he left nine children, who she looks after; her own marriage is unhappy and barren. Laura is 25; her family name translates as 'I had to go through a lot'. Her fields were burnt, her neighbours slaughtered, she ran with her small children to hide in the jungle, her sister and brother were killed. The Congolese army tried to stop her running away but she persisted, pushing through the roadblocks with her children and an orphan she collected on the way. Vivien, whose surname means 'What's new', has 10 children. Her daughter was kidnapped and is gone, lost; her husband got sick and has died. Now she has 11 children. Another Marie: she escaped from an LRA camp where she had been repeatedly raped.

I walk out of the hut, just for a moment, just to collect myself, because I don't trust my emotions or my face. It isn't the pity that gets you, it's the intense dignity of vulnerable bravery. I come across a family of pygmies, they shake my hand and I suppose them to all be Yoda-ishly wise. Someone points at an ill-made, collapsing hut. I duck inside and there, on the floor, a man is dying. He smells faintly of piss, he's wasted away to faded skin wrung over a rack of bone; his hands, with their long yellow nails, are crossed on his chest. He opens his malarial eyes and smiles, revealing his last tooth. A niece sits in the shadows to see him on his way. She asks if I could spare a little sugar. It is a surprisingly calm and comforting human meeting.

In the square in the heart of Ngilima, the displaced and the bereaved and the lost have all collected together to build a marketplace. Hundreds of people carrying baskets of red earth: they dig trenches, cut posts, carry water for workers; a man with a bullhorn directs the crowd, who sing and clap. This endeavour is an act of immense optimism, like the climax of a Russian realist film: build it and they will come, the market will come, the fear will be banished. I go to see Pascaline's son, who returned from the LRA but lost his hand. He has 11 brothers and sisters; he is the most traumatised of all the victims I see. He has bouts of terrible rage and then periods of silent depression. He sits and talks in whispers and three-word sentences: he was taken with his brother to be porters and given impossibly heavy burdens to carry through the forest. There were hundreds of boys used as slaves. The youngest and weakest were taken away and killed with machetes and sticks. His younger brother complained and was slaughtered. After two years, Felicite was the only one of the boys who'd started who was still alive. Then, one day, they were ambushed by the Congolese army and he surrendered and shouted he'd been kidnapped and was shot in his raised hand – he doesn't know by who. I ask what is the worst thing he's done and he pauses for a long time and his family watch him miserably. 'The looting,' he says quietly. There is no joy in the returned son, there is just a different fear and worry. Later I'm told that without his family there, Felicite has said that the LRA made him kill and rape, and there is the wordless worm of suspicion that this lost boy may have been forced to murder his own brother.

The night before I have to start the long journey back to London, Angélique comes to say goodbye. Hard times in bad places are invariably where you find good people and, over the years of travelling, I have met a bright few, but I can't remember anyone as inspiring as Angélique, an embodiment of Agape, the charitable love of humanity: an exceptional woman, called to a place of exceptional torment. This nun has now been awarded the Nansen humanitarian medal by the UN. Congo is the terror that hides in the jungle at the edge of our world; Congo is the name of the bogeyman, the apocalyptic dark heart of the black continent that has fascinated Europe with its distant horror for centuries. But let me tell you, it is also one of the most moving and beautiful and uplifting places I have been to. Not despite its torments, or our shuddering fascination, but because of them. Angélique gives me a doll that the sewing collective have made for my daughter. She says they thank me for coming all this way to hear their stories. Of course, it's not really me they thank, it's you for listening. She smiles and holds up the rather gimpy thing. 'We don't make dolls for children,' she says. 'But maybe we should start.'

November 2013

Lampedusa

On the morning of 3 October, a fishing boat leaves Tripoli. It is a small wooden boat, like a child's drawing, with a high wheelhouse. It is old, worn out, no one can remember its name. Fish are scarce, and its owner would have been happy to get rid of it for a handful of sticky notes. On board are 520 passengers; they pack every inch of the hold, a biblical human catch, and they stand crammed on deck. Each has paid about $1,600 for the one-way trip. It is a calm, warm day, the tideless Mediterranean is blue, the rickety engine warbles and chokes, slowly pushing north. Its destination is Lampedusa.

This is the last journey, whatever the outcome. The boat is a disposable barque with a disposable cargo: Eritreans, mostly, some Somalis and Syrians, with a couple of Tunisians, men and women and children. There are 41 unaccompanied minors – the youngest is 11. They look back at their last view of Africa. The distinction between an economic migrant and a refugee is simple: are you running from or to? All these souls are escaping.

Lampedusa is a crumb of an island that has fallen off the end of Sicily. It is closer to Africa than it is to mainland Europe. It is our Ellis Island, where the huddled masses – the tired, the poor, the wretched, refugees, hopeless and tempest-tossed – come to be free. On a rocky southern shore above a crumbling coastal gun emplacement there is a modern sculpture, a slab with a door called, grandly, the southern gateway to Europe. It's not a very grand monument;

it's not a very big door. Lampedusa is the year-round home of about 5,000 people. Once it lived off fishing, but the fish are all eaten, the coral dead. Now it catches tourists. A baking-hot summer getaway, one and a half hours from Rome, set in the most iridescently clear sea. Someone with nothing better to do has designated one of its beaches as one of the most beautiful in the world. You reach it down a long, rocky path surrounded by wild thyme, marjoram and fennel. A kestrel darts overhead. It's a short curl of soft white sand, where the turtles lay their eggs and the dolphins and whales come up for air. Next to the beach is another bay. This one is surrounded by a steep wall of cliffs and it was here, on the night of 3 October, that the old fishing boat, with its exhausted passengers, ran out of steam and fuel.

They wouldn't normally have expected to get this far: as a practised rule, the Italian coastguard tracks and picks up the trafficking boats at sea and transfers the refugees to the small port in the town. These arks usually call ahead on satellite phones or short-wave radios. It is an organised and familiar run, except not this time. There was no call and somehow no one noticed the blip of 500 Africans on the radar. The boat began to drift towards the cliff. Someone set fire to a blanket to attract help. They could see lights on the shore. The passengers were tired and frightened and so close to the promised land that they panicked and moved to one side of the ship, which swayed, yawed, lost its slippery balance and capsized: 368 Africans drowned.

Giusi Nicolini, the mayor of Lampedusa, spares me a couple of minutes. She's on her way to Rome to talk to the prime minister about the refugee crisis. She smells strongly of nervous cigarette smoke and the frustration of someone who's not been listened to. 'This is not a new crisis. It is not a crisis at all,' she says, emphatically. 'We have been taking in refugees every week for 15 years. They are not the problem. They are not the fault.' Nicolini is exasperated with Rome's maudlin and politically opportunistic reaction to the sinking. 'It's all very well to be moved by nearly 400 coffins,' she says, 'but how do you deal with the survivors? That's what matters. It's not tears for the dead, but tears for the living.'

Lampedusa has a remarkable and surprising relationship with its immigrants. They care about them, they wish them well, they hope for the best. They don't resent them or complain that they don't learn the language or customs. When, at the start of the Arab Spring, in December 2010, around 5,000 Tunisians turned up uninvited, outnumbering the indigenous population, stealing chickens and setting fire to the reception centre, the locals called the rocks on which the Tunisians camped the Hill of Shame. Not the Tunisians' shame, mind, but the Italians' shame: the shame of making the desperate and the needy sleep out in the open.

The people of Lampedusa are good – if slightly unusual – Europeans. When the refugees turn up dead, and an awful lot of them do, the locals bury them next to their own fathers and grandmothers in their little cemetery, as unnamed sub-Saharans, with numbered wooden crosses, and year after year, each has flowers laid beside them.

It's not a sentiment that's shared by the Italian authorities in general. When the refugees are brought ashore they're given a medical check and their names are taken, then they're bussed to a camp on the outskirts of town that's been pushed into a thin, dead-end valley: two-storey blocks of dormitories and an administration building, surrounded by a chain-link fence. There are Italian soldiers with side arms and clubs guarding the door and it's patrolled by riot police.

The dormitories are packed, there is barely enough room to walk between the beds, the walls are covered in hopeful, religious graffiti and names, the place smells of sewage and sweat. There are no dining facilities; refugees squat in the open or eat on their beds. There is a small area set aside for nursing mothers, otherwise there is only one lavatory for 100 women.

A Syrian complains that she hasn't been able to go to the loo for days because the door doesn't have a lock and there are always men there. Sanitary towels are difficult to get and are handed out, two at a time, usually by a man. There is no sewerage system on the island and no standing water. A bowser comes daily from the desalination plant. This facility was built for 200 refugees who would spend no more than 48 hours here, but it is now inhabited by more than 700. Most have been here for nearly a month.

The men sleep on sodden foam rubber in caves outside, under shreds of plastic, wrapped in paupers' blankets, dressed in the bright polyester tracksuits that are given to them. They look like a school production of Montagues and Capulets. They also have a coat, a child-sized blanket and cigarettes. The fags are a bribe to forestall arguments. The North Africans seem, in particular, to suffer nicotine withdrawal, according to the camp's bureaucrat. But they don't get detergent. It's wet and it's cold, the wind snaps and flaps at the hastily tied plastic tents. There is nothing to do. Boys cut each other's hair into silly shapes out of a deathly boredom.

Technically, they are not confined, despite the presence of soldiers and the police – they have committed no crime. However, the authorities won't open the gates, so the inmates escape through a convenient hole in the fence, to walk aimlessly around the blustery, paperblown, bordered, pedestrianised, wet town, dreary in the off-season – Margate on the Med, without the slot machines. Little knots of Eritreans and Cameroonians huddle over their mobile phones in the empty streets, or stare at the brown football pitch beside the graveyard of dead and splintered freedom boats piled in a tangled, rusting pyre of flip-flops, life vests, like the sad bones of beached sea creatures.

The Africans stamp their feet and shout and wait without explanation or expectation. This is as bad and ineptly septically organised a camp as I've seen – worse than Syrians can expect in Jordan, worse than the Sudanese camps in Chad, or for Afghans in northern

Pakistan. It's not run by the UN, because technically it's not a refugee camp, it's a reception centre. The UN is here, but only to inform
the newly arrived of their rights and how to claim political asylum.

The Italian bureaucrat in charge is young, blinking, bad-tempered,
self-important and further out of his depth and disorientated than
his charges. He insists I sign a waiver agreeing that I will identify no
one and nothing, see nothing, say nothing. I refuse. We compromise
on something that says I have understood what he is asking.

Newspaper headlines constantly refer to these people as illegal
immigrants. They're not, they're refugees. They are already victims,
most in ways that sear you with pity and shock. A group of Eritrean
boys in their twenties, survivors of the shipwreck, lounge on their
beds, flicking lighters, sharing fags, and they tell me how they got
here. Natneal Haile carefully writes his name in my notebook. He is
a delicate and handsome boy with a bright smile. He speaks good
enough English. He left Eritrea, like his friends, to escape the army.
The paranoid military dictatorship conscripts all men from the age
of 15 up until they're 50. You could spend your entire life in uniform
waiting for a war or a coup, for barely $20 a month.

After five years, Natneal deserted, crossed into Sudan and worked
his way down to Juba, capital of the new Southern Sudan, where
he laboured for two years. Then he paid traffickers to smuggle him
into Libya across the Sahara. In Tripoli, he was jailed for being the
wrong person with the wrong religion. 'They are terrible people, the
Libyans,' he said. 'So violent. It was very frightening. Everyone has
guns. People have guns in their own homes, can you imagine that?'
His eyes are wide with astonishment. His friends nod and smile rue-
fully. 'They have no pity.'

Natneal remained in jail until his family back home paid a £1,000
bribe to have him released. This is a common story. Most of the
Eritrean men I spoke to have been imprisoned in Libya or held
hostage in the Sahara, all beaten, all tortured. They knew others
who had died of thirst, of beatings, of starvation, the girls who'd

been raped, whole families abandoned in the desert, disappeared under the sand. They tell the stories with a matter-of-fact fatalism. 'Please,' says Natneal, 'tell the world about our people in Libya. They are dying in prison.'

He got a place on a boat to Lampedusa. The boat sank. All told, the journey from home cost $6,000. This figure is corroborated by others. On average, it takes four years to make this journey. Natneal wants to be a civil engineer. Where would he like to go? 'Norway,' he says. 'Or Switzerland.' He smiles with a shy optimism, as if admitting the name of a girl he fancies. Really? 'Yes,' he beams. Switzerland has taken a high proportion of those escaping military service in Eritrea for asylum, but you have to claim asylum in Switzerland. Norway is the most popular country at the reception centre, deemed by Africans a country of liberal opportunity and safety, if not friend-liness. Some say England, because they can speak English, and it's partly, I think, out of politeness to me.

These journeys are far more intrepid and dangerous than climbing a mere mountain or trekking to a pole. They are made by some of the poorest people in the world, who leave their villages, communi-ties, cultures and families knowing, in all likelihood, they will never see them again. They are funded by parents who understand they are sending their children away for ever, that they will never hold their grandchildren, and that they may hear nothing but silence for ever. But still, no one wants to stay in Italy, and that's a problem.

The EU Dublin convention stipulates that people claiming polit-ical asylum must remain in the first safe country they land in – you can't pick and choose (although Greece, Spain and Italy claim this is unduly onerous on them). Refugees have to be fingerprinted to be processed, and most of them refuse. Not being criminals, they can't be forced, so there is a stand-off. Some of the refugees have gone on hunger strike, and not all nationalities are treated the same. Syrians are now almost automatically taken in by other countries because the civil war is hot politics. There is a group of Syrians camping in a makeshift tent underneath rocks: they're cold and furious; each buttonholes me with his grievance then shows me a bullet wound. Everyone has been shot. It is left unsaid that they are deserters from Assad's army. France is very keen not to encourage any more North Africans, while Britain doesn't want this UKIP dinner-gong subject on the agenda.

A few years ago, Prime Minister Silvio Berlusconi came to an agreement with Colonel Gaddafi that the Italian coastguard could simply tow migrant boats back to Tripoli, even though this was illegal and deeply immoral. No other European raised a complaint, or even an eyebrow. The reason the refugees don't want to stay in Italy is because this is the most overtly, casually, critically, racist country, given the least opportunity. It is also operatically sentimental. The sinking of the boat was the cause of a hand-wringing bout of pathos in the Italian press. The centre-right Interior Minister, Angelino Alfano, famous for instigating the law that put the holders of the top four government posts above prosecution, decreed a state funeral for the tragedy that had befallen Italy and held it in Agrigento, which happened to be his home town and constituency. But he wouldn't permit the survivors, their families or friends to be there, nor the coffins either. He did, though, invite members of the Eritrean government from which they had fled. It was a state funeral without any bodies or mourners, a photo opportunity for a politician and an allegory for Europe's engagement with its most needful neighbours. The people of Lampedusa were embarrassed, upset. They held their own service with the survivors and the seekers of asylum on a rocky bit of their island, which looks out to sea. Each planted a tiny tree for every drowned soul.

Mohammed is still angry. His delicate Eritrean features are set in a worried frown of sorrow, shock and a sharp, righteous ire. He's come to tell me what happened that night in the bay. He speaks halting but good English, softly. He would like to be a translator. 'When everyone moved to the side of the boat, it went over quite

fast,' he says. 'They said on the news we set fire to the boat on purpose, but that's not true. People fell and slipped into the water. They
were holding on to each other, grabbing your legs, standing on top
of each other. I had to push people away. It was terrible. The noise,
the sound of screaming and crying.' He pauses. In the silence, he is
hearing it again. 'It went on and on, the shouting, the screaming,
for five hours. Five hours. We swam and swam. Parents held up
their children till they couldn't hold them any more. We could see
the lights in the distance but no one came. It was cold, so cold we
were numb. People beside me in the dark said, "I can't swim any
more, tell my family." We didn't know them, so they said the name
of their villages. "They'll know me," they said. And they would stop
swimming and weren't beside me any more. Do you know how hard
it is to swim for five hours? You're thinking you can't go on, there is
no end. You can't go on so you drown. And then there was a boat.
Two boats came and they saw us and went away. One sailed right
round us and went away. How could someone do that?' He pauses
and looks at me for an answer, as if it might be a European habit.
I don't tell him that it is. The identity of these boats is a mystery.
There will be an inquiry, but sailors in the Mediterranean are in-
structed not to stop for refugee boats. There was no call, no message
to the coastguard. Mohammed was finally pulled from the sea by a
local fisherman. He needs to find the man to thank him.

We are joined by Costantino, 56, a local construction worker, originally from Puglia. He has a pleasure boat, and he went fishing
with friends at 7.30 a.m. and he sailed into the bay at about the
same time as the coastguard got there and there were bodies everywhere. He picked up 11 survivors and thought there was no one
else alive. 'And then I saw this girl in the water, dead, but her hand
seemed to move. She was covered in diesel oil. Almost too slippery
to pull into the boat . . . I cleaned her face with fresh water. She was
alive. She was the last person to be saved.'

Costantino is very affected by her; she was very young. He went to the hospital to see how she was. Her name is Luam. He gave her some money and a phone, made sure her parents knew she was alive. She had damaged lungs and was transferred to a hospital in Sicily, from where she discharged herself and slipped away, disappeared into the great diaspora of refugees in Europe. This is what most of them do: vanish to continue their journey illegally in the hands of traffickers and gangs who exploit, enslave, rape and bully. Costantino says he knows where she is, but he won't say. She asked him for one last favour. Her friend, a girl she travelled with, perished in the sea. Could Costantino make sure she was remembered at the service? He took the number recording her death off the small tree and replaced it with the girl's name, Sigerreda.

Mohammed and Costantino make an unlikely couple, sitting side by side, tensely distracted by the unresolved horror and sadness of that night, the bodies floating beside one of the most beautiful beaches in the world. 'Knowing what you know, would you do it again?' I ask Mohammed. Misunderstanding, he says people are doing it now. 'They are at sea right now.' No, would you go through it again? He looks at me with a pitiful disbelief. 'No, no, I couldn't.'

'I can't help thinking about it,' says Costantino. 'You know, we were meant to go out fishing at 6.30 a.m., but I was late, so we went at 7.30. I can't help thinking how many more could have lived if I'd been on time.'

The reason the Lampedusans are kind and good to these desperate visitors is because they can be. They've met them and they see them; the reason we can talk about 'them' as a problem, a plague on our borders, is because we don't see them. If any of these refugees knocked on any of our front doors and asked for help, we would give it. We would insist they be protected and offered a chance to be doctors and civil engineers, nurses and journalists. We would do it because we are also good and kind. It is only by not looking, by turning our backs, that we can sail away and think this is sad, but it is not our sadness.

The divers went down to the deep wreck and the boat revealed its last speechless, shocking gasp of despair. The body of a young African woman with her baby, born to the deep, still joined to her by its umbilical cord. In labour, she drowned. Its first breath the great salt tears of the sea. The sailors who formed a chain to bring the infant to the light, used to the horror of this desperate crossing, sobbed for this nameless child of a nameless mother that was born one of us, a European.

December 2013

The Rohingyas

Nabin Shona comes into the small room carrying an air of worn disappointment. She offers me her hand. It is limp and light and dry, like briefly holding an autumn leaf. She's been waiting for over an hour, but in a refugee camp every wait is merely the twig on a tree of waiting. She sits opposite me on a plastic chair and arranges her headscarf. She is dressed with a sober, threadbare modesty and tells me her name and her age: 42. She looks older, her eyes are dark rings; in her nose, the tiniest gold stud.

The room is shabby, a clerk's office made of plaited bamboo and corrugated iron. The air holds its breath and hangs like a hot hand towel waiting for the imminent monsoon. A fan creaks in the ceiling, when the emphysemic generator has the energy. I say what I've said many times today. 'All I want to know is what you want to tell me, your story, what happened.' She speaks in a reedy whisper, the translator leans forward: 'They came in the night, the army. They wanted to steal my goat. I was beaten.' I think beaten may cover a more intimately shaming truth. A lot of the women say 'beaten' as if the word tasted of bitter medicine. 'I was taken to the army camp and my legs were trapped between bits of wood.' She calls them *kinda*, a sort of stocks. 'I was seven months pregnant. I had to leave three small children at home by themselves. My husband had already fled to avoid being used as forced labour by the soldiers.' Her legs still hurt. She shows me the scar. When a bribe was paid she came here to the refugee camp. She was 18.

Nabin starts to cry, rubbing away the tears, collecting them between her finger and thumb because she doesn't want to leave them to fall alone in this place. She has been here, waiting, for 24 years. They took her 12-year-old daughter to prison for avoiding repatriation. She's had four more children in the camp. She fades to a halt, sagging under the humiliation of her emotion. I ask if there's anything else she'd like to say. She takes a breath and looks up, fierce in her despair, her voice suddenly clear and brittle: 'Why don't they poison all of us? Or drag us into the sea?'

This isn't an exceptional story. I've chosen it because it is so typical, so ordinary, so banal. Kutupalong is a refugee camp in Bangladesh on the Bay of Bengal, a couple of kilometres from the porous and fractious Burmese border. It has been here for more than 20 years; so have many of its inhabitants. The camp hides off the main road in a landscape of neatly square paddy fields, salt pans and fish ponds. Officially there are 12,000 refugees here, and a further 18,000 at another camp, Nayapara, about 30 kilometres away. Unofficially, there are an additional 200,000 unregistered refugees, many living in makeshift shelters that have mushroomed around the two camps.

These refugees are the Rohingyas, a poor rural minority from Burma. According to the UN, they are the most persecuted people in the world. Think of that: how pitiful your lot must be to contend for that fathomlessly miserable accolade. They have been systematically preyed upon by the majority Burmese: beaten, raped, murdered, abducted for slavery, their goods looted, their crops and land stolen, they have been hunted by mobs, excluded from all social and political life in a systematic and prolonged campaign of intimidation and vilification that is not simply ignored by their government but actually sanctioned, encouraged and inflamed. The most widespread and heinous abuses are perpetrated by the military and the judiciary. It is, though, pretty much ignored by the rest of us. Not only is this the worst, it is the least-known and -reported pogrom in the world today. Compared to all the other degrading and murderous bullying on earth, this has one startling and contrary ingredient: the Rohingyas are Muslim, the Burmese are Buddhist. The gravest, cruellest, state-sponsored persecution of any people anywhere is being practised by pacifist Buddhists on jihadi-mad, sharia-loving Muslims. It doesn't really fit in with the received wisdom of how the world works. The Burmese say the Rohingyas are dogs, filth, less than human, that they are too ugly to be Burmese, that they are a stain, a racial insult and that, anyway, they are Bengali – illegally imported coolie immigrants, colonial flotsam.

In the last census, they were not allowed to call themselves Rohingyas; only if they admitted to being Bangladeshi could they register as existing. Burma does recognise more than 100 other cultural, racial and religious minorities, just not the Rohingyas.

The truth is they have lived peaceably and happily alongside Buddhist peasants for hundreds of years. It is said they derive from early Arab traders who converted the locals to Islam before the Mughals ever got to India. They had their own language, they were a part of the ancient Arakan Empire and they are very similar to the Bangladeshis along the border because, under the British, the border between India and Burma didn't exist. The current military government, as if wiping dog shit off the sole of its shoe, decreed the Rohingyas were no longer Burmese and they were made stateless. Consider that: what that means. You have no rights, no access to law, to education, no healthcare, no protection from the police, the army, the courts, no passport.

Abu Kassim was beaten by soldiers who took his ID card, confiscated his fields and his house and gave them to a Buddhist. He went to the administrator, the magistrate, and asked for fairness. The judge took him by the neck and threw him to the ground and said: 'Your home is in the clouds.' He cries at the memory.

The stateless have no voice, no civil rights at the tap of the computer key, they were made unpersons – vulnerable, despised and loathed; criminals in the only home they'd ever known. Their children are never safe, their daughters are objects of careless lust, husbands and sons are feral beasts of burden. They can't complain to international law, only God listens. It is a humourless mockery to know that technically making people stateless is illegal.

Amir Hamja is 77, an old man with a long beard, a white skull-cap, funereal eyes. He remembers colonial Burma. 'Things were better with the British. There was law. When the Japanese came, we Rohingya fought with the British. The Buddhists wanted independence. They thought the Japanese would get it for them.' Amir was beaten and humiliated. Humiliation is a word that comes up repeatedly. For people who have very little, respect and dignity grow as precious possessions. He too begins to cry: 'They humiliated the imams. They made them lie down and the soldiers walked on them. They stripped them and did their washing on their backs. Men were made naked so they said they would be more like humans.' Still, two decades later, this casual theft of dignity is more than he can bear.

Orafa Begum is 19. She was born in the camp. She wears the hijab that covers her face. More and more girls are wearing full veils and long black dresses – it isn't their tradition, but fathers are insisting, frightened of the awful humiliation of a molested or raped child – and they are being made to stay in their tiny, dark hovels.

Orafa pulls down her veil so she can speak face to face. She has a beautiful young face with dark eyes. She helps in the school here. She had a brother who died from an eye infection, another brother has an untreated urinary infection, her mother is deaf, her father – an imam – was beaten and is now mentally handicapped. Orafa supports them all. In her beautiful eye, she has a cataract.

The camp itself is a miserable, collapsing, higgledy-piggledy, stinking sty of a place. The huts are tiny, made of mud and blistering corrugated metal with ripped, rotting, plastic-sheet roofs, augmented with leaves. Along each of the little alleys that separate the dark huts are deep gutters of sewage, in which chickens and bulbous, mangy, muscovy ducks dabble for sustenance. Come the monsoon, it will be an impassable mire of filth that seeps into every room, clings to every foot.

There is a problem here with water: there's nothing like enough. The water table is brackish. The women and children spend hours waiting to fill tin gallon-jars around an emetic pump. I crawl in through a hobbit door of a hut that is Stygian-dark, the only light coming from a tiny low window and the smouldering wood under a clay stove. There is nothing here: a roll of blankets and the dirt floor, a few rags hung from a string slung between nails.

These two rooms, barely the size of a pair of Portaloos, are each home to a family: one of six, the other of four. As a temporary stop it would be vilely uncomfortable, but the families have lived here for more than a decade.

Khalija Khaeun is 65, her face deeply lined under her hijab. 'I have a beautiful daughter; the soldiers came to rape her. My husband died in the military camp, where he was taken to be a slave. He was beaten to death for being too weak to carry bricks. A few months ago, my nephew was hacked to death in Burma. My son was attacked in a bazaar. In my life there is nothing but sorrow and suffering. Even the birds can make a nest. We have nowhere.'

In the rudimentary medical centre I'm shown the birth room: two iron beds with thin, crumbling foam mattresses and a birthing chair with stirrups that looks like a piece of angry feminist art. A baby is born here almost every day: only those who have enough, and can harbour plans for the future, worry about having too many children. To those with nothing, children are the only hope, their only means of production. The Rohingyas are making children at a cataclysmic rate.

The children born in these camps don't count as refugees, they are not registered and therefore no provision is made for them. The nurse tells me they have no anaesthetic, no oxygen, no gas.

'What do you do if someone needs a caesarean section?' I ask. 'Well, we have to phone for an ambulance from Chittagong,' she offers hypothetically. 'That would be two hours away on a good day.'

She smiles and takes me to meet the doctor, past a queue of young mothers with their babies. He is an effusive and ebullient man in a jacket and tie. I ask him what his main medical concerns are: some infant diarrhoea, there is a constant fear of polio, meningitis, cholera, but the biggest problem is respiratory disease, he says. 'You know, smoky huts, lots of asthma, bronchitis.' He smells strongly of cigarettes and the pack that was on the desk when I came in has been surreptitiously hidden. 'You smoke over the mothers and the children.' It comes out as an accusation rather than a question. He grins sheepishly. 'Well, you have to have a little pleasure.'

There is precious little pleasure here for the inmates. There are no amenities for fun, it's too hot to kick a ball or play cricket. Some lads huddle over a home-made board and play a game which is half Shove Ha'penny, half pool. In a dark room, women who have been raped or abused or divorced press cakes of carbolic soap. They work in silence. The smell of cleanliness is overwhelming, as is the finger-wagging parable of their dirty humiliation. In another room young girls sit sewing sanitary pads and pants. There is no childhood to be had here.

I walk past a hut and can hear rote chanting. It is a mud madrasa. The young imam beckons me to come in. Neat lines of tiny children are repeating pages from the Koran. A little girl, about my daughter's age, is bidden to stand and recite. In sing-song voice, like an echo of distant bells, the Arabic pours out of her, her eyes stare at something unseeable: it is both gossamer-fragile and profoundly strong. The stream stops, we clap, she stares at the floor and goes back to sit with her friends. My translator says, 'That was the story of Noah, the flood that washes away the wicked world.' Education means everything here; it is the only value that's convertible into a future.

Before I was allowed in to visit this camp I was summoned to the Bangladeshi Foreign Ministry. I sat in an office for 15 minutes and watched a civil servant in an elaborate sari and coiffured hair with a monochromatically pale face talk on the phone and tap at her computer. 'Sorry,' she says with exaggerated politeness. 'Let me say that you are the first journalist who has been given a visa to visit the camp. This is a test. What happens in the future depends on what you write. You understand our conditions?' I've been told previously I must never refer to the Rohingyas as Bangladeshi, that I must only visit the two official camps and not mention any of the unofficial ones, that I must be accompanied at all times by two government officials who will sit in on all interviews. The two minders never appear, I suspect through incompetence rather than second thoughts. However, I am made aware of secret military policemen who shadow our movements and hang around in the crowd listening. 'They are the ones who smile,' says a refugee helpfully.

Official Bangladeshi policy is that the Rohingyas are Burmese and Burma's problem, that they should be encouraged to return. Often they are forced back, which international law says is illegal. The camps are kept basic so as to not attract more refugees and because they are sources of irritation and jealousy for the surrounding Bangladeshis, who are not much better off. I have some sympathy for Bangladesh: this is one of the most crowded, beset countries in Asia, it doesn't need an influx of new mouths who will undercut the already barrel-scraping wages that Bangladesh pays. 'It's all Burma, Burma, Burma now,' says the civil servant. 'Everyone in the West wants to do business there. There's so much money to be made in Burma. No one wants to confront them over the Rohingyas.'

Abdulla is 68. He looks stern and angry. He tells me about his son. The tears roll down his face. Nea was 18, he spoke English and translated for the UN aid workers. The Bangladeshi police came to the camp to put down a demonstration against forced repatriation and they brought local villagers in to help them. The villagers looted and beat the refugees. Nea was accused of telling the UN what was really going on. He was dragged out into the street and the local peasants stamped him to death.

The unofficial part of the Kutupalong camp, the one I'm not allowed to see, marches right up to the edge of the official one. There is an invisible border; it is the same but worse. There is no rudimentary medicine, no insufficient food, no carbolic soap or sanitary pads. The stink is fouler, there is less water, the huts are meaner and filthier, the alleys between them narrower. Only the people are the same: stone-faced, ragged, veiled, xylophone ribs and pot bellies, exhausted by boredom and disappointment, doubly stateless, unregistered, unrecognised, unconcerned, hopeless. It is not difficult to escape the camp. There are no walls and there are Bangladeshi gangmasters who, for a cut, will take them to labouring work in Chittagong where they are paid half of what the pathetically paid Bangladeshis get. If they're caught by the police they're pushed back across the border. Other gangs promise to take young men to Malaysia, a Muslim country where they can find work. It is a long journey via Thailand. The Thai navy used to pick up the boats, take them ashore, feed the refugees, give them water, then tow them back out to sea, saying they had done their humanitarian duty. No one knows how many Rohingyas drowned. It is probably thousands. Halle Mustafa is 17. 'My brother was arrested in the bazaar. We borrowed money to pay the bribe to get him out of prison. He ran away to Malaysia. We haven't heard from him in two years.' My translator whispers he is definitely dead, thrown overboard at sea. It happens to a lot of the boys. Halle sews intricate beadwork. She is the only earner among four sisters and two brothers and is still paying off the ever-steepling debt for the missing brother's freedom. Rohingyas are also used as cross-border mules for a drug called yaba, a violent hallucinogenic amphetamine invented by the Nazis that has been growing in popularity in the East for both work and play.

What they haven't done yet, the Rohingyas, is fight back, become terrorist suicide bombers or call for jihad. They pray and they hope and not one of them can tell me why the Burmese turned on them with such implacable violence and hostility.

The Rohingyas aren't allowed to travel outside their villages without permission, making them ghettos; they are forbidden further education, there is a curfew and a ban on groups of more than four people, making worship in mosques impossible; there are restrictions on marriage – they must get permission, which can take years – living together without being married is punishable by imprisonment; there are petty laws on things like the cutting of beards and there is a two-child policy that doesn't apply to the Burmese.

And the rest of the world has the historic repetition of turning its back on the problem that isn't loud or gaudy enough, that doesn't fit the current plot or threaten anything we want and is too small, too distant and too awkward to try and fix. It was after the military coup in 1962 that the violence became systematic: bullies bullied frightened peasants who turned on their neighbours and bullied them as catharsis.

Mustafa Shafial was a photographer for the National League for Democracy: Aung San Suu Kyi's father's party. Many Rohingyas supported them. Mustafa's business was burnt by police. In desperation she gave her house to a Buddhist neighbour on the understanding they would give her back half of it when things got better. Aung San Suu Kyi's silence about the persecution and the plight of the Rohingyas who supported her vaunted father is deafening, shaming and telling. 'Aung San Suu Kyi has done nothing for us,' says Mustafa. 'Rohingya died for her party, but she can't even recognise us.' Narul Hakim is 55. He spent 13 years in a Bangladeshi jail, unable to raise the bribe for enough space to lie down: 'We slept squatting in a line of prisoners.' In Burma he was a village headman and he organised a demonstration in the camp against the forced repatriation. The police falsely accused him of the murder of Rohingyas who were shot in the riot. He has yet to face more trials. 'Our lives are over. There is nothing for us now. We only fight for our grandchildren, that they can belong somewhere, have a home.'

He takes a little package out of his pocket and says, through tears, 'Look here,' and unfolds a handkerchief. Inside are worn and tattered cards and passes, official letters with inky stamps. They are the remnants of his identity. 'This is me,' he says, offering me the little slips of card and plastic that accredited his existence: that once connected him to hope, to ambition, to a future, just to belonging. 'When I die,' he says, 'someone will have to write a certificate, they will have to say that I was here, that I lived.' Later, in the cool of the golden afternoon, I see him in the camp holding his grandson, a little boy born here with huge, solemn brown eyes. Narul hugs him tight and stares at him with a terrible, intense love.

June 2014

Lebanon

———

This is not much of a town. A hushed higgle of neat streets and dusty whitewashed shuttered windows, gardens and bright winter flowers. A mosque, a church, a little café, a sleeping cat, an old woman shaded at an upstairs window. A rural town that's too quiet, with bated breath. A high-noon Ambridge. There's a vegetable market at the weekend. We're surrounded by vineyards and claggy fields of rich brown tilth that stretch away to a ridge of hills that simmer in the milky sunlight. On the further side is the Syrian border. The mayor of Al-Marj, Nazem Saleh, sits behind his heavy, ornate desk, a sarcophagus of civic good intentions. There is a flat-screen TV that plays silent news and another that shows silent football, there are basketball trophies on the shelf and a sidekick on a low chair. All Middle Eastern mayors come with a straight man. Saleh laughs as he waits for us to be served coffee: Nescafé and then thick Arabic in little cups.

He laughs, not because anything is funny, but to put us at our ease. Nothing here is funny. 'We need help urgently.' He runs his fingers through his purple-black hair and strokes his moustache. 'We need money and resources from government, from outside, from charities. The situation is critical.'

Al-Marj has a particular and pressing problem that is repeated up and down the border. It is the *reductio ad absurdum* of the nightmare of countries, villages, streets, suburbs, slums, crescents and cul-de-sacs all over the world, that the indigenous population will be outnumbered by the other – incomers, refugees. The inhabitants are now a minority in their own home. It is the ancient and contemporary terror that is always evoked by fist-waving politicians. 'We can't cope,' he says and tugs a cuff. 'It's not safe. I want a curfew. We need police, soldiers.' 'Have there been incidents?' I ask. He shrugs and waves a hand, indicating not yet. 'But there are our women,' he says obliquely. 'And they break into the water pipes and they become polluted. There is no sewerage system. They steal electricity from the pylons. There is a great danger of disease and wages are falling. Refugees will work for very little. There is no work for local men.'

He talks of what the town once was. What does he think will happen to it now? Again, the laugh. 'That is politics beyond my responsibility,' he says. He has opinions, of course, but they're personal. OK, what sort of town does he think his son and daughter will inherit? The smile fades, his baggy eyes grow tense and hard and angry. 'They are already planning on leaving,' he says.

Lebanon has an indigenous population of about 4 million. There are now 1.5 million Syrian refugees, add that to 500,000 Palestinians who have been here for a generation and a sizeable population of Iraqis and Sudanese. This gives it the highest proportion of refugees in any country on the globe. If it happened here, it would be the equivalent of the entire populations of Norway, Nicaragua, Denmark and Croatia turning up penniless on the South Coast, mostly made up of women and children.

If refugees were valuable, Lebanon would be the richest nation in the world. But they're not. The largest industry was once tourism. They've swapped holidays for disaster relief, and the World Food Programme, which is feeding most of these incomers, has announced it is going to have to cut rations because the First World has reneged on its promises to support – although the UK has actually stumped up most of the help it pledged.

Winter is coming and this little nation is floundering and sinking into something dire, and here's the punchline: Lebanon has no government. There is no one on the bridge. Its reaction to the crisis has been to agree to disagree. There is no president. The nation bobs in the swell of the most turbulent politics in the world, surrounded by enemies, anarchy and draconian fundamentalism, not just without a Plan B, but with no Plan A to begin with. But maybe a non-administration is preferable to any of the practical alternatives in a region where a century of hardline conviction and absolute certainty has spread the misery thick as hummus.

On the edge of a fallow field, a child reclines on a pile of rubbish. His mother, aunts and sisters are sifting through the stinking garbage. They pull apart remnants of cotton and spools of lace trim. It might, for a moment, be a mad bridal fitting, but they're looking for things to burn. There are no trees. Tiny bundles of kindling are prohibitively expensive. They need to heat their plastic-sheeting huts and cook their potatoes. A woman sits in the thick mud of a ruined onion factory and makes flat bread on a tiny rubble oven. The gagging aroma of burning plastic masks the comforting smell of baking.

Syrians have always come to these fields. They arrived as agricultural workers and built seasonal huts to pick grapes. The civil war has sent them back with their families, their neighbours, their communities, whole towns. The shanties have taken over the fields. They pay a little rent to the farmers, who now make more money from growing humans than they did from the onions. The makeshift camps are squalid affairs, built from borrowed, begged and found materials. Sheets of corrugated iron and plastic, billboards held down with old tyres. Here is one made from a Bentley advertisement, another from a poster for dream flats. Here is the mascaraed and blonde provocatively vacuous face of a Lebanese soap star sheltering a family from Homs.

The tiny alleys between the shelters are slimy quagmires of muddy sewage. Children's feet are boluses of sticky mire. Their faces rimed with snot and filth. A little girl sits on a chair of detritus watching an empty TV without a screen, describing imaginary programmes to her muck-dressed doll. Her fantasy game is to imagine peace, home and normality.

These camps are unofficial and vulnerable, monitored and rudimentarily tended by NGOs and the UNHCR. Lebanon won't allow official camps, wary of what has happened in Jordan, where the huge Zaatari camp has become an unpoliced city of gangs, anger, despair, violence and insurgency, and its own experience with the Palestinian camps, which precipitated its civil war in the 1970s. Large concentrations of refugees have political momentum, power and gravity. These small, insecure pockets salted into the population keep their heads down to avoid problems.

Lebanon has had a left-hand, right-hand attitude to the refugees: officially they have been strident and tough, offering little help or consolation, but the Lebanese individually have been astonishingly generous and welcoming. A million and a half displaced souls have been given shelter and charity. There has been little open hostility to them. Almost everyone I ask says locals have been personally kind.

Nasreen is 35. Her husband, a carpenter, is still in Syria. She found a small shop front in Saida. The war has been bad for business, so, like the farmers, landlords now stock people instead of frocks and tourist tat. In one small room, she lives with a pile of mattresses, her three daughters – 15, 13 and 8 – and a one-year-old baby. Nasreen was gassed while pregnant, her health is bad, she worries about the effect on her sleeping child. She also has two boys, 10 and 9. She is given food vouchers every month; she spends it all on biscuits and the boys sell the biscuits on the road. She has to make £80 a month in rent. She's quiet, close to tears. The girls sit as silent owls in their tight hijabs, close like buffers against a wind of sorrow. She worries about the boys. People shout at them for begging and the roads are dangerous. Just imagine being a nine-year-old lad and knowing that every morning you're responsible for the lives of a family of seven.

The milk of human kindness is growing sour in the Lebanon, though. Tired out by the huge weight of the refugees who have been here more than two years, and the way back looks even further than it did at the start. The horror of the war is leaching across the border with them. Isis and the al-Nusra Front have kidnapped Lebanese soldiers and are executing them. In the cafés there are comically grim comparisons between al-Nusra, who shoot their victims in the back of the head and tweet the death notices, and Isis, who saw heads off with Bear Grylls knives and plaster the verities on YouTube. There is a palpable hardening of sympathies. The Lebanese were furious at how many Syrians went home to vote in the fixed, face-saving election of President Assad. It seems an affront to their hospitality. And there's Hezbollah, crossing the border to fight on behalf of the Syrian government, which has plainly helped to turn the tide and elongate this war. Lebanon's relationship with Syria was ever domestic and abusive. I ask refugees in huts, in fields, in alleys, in queues, squatting in underground car parks where it is more profitable to rent space to them than to cars, where they thought they would be in 10 years' time. No one, not one, had a hopeful answer. Mostly they shook their heads and shrugged and stared at their hands, and offered a doubting 'inshallah' that they'd be home. Very few wanted to stay here. Even fewer wanted to move to the West, and only then to glean an education for their children. 'I would give everything to lie on the dirt my home and my business stood on,' says one man, close to tears.

Driving back from the Bekaa Valley, past the mountain villages, under the Shi'ite martyrs' flags, past the wayside Madonnas and the snow-dusted mountains, Beirut appears as if a magician's trick. Seen through the trees, surrounded by the mountains – tada! It is a great shining city, wearing the veil of the pale Mediterranean, a miraculous place. In this region, there is no other like it. Beirut twinned with nowhere, a paragon, an impossibility, a civic tautology. Homogeneous, sophisticated, amused, garrulous, epicurean, safe. Surrounded by an angry, hunched and increasingly fractious state. Within an hour of sitting in onion fields with the despairing Bedouin who have been given the worst choice of the twenty-first century, between, on one hand, Assad and, on the other, Isis, I found myself in a soigné street party of boutiques where everything cost £1,000 and came with a knowing chic irony. Where a band played and there was champagne and delicious things on sticks and folk wandered past and chatted and air-kissed and were as glamorous and interesting and studiedly starry and beautiful and sexy as any media, fashion, moneyed or international gaggle you'd find anywhere in the cordoned, red-carpeted rest of the First World, except that these were better-looking. Beirut is a very handsome city: wide, knowing, dark eyes, invitingly arched eyebrows and a discreet addict's taste for plastic surgery. I'd see coveys of expensively animated nubile women with hot, hot Semitic faces all looking down identical retroussé little oriental noses.

'Look at her,' my Shi'ite Hezbollah-supporting driver said at a blonde with cleavage popping in a tiny bum-clutching dress and vertiginous nude heels as she sashayed past. 'Can you tell if she's Christian or Muslim?' This is a city where everyone can tell and no one says. This is a city that was riven by religious divide in a vicious civil war where the Palestinian refugees were massacred by the Christian Phalange and the Israelis, a war that cost this tiny country 150,000 lives, where the buildings are still shrapnel-dashed and everyone remembers a dead relative, a lost home. But it has managed to take a civilised breath and revert to being a liberal, sybaritic, separate but encompassing city, where mixed marriages are boringly regular and women can wear miniskirts next to their sisters in burqas.

'It has managed it by doing the opposite of the South Africans,' says a BBC reporter. Instead of a truth and reconciliation commission, where they talked about everything as therapy, here the Lebanese never talk about history. Like a fractious family, they maintain a fragile peace by pretending there's nothing the matter and never mentioning the war. It's really very English of them. 'What is the prognosis for Lebanon?' I ask an American analyst of Lebanese extraction. 'Well,' he says guardedly, 'it's not looking good.'

The politics works on the principle of a three-legged stool: it doesn't matter how uneven the ground is, the stool doesn't rock. There are 17 recognised confessions here, but three main religions. There are about a million Christians, a million Sunni and a million and a bit Shi'ite. The president is always a Maronite Christian, the prime minister always a Sunni and the speaker always a Shi'ite. There is also the Druze, a Muslim sect who believe in reincarnation. Their population is growing, which is difficult to explain theocratically. Their leader is the ever-amusing Walid Jumblatt, who sounds like a character from the Cartoon Network.

The Christians lost a lot of their power after the civil war and no one really knows what their strength is because the last census was taken in 1932. The likelihood is the Shi'ite are the majority, but the influx of Palestinians, and now Syrians, increases the number of Sunnis in the country. The Sunnis are supported financially and politically by Saudi Arabia and the Gulf, the Shi'ites by Iran, and they support the Assad government because he is a member of the Alawites, a Shi'ite sect. The Christians have traditional links with Israel and Europe and the wider world. There is a Salafist movement that is extreme Sunni with a bad look of short trousers and beards without moustaches. Hipsters with attitude.

At the moment, no one can agree on a president and their differences are becoming stronger than the imperative of getting along. The country is staggering under the economic, social and theocratic weight of the refugees and the neighbours from hell. So what's the prognosis in 10 years, I ask the analyst. 'If you force me, I'd have to say it looks unlikely that there will be a recognisable Lebanon in 10 years.'

'Where is Israel in all of this?' I ask the resident Middle Eastern correspondent for an American newspaper. 'Well, interestingly, Israel is almost irrelevant at the moment,' she says. 'Driving the Israeli occupation out of Lebanon was seen as being down to Hezbollah. They are the only regional force that ever beat the Israelis and they gained a lot of military bravado from that. They have a reputation for supplying grassroots community support: food, medical attention, setting up schools.'

All the religious factions do this. Lebanon has virtually no civic infrastructure, it's all run piecemeal, by interested groups. 'But did you know that when the LGBT community held its first ever press conference and rally in Beirut, Hezbollah supported the brothers and sisters. That wouldn't have happened anywhere else in the Middle East.' So where does she think Lebanon will be in 10 years? 'Oh, I don't think there will be a Lebanon in 10 years, not as we know it.'

In the cafés, couples smooch on dates, girls sit on their own, writing novels on computers, gangs of men watch football and talk about politics. Everyone still talks about politics, but only in the present tense. It's a perennial obsession. Listening to Lebanese politics is like being pitched contemporary adaptations of Shakespeare: all the tragedies, histories and comedies are mirrored in contemporary Lebanese life. There are Caesars and Henrys, Shylocks and Romeos and Juliets, there are Lears and any number of Hamlets. It's as if 400 years of European history was edited into a single lifetime in Lebanon.

The pivotal event here, which they return to again and again, is the assassination of Rafic Hariri on Valentine's Day, 2005. A huge bomb in the middle of Beirut blew up the former prime minister and 22 others. Hariri had been the richest man in Lebanon, a property developer supported by Saudi Arabia and an opponent of Syrian interests in the country. A deified hero of Sunnis, his reputation and his family still guide his Future Movement Party. No one has ever claimed responsibility or been charged with his murder, but there is a general belief it was perpetrated by Hezbollah on behalf of

President Assad, although my Hezbollah driver gives me a detailed and Lebanese version of how Mossad was definitely responsible, using drones. If it was an Assad plot, then it backfired. There was an enormous popular demonstration against Syria, the Cedar Revolution, and its troops were forced to withdraw back over the border.

In the centre of Beirut is the café where Hariri had his last cup of coffee. It keeps his table and chair as a shrine. This area, with its Rolex clock tower and its new parliament, is despised and avoided by the locals because it was built with Gulf money and no taste. 'Look at this city, look at it.' A Lebanese journalist waves his hand. 'What keeps it going? What keeps the boutiques, the restaurants, the beautiful apartments? What do you think keeps all of this aloft? Lebanon makes nothing. Do you drive a Lebanese car? Have you a Lebanese computer? No. Is there oil? No. Or gas? No. There is barely any water. What keeps this city bright and bustling? Our biggest business was tourism, but that's gone. It is the diaspora. There are 10 million Lebanese abroad. We are the Phoenicians. We have always travelled and done business. West Africa, Latin America, Asia, Australia, you find Lebanese businessmen everywhere. We are very good at it. They send money home. It is an irony that we are a nation of rich refugees. But that's not it.

'Have you heard of Lebanese banks? No? That's because no one wants you to know about Lebanese banks. One or two are the most discreet and trustworthy in this part of the world. All the Saudi money, the backhanders, the baksheesh, the gifts, the skimming, comes here. It is laid to rest in these select Lebanese banks, no questions asked. All the graft and the untraceable greasing of palms from the Gulf ends up here, all the opium money from Afghanistan comes here. The business of Beirut is a giant money laundry. We take in dirty laundry and hand you back clean sheets. That is why property prices are as high as New York.'

Another journalist, a television pundit and longtime observer and conspiracy theorist, joins in. 'You want to know what will happen to Lebanon? You and the West are so self-obsessed. Americans always think it is all about them, for them or against them. The big regional conflict here is between Saudi Arabia and Iran. In Saudi Arabia with the Wahhabis, the king is ancient and the crown prince decrepit. The old ruling class is ossified, a crust on a putrid stew of discontent. And then Iran: Shi'ite, expanding, energised, conservative and cosmopolitan, wanting to take its place to exert its power.

'That is the struggle: Saudi and Iran, Sunni and Shia. And in the end, you want the real conspiracy theory? Let me tell you. America will support Iran, tacitly. The region will fall and collapse. The old colonial Sykes-Picot lines drawn in the hot sand by cold men will be blown away. We will revert to bastions of mutual interest and belief: a Kurdish state, a Shia Iraq will be a client of Iran. Sunni Iraq and much of Syria will be a fundamentalist caliphate. Assad will have a garrison and an inner truncated country that relies on Russia and Hezbollah. And Lebanon, poor Lebanon, will disperse into its constituent parts. In 10 years there will be no Lebanon.'

'But what about this city?' I ask. 'This Beirut?' He shrugs. 'Maybe Beirut will find a way to float, like Monaco or Constantinople, held aloft by magic and money.' The table falls silent and another voice says, angrily: 'You, from the west of the Mediterranean. You see refugees as the problem. They aren't. They are a symptom. You see them in our fields as weeds, invasive species, but you never ask, what is a weed, but a flower in the wrong garden? That is the real problem with Lebanon, and the whole Middle East, we are all flowers in the wrong garden. You English should understand this; this is the garden you planted.'

And I realise that round this table there is me, a Brit, Rena the photographer, who is Azeri, my travelling companion from the UNHCR, who's a Croat, a visiting aid worker, who's an Afghan, a Shi'ite Lebanese, a Christian Lebanese, a Sunni Lebanese and an American, and we're all perfectly at home in this place, with each other. 'What would you have said,' I ask of the journalist, 'if I had asked you the question 10 years ago: "What will happen to Lebanon?"' 'Ah!' he laughs, and throws his hands in the air. 'The same thing, of course. Lebanon can't possibly survive.'

January 2015

Refugee Journey

Kos welcomes migrants. The plane from Gatwick is full of them. The British, back to enjoy the fruits of their professional provincial labours, a second home in the sun for folk who think Spain too cabbie-common but can't afford the Caribbean. Kos is just pretty enough. The beaches are thin and coarse, there's English breakfast and pizza and cheap beer. It's safe, it's lazy and its main commodity, which it doesn't own, the sun, is dependably sultry and shiny. You can see Turkey from the beach. It's just there. The lights of Bodrum flicker in the heat, its khaki hills rising out of the pale, bored, flat water. A fit swimmer could butterfly and backstroke it in a few hours. You wouldn't know it had claimed so many hopeful, thrashing, gasping lives, but that's the thing with the sea, it never looks guilty.

The refugees are arriving in their hundreds every night. The beach is littered with discarded life vests and scuppered rubber dinghies. The pasty, paunchy English, part-time economic migrants, pick their way through the tangled trash of desperation, spilt bags, discarded flip-flops and nappies, and gingerly sag into their sunloungers.

Beside them, the refugees sink onto stained mattresses and beds of flattened cardboard, or cheap festival tents put up along the promenade. Children curl and splay exhausted, or run to play in the sea that they just survived, their parents hunched by sadness and relief. Finally, they're in Europe.

The British tourists wear shorts, T-shirts and trainers. The Syrian refugees wear shorts, T-shirts and trainers. They regard each other without irony. We have paid £50 to get here. It has cost them £900 each. Here on the beach, the myth of evil gangs of traffickers is also abandoned. The facilitators of this crossing are simply opportunistic, just poor people exploiting a pressing need, charging a fortune for a rubber boat. Trips are set up like illegal raves on Facebook. Even the French honorary consul in Bodrum was doing it. A muscle-bound blond boy, his VW Camper parked nearby, kitesurfs through the floating detritus of exodus, skipping over the spume of abandoned lives. It's an image of such vain, vaunting solipsism that it defies satire.

The exploitation of the refugees doesn't stop at the shore, where locals scuttle down to nick the outboard motors and oars. Many of the incomers, particularly families, rent cheaper hotel rooms; well, they were cheaper, but prices have doubled for Syrians.

I listen to a BBC reporter say that these are middle-class migrants. The British press continues to call them that, which may seem like semantics, but makes a world of legal difference. They suffer for a name. The United Nations High Commissioner for Refugees (UNHCR) is unequivocal. These are refugees, and to say they're middle-class is laughable. Nothing is as dystopianly egalitarian and classless as a huddle of refugees. Many of them were professional, land-owning, business-running. These were the last people to leave, those with the most reason to stay: professors and engineers, opticians, shopkeepers. When they go, it means the infrastructure has irretrievably collapsed. They're not here to better themselves – the best they can expect is to be a German cab driver or caretaker or shelf-stacker. They go when there is no light left at the end of the tunnel, because the tunnel has been blown up. Offices and shops here have found that they can demand a euro to charge the mobile phones of the homeless. The mobile phone is the one indispensable must-have of the diaspora. Greece has its own troubles.

Refugees are an added burden, but they are also an opportunity, a resource. The UNHCR has asked local cafés if, for a down payment of €1,000, they'll let the Syrians use their washrooms and perhaps offer them water; I am told that they've refused. But many people here are actively helping. They hand out food and drink. There are the hastily made-up little NGOs from all over the world, turning up with cars full of eBay clobber. A smiling Dutch family hands out T-shirts with cheery fashion advice. A local physics teacher and his wife have set up a committee to distribute food and organise sanitation. She fears that they're being watched by Golden Dawn, the ultra-right-wing political party, which has a following here. There have been attacks on sleeping refugees. Provocative boys on the back of scooters shout abuse and offer punches and graffiti. The physics teacher suspects that the mayor and the union of hotel owners are tacitly sympathetic to the right, resisting any infrastructure that might offer the refugees comfort or safety. Temporary camps could, all too easily, become permanent, and the less done to offer succour and encouragement, the better.

Out of town, in a foreclosed, deserted hotel, refugees are being evicted; they're handed fruit and tinned food by a furious pair of French *faire bien*-ers who are trying to impose the democracy of a queue. The air is filled with the smell of peeled oranges. Inside, it's quiet and sad; the walls are covered with children's drawings of families. There's a birthday cake with balloons and candles drawn by a grown-up, in lieu of the real thing, and a simple statement carefully, ornately, written in English: 'I miss you.' The refugees themselves are gentle, quiet and mostly relieved to have made the crossing, to be safe. Yet everyone is also bereft, missing a brother, a son, aunts, parents, grandparents, whole generations. Their stories have the simple, monosyllabic banality of grief. They are polite, sad and hopeful. They smile when you say hello, and are content to repeat the mantra of barrel bombs and crumbled homes, of the viciousness of torture and loss. They'll show you fresh scars, but not a single person begs or asks me for anything but advice. But then all I have to offer is good wishes. The first thing they have to do is register with the police. This is not, underlined not, a registration as a refugee – it is a simple piece of paper that says the authorities in Kos won't exercise their right to arrest and charge the refugees as illegal immigrants for a fortnight. When they have this, they can buy a ticket for the ferry and go to Athens. Refugees queue behind the police station. It's very hot. A British woman with rather mad hair, wearing an odd collection of holiday clothes, says: 'Are you in charge here?' I tell her I'm not. 'Why is there no shade for these people? I put up that tarpaulin.' She points to a limp groundsheet tied to a tree. 'The police won't do anything; it's monstrous. I'm going to chain myself to the railings right here. You're a journalist. Write about that. I'm protesting at the way they treat animals. It's quite disgraceful. I want to get a man arrested for being terribly cruel to a shar pei. I've got photographs.' The police try to organise the refugees into groups. They are loud, abusive, furious and irrational. Everyone talks in English, which is no one's first language. The chief of police is a fat, incandescent bully who stomps around screaming, shoving and jabbing at the refugees. They, in turn, do their best to placate him, like small grandparents calming a huge, hysterical toddler. I have noticed that, right across Europe, the refugees bring out either the very best in civilians or the very worst in people in uniform. There is a barely contained racism, aimed particularly at black Africans. The powerless and enfeebled state of individual refugees incites or triggers a disgusted intimidation and bullying in policemen, while the obvious power and collective purpose of the crowd frightens them. It's not a combination that is open to rational argument or calm sense, let alone kindness.

A man comes over and asks me to come with him. He's worried about his friend, who has threatened to kill himself. I collect a UNHCR worker and we're led to a young chap I recognise; I saw him the day before in tears. I buy him an orange juice in a café and ask him to tell me his story. His friend has to translate. They're Iraqis from Baghdad. The boy is beautiful, with large, tearful eyes and hands that flutter to his face. The words tumble out in gasps. I had to stop him so the translator could catch up.

'He has – how do you say? – got too many female hormones. In our community the men abuse him very badly, all the time. Whenever he goes out they – how do you say? – the men f*** him and beat him. It's very bad. His family, mother, father, uncles, cousins all sold things so he could get the money to escape. Now he's here, alone.'

'He's not travelled with you?'

'No, we just saw him. I'm with my family.' The UNHCR says it will make sure he gets his papers.

'Will you look after him?' I ask the man. He says yes, but his eyes flicker away.

The boy smiles at me, shakes my hand and walks off with a delicate, swaying gait. He's 22, alone and frail. This isn't how anyone should have to come out. There are noticeably quite a lot of gay men here, fey and camp, displaying small and exuberant flourishes of aesthetic pride: a scarf, glasses, a bit of a hairdo trying not to draw attention but unmistakable. I'm told the owner of the café we're sitting in is a Golden Dawn organiser. I ask the woman who seems to be in charge what she thinks about the refugees filling her town and till.

'Why are you asking me?' she says, with smiling anger.

'I'm asking lots of people.'

'Well, go and talk to them, then. I have nothing to say, nothing.'

We are standing on the little hill where Hippocrates codified medicine 2,400 years ago under the shade of his plane tree, where the Hippocratic oath was first declaimed: 'I will take care that they suffer no hurt or damage . . .' That night I stand at the door of the docks where the policemen rant and the refugees who have managed to buy tickets file onto the ferry to Athens and the mainland. I see the gay Iraqi boy; he smiles and gives me a shy wave. He's on his own, on his way.

Idomeni station is on the border between Greece and Macedonia. The Greeks, even sensible, liberal, charity-working Greeks, can't say 'Macedonia': it physically sticks in their throats. They have quarrelled over the territory for more than 2,000 years, so they call it FYROM, the Former Yugoslav Republic of Macedonia.

The border runs through sparse farmland. We walk up the railway track. Each side is decorated with plastic bags, bottles, soiled sleeping bags and raggedy shoes. The refugees leave swathes of discarded stuff behind them. They have to carry everything; many men are piggybacking children across Europe. Every unnecessary ounce is a stone within a mile and, at the end of a day, a ton. The refugees are again screamed at, then pressed into groups of 50 so they can be walked across to the unmentionable Macedonia. They wait to be singled out. Here is a young man holding hands with a girl. They are in love. Another boy stands beside them. They are Syrian. He has the confident look of a young intellectual. She looks at him adoringly. She says he's a playwright and a poet and a writer of short stories, all as yet unpublished or performed. He is barely in his twenties, his girlfriend is 17, the boy beside him is 15. He is her best friend and she wouldn't leave him behind. The poet smiles at him. The lad looks shy. At 15 he counts as an unaccompanied minor. The UNHCR could make special provision for him, but they decide he is better off in this makeshift troubadour family. I walk away and I turn to see them standing on the railway line, a tight triangle straight out of a school production of *Romeo and Juliet* with a little Mercutio. At the station there's a broad, confident chap with a couple of his mates. He asks me to sit down for a cup of coffee in a thick Yorkshire accent. They've driven from God's own county to deliver well-meaning, but mostly unnecessary, sleeping bags and more water. He calls himself a philanthropist and shows me a photograph of his Rolls-Royce. He tells Andrew, the photographer, that Andrew's wife can't be a proper Muslim (she's from Kosovo) because she's married a kafir (non-believer). Interestingly, in our trudge across the Balkans, in all of the provocation, the only instance of religious intolerance I hear is from a Pakistani Yorkshireman.

Macedonia is a tense and rugged country, bitter and surrounded by ancient vendettas. It is roughly two-thirds Orthodox Christian and one-third Albanian Muslim, and in 2001 they fought a miserably cruel little conflict against each other. The camp here is basic: tents, a line of stinking vile portable loos. Across fields alongside the railway line, evening creeps up like a premonition. It grows sinister in the darkness. Again, refugees with exhausted, fractious children and with a growing sense of powerless panic are being pushed and bellowed at by Macedonian special-forces troops with handguns and truncheons.

They are lit by searchlights, bleaching the colour from everything. They look grainy and black-and-white. The train pulls in. It's an ancient, battered, European, defeated thing. The pale-yellow light seeps in through the stained and smeared windows, bathing wide-eyed faces. The refugees are marshalled into lines. They have bought tickets for €25 each. Last week they were €6.

The soldiers load the carriages with vile, goading contempt and ferocity. They seem to take pleasure in the lottery of escape. The carriage is filled to crushing until people shout from inside that there is no room, that they can't breathe. The soldiers shout back that it's their fault for sitting in the corridors. One sergeant leans in and grabs a politely remonstrating boy and pulls him roughly out of the train. His family cry in terror. His mother screams with a terrible agony. The loading goes on; the soldiers strut, smirk and joke with each other. There is something about this moment, in this filthy field, with the clutching of children and luggage, that conjures a ghostly remembrance.

Not mine, but ours, the continent's. This was never supposed to happen again. Never. Soldiers cramming frightened and beaten, humiliated and dehumanised others into trains, clutching their mortal goods, to be driven off into the night. The train pulls away, its dirty windows showing bleak, frightened faces. They roll past like newsreel. We're left in the dark and silent field with just the rubbish and their shoes and the distant barking of dogs.

We drive across the border, a cursory glance of passports, and meet the refugees again on the Serbian side of Hungary. The trail is easy to follow: a broad swathe of rubbish, corn taken from fields and roasted on little fires on verges. Straggling groups walking up motorways, exhausted fathers with sleeping toddlers on their shoulders.

At the road crossing, the mood has changed. The Hungarians have built a razor-wire fence that leapfrogs the refugees down their border. They've blocked the railway with a goods wagon and they stand behind it, grim-faced, heavily armed and armoured. The hope and the relief is all gone now, replaced with a stoic determination, salted with despair. There is a spilling-over of anger and the Hungarians spray water cannon and teargas through the wire like demented cleaning ladies trying to remove stubborn stains. The refugees shout their frustration, children and mothers cry, young men chant: 'Thank you, Serbia, thank you, Serbia.' It is possibly the most unlikely slogan ever heard at a European demonstration. The news reporters, blinking back chemical tears, draw hysterical allusions to the Cold War, the Ottoman invasion of Europe, to Nazis and communists. And the plain truth that, in 1956, the world took in thousands of Hungarian refugees fleeing their own failed and bloodied revolution. Within a day the border is deserted. It's just the rubbish and the lost shoes and a five-mile queue of lorries. The refugees have moved on. They are like water, they find the point of least resistance. The iPhones tell them that that is Croatia, where they'll get shoved onto buses again to Austria, a step closer to somewhere where they can find a bed, be safe and consider nurturing a small new life.

In Budapest's laughably grand station, which is all front and no platform, the thousands of refugees have moved on, leaving piles of mattresses and touching notes stuck to walls and pillars, scribbled in interrupted school English, thanking the locals for their help. The tide has ebbed to find another shore. The truth of this exodus is that those who steeple their fingers and shake their heads and claim to have clear and sensible, firm but fair, arm's-length solutions to all of this have not met a refugee. It is only possible to put up the no-vacancy sign if you don't see who's knocking at the door. For most of us it's simple. We couldn't stand face-to-face with our neighbours and say: 'I feel no obligation to help.' None of you would sit opposite a stricken, bereft, lonely, 22-year-old gay man and say: 'Sorry, son, you're on your own.' Or not take in a young poet and his delicate Juliet and their awkward, gooseberry friend. The one thing the refugees and the Europeans both agree on is that Europe is a place of freedom, fairness and safety. It turns out that one of us is mistaken and the other is lying.

On the banks of the Danube, outside their grandiloquent gothic parliament, there is a small memorial. Jews were lined up here and shot so they would fall and be washed away by the great European river. They weren't killed by German Nazis, but by fascist Hungarians. But first they were told to take off their shoes. And here they are, made in bronze. People come for remembrance and leave stones in them. Hard stones in lost shoes.

October 2015

The Jungle, Calais

Even refugee camps must succumb to urban planning and gentrification. The French are taking a brutalist broom to the tangle of Calais and putting up white Le Corbusier portable cabins. The French are also replacing the urban gravel, all fenced in with discreet barbed wire. Not so much the Jungle as municipal allotments. The refugees are resisting moving, even though the new accommodation will have electricity and plumbing. At dozens of borders for miserable months the refugees have stubbornly resisted being identified as packages that can be returned to sender. The one thing they share with the mayor of Calais is that they do not want this place to be permanent. You could be quarantined here for years, ignored for ever. It's ominously gulagy, like the end of the road.

The refugees would rather stay in the donated festival tents that have turned this site into a dystopian Glastonbury because that feels temporary; a pit stop, a moment in a journey that will end with a cousin in Swansea, a mother in Southampton, a school anywhere. The Jungle is freezing. A wet and miserable lattice of duckboards wobble on the foul jelly of mud like a cameo of the trenches that rutted this bit of northern France 100 years ago.

Like all refugee camps, this has grown little excrescences of probity and utility. Along with the portable toilets and the communal trough and tap washing facilities are bins provided by charities, all pristinely empty while the ground is a mire of discarded junk.

There is a street of restaurants where you can recharge a phone to call some distant former home. Or smoke tight roll-ups or drink Nescafé. The first refugee story I covered was a famine in southern Sudan. An editor on the paper (now departed) implored me not to go. Sending a food critic to report on a famine was just bad taste. But who would you trust with bad taste if not a food critic? I was reminded of this by a trio of doers-of-good, who were walking up this muddy main drag when one of them saw me and did a theatrical double take. 'My God, I was just saying AA Gill should come here and do a review. And here you are.'

The camp has a touchingly divine Ethiopian Coptic church, built from tarpaulin and bits of lost wood, painted with the clear, strong and bright fresco saints of Africa. There was a boy, pressed tight against a bold St George. I think the church has just been bulldozed. There is a street of small tented cafés, most of them run by Afghans or Pakistanis from the North-West Frontier. There's one called 3 Idiots. A man stood grinning in the door. 'I'm one of the idiots. We're all called Khan.'

Next door, a Peshawari man makes rotis in a small bread oven, taking the tennis-ball-sized white dough, patting it and flipping it onto a cushion and then sticking it to the inside wall of the stove. Some of the best unleavened bread I've ever eaten was in Peshawar, and this was as good as I remember. I bought two for €1. The baker made the long and difficult journey across to Libya, got on a boat over the Mediterranean and ended up in Bari in Italy. I asked where he wanted to get to.

'Oh, I live in Bari,' he said. 'It's lovely there, nice people, wonderful weather, good food.'

'Well, what are you doing in a freezing, wet refugee camp in Calais, then?'

'Well, the only problem with Bari is that there's no work, so I come up here for a couple of weeks at a time to make bread.' He makes about 400 roti a day.

'Where is your oven from?'

'Ah,' he laughs, 'that came from England.'

Next door is a caff without a sign. I ask the owner what it is called. It has no name. Everyone knows it's here. A name would imply permanence. 'My name is Mohammed Ali. But I am not Cassius Clay. Don't be mistaking me for him,' he laughs.

Mohammed is also from Peshawar. Today, for lunch, he is offering red-bean curry, reheated fried chicken and a stew of chicken livers. I'm here with Natalie, an absurdly and insouciantly brave doctor from Médecins Sans Frontières; Jon, my photographer; and Bana, an optometrist, translator, Kurd and child of refugees. The room is a tent, with a make-do kitchen in one corner, a couple of gas rings, a banged-together counter, a kettle, some pots and pans. There's a television and a deep bench around the sides where a handful of young men recharge their phones, text and scroll, the unchecked great diaspora of displaced information. The phone is everything for refugees, and anywhere that wants to attract their business must have charging points.

The dishes come hot and generous, with fluffy, nutty white rice. Bana is a rice stickler – she's particularly appreciative. The red beans are a great, solid, aromatic dose of slow-release carbohydrate, as warm and uncomplicated as a hug. The surprise, the great surprise, is the chicken livers. They are perfect. Soft, with that mysterious, renal flavour that is medicinal and industrial, but also like earth and grass and licked copper. The sauce is pungently hot, but still a negligée, not a shroud, for the meat. This was a properly, cleverly crafted and wholly unexpected dish, made with finesse and an élan that defied the surroundings, but at the same time elevated them. Ali smiled with a rare pride. 'Where do you want to go?' I asked. He shrugged and the smile became sad. 'You know, you know.' As if to say the name out loud would be inauspicious.

A cup of coffee – Nescafé, with a lot of milk and even more sugar. After years of po-faced hipster coffee, the sweet, thick Nescafé comes like a mouthful of remembrance. It is the taste of the south, of the Third, left-behind World. I have sat in the make-do shade on the red earth in so many refugee camps and roadside temporary halts and sipped this bittersweet, mothering coffee. So many slow, hopeful journeys.

There is a domed tent run by two British playwrights – Joe Robertson and Joe Murphy – called the Good Chance Theatre because refugees say: 'There's a good chance I may get away tonight.'

Robertson and Murphy have crowdfunded it and got support from the Royal Court Theatre in London, among others: 'Do you know Stephen Daldry? He's our chairman.' 'Yes, actually, I do,' and I am handed a phone and I am chatting to Stephen and he agrees this is all just wonderful but it is a bit surreal. Now you may roll your eyes and think it is a lot of luvvie vanity to take Shakespeare to refugees, but there is no human experience that is beneath, or does not deserve, the expression of art. There were orchestras in concentration camps; there are poets on death row.

This is not a benign hippie commune of good intentions, however. The Jungle is a dangerous place, particularly at night. We see few women and never on their own. It is mostly men, frustrated and resentful, weary and stoic. I stop a boy; he has a handsome cockiness, the worldly, caged look of kids who fend for themselves. He is an Afghan. 'Who are you here with?' I ask. He shrugs. His mother is back in Afghanistan. He came with his father, who has gone on ahead to England. 'How old are you?' Eleven. This 11-year-old lad has been abandoned, cocky as an Artful Dodger. My translator Bana asks quietly: 'Are you frightened?' He looks away. Again, gently, she repeats: 'Are you frightened?' And the mask of aged competence slips away revealing a heartbroken, terrified 11-year-old, thousands of miles from any home, abandoned in the most desolate place the First World can construct.

Walking through the dense, slimy alleys of tents, a trio of young Egyptian boys come up to me. One shakes my hand: 'Hello, brother.'

He too wears the mask of a young teenager trying to look tougher than he feels, but here I am aware of an insincerity in his coldly grinning look. He hugs me: 'Brother.' And I am aware that his mate is standing close behind so I grip his elbows and push him away, his hand searching for my pocket. I turn and push his friend. There is no pretence now. 'Give me that.' He grabs for my jacket. The friend in front now, wearing a look of bewildered bravado, pulls a Stanley knife from his hoodie and says: 'Give him, give him.' I start to bark orders with a colonial authority as insecurely phoney as their bravado. Joe the photographer arrives, bellowing and jabbing. The three of them slink off ahead of us. The boy with the knife says: 'Give me this thing' as if it were a negotiation and he deserves a conciliatory prize. He points at my Islamic prayer beads that, absurdly, I am still holding and adds pathetically: 'I want them to pray.' Afterwards I look at Joe's snaps and I wish I did not quite so resemble the Duke of Windsor visiting the poor.

Many of the refugees are leaving the Jungle because their chances of getting to England are vanishingly small. We should be absolutely clear about this. The estimates of people actually getting to Britain is perhaps a dozen a fortnight. Security is very tight, the risks are exceedingly high, a lot of boys die. Nobody prints the numbers of those crushed under trucks, nobody wants to talk about it. I spoke to a man who had made 20 attempts in 28 days: 'It is very dangerous. I am frightened of dying. Look at my life here.' He waves at the soggy garbage. We know the figures are tiny because the price the people-smugglers charge to get them onto a truck are enormous. Between £9,000 and £11,000 to guarantee a drop in England.

They are decamping to Dunkirk, a strip of fetid, undrainable municipal spinney opposite some of the ugliest detached houses in Europe, guarded malevolently by the CRS, the French riot police. If Calais looks like the First World War, this is the Hundred Years War; medieval in its squalor and poverty. Slime-coloured men collect sodden wood from the trees and burn it in makeshift braziers.

They huddle around like extras from Agincourt. No theatres here, no cafés, no semblance of any pleasure or home.

I meet a woman, an Iraqi Kurd, holding a baby. He has the beautiful, open-faced grin of a Down's syndrome child. Lawey, three years and eight months, blows an exaggerated kiss. He has a throat infection. His mother stands bowed; her back is bad. A visiting doctor told her to get a massage, a prescription of such astonishing, wilful insouciance it takes your breath away. She was a civil servant. Her husband was a civil servant. Daesh came and they had to leave. She lost her husband in Turkey. His phone is dead. Tears start to fall down her worn face. 'I don't know what to do. I would never have come here if I had known.'

She has a brother in Sheffield. 'He will look after us. I don't want anything. I don't want any money,' she says. 'I just want to see my brother. I just want . . .' Her voice fades. Her daughter, Hero, is standing by the fire watching her mother. She wants to go back to school to be a doctor.

Every child in every refugee camp in the world wants to be a doctor. What they mean is they want to make things better. They want to heal.

January 2016

Mexico

Border towns all seem to be looking over their shoulders: they have secrets, places to be. This one squats on a river at the edge of Mexico; the main street runs into the scrub on the bank. There is a mural of a grinning coyote chasing a chicken – a dark joke for people who don't have a lot to laugh at. Coyotes are the names given to smugglers; chickens are the people they trade in.

It's early, but already the day is hot. On the riverbank there is a smell of charcoal, frying tacos and sweat. Men in dirty vests and shorts struggle to deposit goods onto makeshift jetties, where rafts of planks lashed to inflated inner tubes strain on skinny ropes. The business here is running cornflakes and motorbike parts, ketchup, tampons, probably a few drugs, a little light armament, information, messages of regret, apologies, threats, promises, despairing love and, of course, people.

They smuggle lots and lots of people here. No questions asked, they'll smuggle anyone: me, for instance. For a handful of pesos, a coyote will take me over the border. I've never actually met a people-smuggler before. Mine's briskly friendly, a plump man, benignly Mexican, with a droopy moustache. He doesn't look like a kidnapper, another favoured local profession, but I've never met a kidnapper, either. He has hard, hairy hands and a gondolier's boater. The hat may be ironic.

The river, broad and viscous, shimmies and curdles in clay-coloured swirls of sticks and dead stuff. The little barque is precariously un-stable. I squat among the boxes of snack food and sanitary ware as we pole out into the current. My smuggler strains and grunts, punt-ing for the further shore as we spin downstream.

A quarter of a mile on, there is a bridge that is the official border. Guards must be able to see us, but are unconcerned. This is not the Rio Grande, I'm not being smuggled into the United States; we're at the other end of the country, in the southern state of Chiapas, where Mexico meets Guatemala.

The Guatemalan border town is a mirror of the one I've just left. It is perhaps a little seedier, the wailing music a bit louder, with dozens of shops selling charitably cast-off American clothes. After half an hour, I walk back down to the river and find another coyote to smuggle me back to Mexico, this time with a huddle of giggling Guatemalan women, going for a day's duty-free shopping.

The story about Mexico and migrants, as seen from the US, is all about Trump and his wall and wetbacks; but the truth is that the crisis is down here in the heat, unseen, unnoticed. Last year, an estimated 400,000 people came across this border, fleeing the mur-derous triangle of Honduras, El Salvador and Guatemala. Mexico is a net recipient of refugees, but few outside this unforgiving place know or care that it receives almost the same number of desper-ate souls who fled Syria for Europe last year. There is nobody here handing out bottled water and fresh fruit, offering festival tents and Instagram selfies with National Theatre actresses.

Licho is a big man who seems to be folded up in a corner of his own body. He has solemn brown eyes, a downturned mouth; I have to lean in to hear him. He works on the illegal dock humping goods, people. Back home in El Salvador, he was a butcher.

'A gunman came and shot my father in front of me. I picked up a machete and killed him.'

'Why didn't he shoot you?'

'No more bullets.'

Licho was 18. He went to jail for seven years. 'I'm pleased,' he whispers. Maybe he means proud. 'I paid for my crime. I had to kill for the memory of my father.' He came to Mexico with his wife to escape the inevitable retribution. He has two children. It's hard, he'd like to go back to see his mother. He'd like to be able to teach his son to be a butcher. Mauritzi, a spindly, handsome boy, spends his day neck-deep in the thick river. A human tug, he pulls the rafts to shore for a few coppers. He, too, would like to go home, but can't. His brother was killed because his cousin was in trouble with the gangs. Then they came for him.

The crisis in these three Central American states has been caused by the carcinogenic spread of gang violence. All of them had systemic problems with corruption and coups in the past; but, contrarily, the gang pandemic was inflicted after the political violence was over. Once the Salvadoran Civil War had come to its exhausted end in early 1992, the US government deemed it a good time to return Salvadoran political refugees and criminals, in particular members of gangs – or maras – that had taken over areas of Los Angeles. Two gangs in particular: Mara Salvatrucha, also known as MS-13; and Barrio 18, or M-18. The gangs quickly took root in the three capital cities: San Salvador, Guatemala City and Tegucigalpa, the capital of Honduras. They don't deal in drugs in the way that the Colombian or Mexican cartels do. They may sell a little marijuana or cocaine on the street, but mostly make their living from protection, backed by operatic violence that would beggar the imagination of the mafia. They are constantly at war with each other.

Carlos Umberto, a carpenter, sits in a dingy concrete room with a mattress on the floor, a lavatory in the corner and ragged clothing hanging from a sagging string across the wall. He is here with his wife, Oldin Michele, and two sons. He looks shocked, his face far older than its 38 years. He paid protection – he calls it rent – of $15 a week. It was a lot. Then the gang demanded $50. He sold his tools to pay it. He borrowed more money to buy more tools, and they stole them because he must be rich. Then they demanded his eldest son. He strokes the lad's head. The boy, no more than nine years old, curls next to his father, who says: 'They said they would kill me. They demanded sex from my wife and told her to smuggle drugs into prison inside her.' He blinks back the tears. 'I ran one night. I got the children and my wife, and we left everything. We have nothing.' The boys cling to him with tight, solemn faces.

The cruelty of the maras is so terrifying that anyone running from it has the right to claim asylum in another country. These people are the first in the world that the UN has designated as refugees from gang violence. But once across the border river here, they are not safe or secure. They have to register as refugees at an office a couple of days' walk away, and the road has police checks. If they are caught, they will be locked up as illegal immigrants in detention camps. Husbands will be separated from wives, teenage children from their mothers, and there is no hurry to process paperwork. The detention centres are violent and frightening, so most refugees make their way across country as best they can. Chiapas is rural, it's the mango season and the great plantations of trees are heavy with pendulous fruit, picked by teams of wiry men. The land is sparse and dry, dramatically bleached. Above us there is always a spiral of zopilotes, the black vultures whose carousels mark the thermals and corpses – reminders of the constant presence of unlamented death. Chiapas has had its own troubles: this is the home of the Zapatistas, peasant revolutionaries who are in a permanent stand-off with the government. Many of the people are Mayan; there's a lot of army, a lot of police. Everyone is poor. The refugees make their way through this baked, bitter landscape aiming for the very few charity-run safe houses and the railway. The train north is called the Beast.

Jose and Juana sit in a little courtyard of a safe-enough house with 16 members of their family. Jose's face is taut and pale in deep misery. Children go through the motions of play, but quietly, as a comforting memory, or they just sit and stare. Juana, straight-backed, takes a breath to slip into the terrible depths of her story.

Henry Alberto, her eldest boy, went to school and was brilliant, diligent and good. She has his reports, but she can't read them; she is illiterate. Gangs came and told him to join them. He refused. He wanted to carry on going to school, and then to college. He graduated from school. He had his 18th birthday, and then they came back for him and killed him: graduation, birthday and funeral all in the same week. Juana dissolves. She sinks under the weight of her story and drowns in tears; her hands reach to touch someone who isn't there. Gaping, salted grief washes over the room. The others drop their heads, turn against the pain. Henry Alberto will for ever be the best of them, the exception, unsullied by experience. He was killed by his friends, boys he'd known all his life. She gets his graduation photo: Henry Alberto, looking like a million school pictures in his borrowed robes with a rolled certificate, smiling, proud, relieved, hopeful. His mother's breath is sodden with mourning. The gangs have a relentless need for children. The attrition rate in their endless turf wars is trench-terrible. Children hold their own and others' lives in such scant regard: the gangs send kids to kill their friends and neighbours to prove loyalty and mettle. If they refuse, their own families are victims of the next child desperate for peer approval and purpose.

Further up the road, now, in the state of Oaxaca. Here is the railway where the Beast rests. It's just a track with dusty boxcars, the rails strike straight ahead into a vanishing point at the foot of shimmering mountains. Horses graze at the weeds between sleepers. This town is featureless, no one stirs, there is no café, no bar, everything is shuttered, dead. There are people here; I can hear muttering, a tinny radio, but nobody is out in the street.

At the edge of the town, there's a Catholic shelter for refugees; a handful of exhausted Salvadorans sit in the shade of a painting of the suffering Jesus. I knock on the door, the panel opens and, behind

75

the grill, there's a bad-tempered face wearing cobble-thick glasses, saying: 'No one is here. The hostel is closed because there is no water.' The man who runs it finally appears. He talks to me guardedly and says that outside of town is one great unmarked grave. There are countless refugees buried there, who were robbed, raped and held for micro-kidnapping, one of the world's fastest-growing illegal businesses. It is done over mobile phones, demanding a wired ransom, usually no more than $1,000. Killing is the simplest option for non-payment.

In Mexico, almost 95 per cent of crimes go uninvestigated, and you are more likely to be banged to rights for a parking offence than to be found guilty of a murder. No one really knows what happens to many of the 400,000 refugees who come here. We do know that 170,000 Central American migrants were detained in Mexico last year, and 134,000 were stopped at the US border. Yet only 3,423 asylum applications were made in Mexico. The police and army are regarded as impossible to challenge. Salvadorans mutter that this hostel is not a good place, things happen here, people have vanished. A disproportionate number of refugees are women and children, but many are also gay or transgender.

Alejandra is in a women's refuge. Her exaggerated, theatrical gestures and expressions show a world-weary but amused sadness. She is transgender, has long, thin hair and a fine-boned face, etched by cigarette smoke and moulded by low expectations. She is also missing a number of teeth. Alejandra had the most humiliatingly dangerous job in the world. As a street prostitute in terrifyingly macho San Salvador, she was threatened, spat upon, beaten, abused, raped and robbed. 'The police locked me up in the dark without food or water for 15 days.' She was the lowest form of human life, with no one and nothing to turn to. She waves a dramatic hand through her hair and grins, in the manner of someone practised at defusing fearful situations with submission. She is here in a refuge with her niece, Gabriela, who also used to be male. (What are the odds?)

Alejandra is 41. She says what she really wants is to make a wedding dress, one beautiful, beautiful wedding dress. For herself? 'No, no, it will never be for me.'

Gabriela, now 19, dressed as a girl and went to school in an act of amazing bravery. 'They beat me like a piñata,' she giggles behind her hands, her eyes filling with tears. 'My brother beat and bullied me constantly. I tried to kill myself, then I ran away, here, with my aunt.' She wants to be a cook. They pose for photographs, damaged and lost but made incandescently beautiful by their survival and self-belief.

William, a farmer of 58, has been married for 43 years. His wife was nearly 14 when they tied the knot. He stands and declaims about the farm he lost. Caught between two gangs, he took a gun into the night and fired and fired and fired until he ran out of bullets. He chants a litany of the things he used to cultivate: cucumbers, parsley, coriander, berries, hens, turkeys. He fled only because he knew his sons wouldn't leave without him. Then his strong voice shreds: 'I am in hell, I want to go home, I know I will die.'

None of the refugees I spoke to said their goal was to get to the United States. Almost all said they would like to go back home, to be safe. There is a passing assumption that most of these people may be refugees when they arrive at the Mexican border, but they'll be economic migrants by the time they reach Texas; that they are on a long conveyor belt, drawn to the land of the free and the fat. Many have relations in America, and certainly they would be safer there than staying here, but the odyssey, with or without coyotes, is still an Everest of hardship and danger, months fraught with anxiety.

I met boys on the road who had lost limbs under the wheels of the Beast, men sent home after years in US internment camps or prisons, who are trying to get back to the States to be reunited with wives and children they haven't seen in months. And MS-13 and M-18 are spreading across the border like an invasive species. You see their tags graffitied across the walls of hostels and phone boxes.

They've come to settle scores, to exact their executions. They circle like the vultures.

There is another tale that is the most extraordinary I think I've ever been told: the story of Romero and Rebeca. Romero is a young man, serious and naive, self-effacing to the point of shyness. He grew up in San Salvador; his father died when he was young. He and his elder brother were brought up by their mother. He looked up to his brother, who looked after him until becoming a local gang leader with M-18.

Romero grew friendly with the woman next door, Rebeca, who was older than him, a political activist from a centre-right party. When he was 15, they began an illicit affair. It wasn't straightforward: Romero is gay, Rebeca is transgender. She was an activist for LGBT rights.

Then M-18 began social cleansing, killing gay and transgender people. Rebeca's boss was uneasy about her sexuality and told her to bind her chest, stop wearing make-up and dress like a man. She refused; the politician sacked her and arranged for the gang to have her cleansed. A man came to her in the night, a man she knew – it is always a man you know – and shot her twice in the stomach, missing her spine by a fraction. She didn't die, but had 45 stitches.

As soon as Rebeca could walk, she ran.

She told no one, couldn't tell Romero – to protect him, and because it was too sad and for the best. But Romero's brother came and found him, and said he knew he was queer and nobody in their family could be a deviant. The boy who had been his protector and a surrogate father now held a gun to his head. He must leave for ever, never return, 'never see our mother again'. And then he shot him, shot his young brother through the kneecap.

An hour later, their mother returned to find her son bleeding on the floor. He told her that he was gay and heartbroken, that his love had left without a word, and his brother had shot and banished him. His mother said she knew, had always known; she loved her sons, would always love them, but he needed to leave, to flee the country, as his brother would return as good as his word. Imagine, for a moment, being that woman.

Romero fled into the dark, made his way up the most dangerous road in Latin America, to the Mexican border. He found a coyote who would take him across the river. He made his way to the little regional town of Tapachula. He begged in a municipal park, police took whatever money he gleaned, local Mexicans beat him up. He slept on a bench and, one morning, he woke and saw a figure – 'a vision'. He shouted. His exact words were: 'Oh my love, my love it's you!' It was Rebeca. She turned and saw him.

I speak to them in the small room that is paid for by the UNHCR, by you. It is their home. She is still an assertive, dynamic, angry activist; committed, protective. He is quiet and demure. They constantly look at each other, as if to confirm the star-crossed truth of their odds-defying presence. They have a mattress, two chairs, a lot of cosmetics, some elaborate scars – and each other.

'Rebeca is your first love, then?' I ask. 'And my last,' he says gently.

June 2016

OUT THERE

Travel Books

I've always said that the first half of a peripatetic life should be devoted to visiting and the second half to revisiting. If someone said, as I'm sure at some point someone will, 'You've just enough time for one more trip before we sit you in front of the telly with the sound turned down and make your meals in a blender,' I will want to return somewhere and it'll be a city.

One of the great lessons of travel is there's not a wilderness in the globe that can compare with the excitement of a new city. And there's only one beach – all beaches are the same beach. A beach is a really, really good-looking, sexy, hot-bodied, nubile kid with no conversation. For an hour you just want to look at it, be with it, lie next to it, but all it ever says is, 'Hi, I'm a hot beach.' It's so boring you have to go and search for washed-up junk just to keep from drowning yourself.

So my final visit would be a city. Rome, perhaps, Calcutta, Catania, Paris, or just where I started, Edinburgh. OK, perhaps Sydney. But I haven't been told I can just do one more place yet. I've been reliably informed I've got about a decade or two and I'm nowhere near finished visiting. I feel like a manic delivery man with a vanload of packages and it's already five o'clock. I've never seen Baku or Ulan Bator. I've never been to St Petersburg for God's sake or Lagos or Honolulu. And if I'm honest, the truth is I'm not going to make it back to Bukhara or Buenos Aires. I said I would when I waved goodbye. I

118said, 'This isn't goodbye; it's au revoir,' but actually it was goodbye.

I won't ever see Mo'ynoq again, the strange lost fishing port at the edge of the vanished Aral Sea, or the abandoned Cold War early-warning beacon up the hill at Ammassalik on the coast of Greenland, or that surprisingly good restaurant at Longyearbyen, the capital of Svalbard in the Arctic Circle, nor Djenné, the silent, sand-blown oven in the Sahara with its huge mosque. But then, on the bright side, I'm not going to have to go back to Wolverhampton either, or Benidorm, and that's a relief. I've just been sent a catalogue from an old and venerable antiquarian bookshop (are there any other type?). It's called Sotheran's; it's in London. Do you know the difference between an antiquarian bookshop and a second-hand bookshop? About 500 quid.

Sotheran's has a marvellous travel section, and every so often they bring out a catalogue and they send it to me, and I'm entranced by this one. It's replete with the cussedness, optimism, excitement, vanity and arrant lunacy of exploration and travel.

Randomly, I found my favourite-ever title for a travel book. In 1899 Burr McIntosh wrote *The Little I Saw of Cuba*. I'm desperate to know. But here again, by further chance, next to it is my second-favourite title. In 1874 Sir Clements Robert Markham wrote a book, presumably his magnum opus, and when people asked him what he was going to call it he took a deep breath and said, 'A Memoir of the Lady Ana De Osorio: Countess of Chinchon and Vice-Queen of Peru (AD 1629–39) with a Plea for the Correct Spelling of the Chinchona Genus.' Down the years and through the mists of time the true living character and spirit of Sir Clements comes to us as clear as morning. The haiku of that title tells you exactly what he was like, but the synopsis of the book tells me that he led the expedition to Peru to find the seed of the quinine tree to transport it back to India as an imperial cure for malaria. Fascinatingly, he changed the world. Here is the record, a rare volume with a ridiculous title on a shelf in Piccadilly.

As someone who has written travel books himself, I feel a kinship with the volumes. I want to bring home Field Marshal Roberts' *Forty-One Years in India: From Subaltern to Commander-in-Chief*. I don't want to read it, along with Raul Valdez's *Wild Sheep and Wild Sheep Hunters of the Old World*. If you haven't discovered for yourself, let me warn you against the hunting memoir. They plumb depths of tedium unknown in any other subgenre. I once kept a civil servant's exhaustively detailed memoir of oryx-hunting in Betuanaland beside my bed for sleepless nights.

All these books are now rare. At the bottom of their synopses are brief citings of other copies: one held in the British Library, one in the Royal Geographical Society, and apparently the only other copy of the first edition of *Packing Predicaments* by Austin Reed is gingerly held in the University of Alberta.

Writing and travel have always gone abroad together. Very few explorers failed to take a notebook, and somehow a travel memoir doesn't have to be particularly well written; it just has to be well travelled. And we do it because, well, partly because it's how travel is traditionally financed, but mostly because it's a basic human need to tell someone what we saw, where we've been. It is virtually impossible to travel in secret or in silence. These books have become as rare and fugitive as the places the authors visited. They are now difficult and delicate and beautiful destinations in themselves.

The innovation of printing was to make the knowledge of the world ubiquitous, but it is amazing how quickly the books revert to being as rare as medieval illuminated manuscripts. They are intense, guttering glimmers of light in the darkness. When I can no longer visit or revisit, I will embark on the last great journey through the rare and difficult land of obscure travel books.

September 2014

The Forest of Dean

———

The forest was different here: darker, weightier, with an old lethargy; the trees crosshatched and stippled, inky green barbs of yew, the flickering scales and tense, pale trunks of beech, thick-ankled cudgels of long-neglected coppice. Ivy and moss clagged and fretted the branches, and the ground was rotting, soft, embroidered with hart's-tongue fern, bracken and brambles. The earth heaved and sagged into burrows and deadfalls: the holes and hacking of mines, the ancient pocks and scrabbling of Celtic and Roman ironworks that formed dank caves in gargoyle-faced rocks, painted with ferrous stain. The track is a single-file ghost through the dappled litter, marked with the fearful feet of fallow does.

I walked on, leaving the deadened voices of the others behind, until I was enveloped by the soft, secret sounds, the creaks and canny sighs of an old, old wood. Slowly, separating the senses, I became aware that something else was here with me. Something walking parallel in step, stealing in stealth, just there under the dark cover of the trees. I swallowed that sour lump of fear that is always in forests, the whispered, sing-song, deadtime terror that rises like smoke in wild places. I went on, big-eyed, and the Other came with me until we reached the edge of a meadow, bright in the afternoon sun.

I hung back in the protective gloaming. Beside me, a man's five o'clock shadow away, a long, ruddy, thick-brushed fox high-stepped into the sunlight. He paused and looked back at me, dark mask held high, the black eyes unsurprised at our propinquity. If there was a message in his gaze I wasn't sensitive enough to glean it. So the fox continued on alone, dainty in the high grass. I watched him till he slipped into the shadows.

Retracing my steps I got back to the coven, where a witch in her velveteen cape was holding high a chipped crystal cup in a pool of bright sunlight, under a dusty yew that must be at least a thousand years old and grows out of a cleaved rock. I told the witch about the walk and the fox, leaving out the fear. 'There you are,' she said with a Gloucester twang. 'I said he had it in him. The knowledge, the sight. That was your familiar, my love, that fox. He came for you. Where else would a fox walk beside you in a wood, except in this magic place?'

The Forest of Dean is a mercurial place.

It has form. Caught between the Severn and the Wye, it is neither English nor Welsh. It is an inverted, secretive un-place; apart. Many people who come here once vow never to return, mention its name with a shiver. Its atmosphere is too thick with malevolence and superstition. Somebody warned me that it would be all six-fingered banjo-pluckers and cousin-coupling salt-lickers. It was the inspiration for J.R.R. Tolkien's Ents, and J.K. Rowling's Forbidden Forest. But for many more it is a great, green resource, an eco-soup of renewal, calm and excitement, a connection with something that has passed through the periphery of our lives, that we see only in the corners of memory, a place redolent of a nation purged and persecuted by mercenary business and modernity.

It is the front line in the fight against the future of our wooded, wild places, and the government's plans to sell off publicly owned woodland, which have been thrown back into the undergrowth for some committee to whittle away. Forests, and this Gloucester A48 one in particular, are camouflaged and duplicitous places. They are never what they seem.

This is the story of one day in the Forest of Dean.

Tom, the photographer, and I arrive at the campsite around tea-time. The women in the smart information centre plus deli and gift shop tell us to park the borrowed VW Camper van under the trees and plug in. No fires, no loud music after 11, children are trying to sleep. The site is a broad, sloping field on the edge of a small town. There are electricity and lavatories for hobos, newspapers and cappuccinos for bank-holiday gypsies.

The campers take their vagabond status with varying degrees of self-imposed austerity. There are small, domed, 20-quid festival tents – humping holts for rutting teenagers – and elaborate nylon bungalows with separate bedrooms and annexes, lights and aerials, and collections of folding chairs with cup-holders. There are the gravid camper vans for men and women with beards. In the early-evening light, through the barbecue smoke, children play one last game of tip and run, and despite all my snobbery and squeamishness, it feels rather blissful; an amateur Eden, acutely British.

We are not one of the great outdoors nations. We don't go walk-about; camping is not in our blood. For us, camping is a comfortable national joke: collapsible tents, sodden sheets, burnt beans, malevolent cows and flashed buttocks. The point is to cram as much of the convenience of home into the outdoors as possible. It's a cross between a car boot sale and a big girl's game of make-believe house. In the toilet block, fathers hold up infants in Spider-Man jimjams to brush their teeth. You get the feeling that most families won't stray far; the tent or the caravan is accomplishment enough, a small but significant annual Everest. They're happy to have moved the familiar chores to a new setting, surrounded by trees and each other. As I lie in my sleeping bag in the roof of the camper, I can see the flicker of light and smell the congealing sausages, and hear the lowing of chat and the bursts of giggling that are the natural sounds of the British under canvas.

The next morning, we're out with the rangers. Thousands of

people visit this forest on a summer weekend – over a year, hundreds of thousands – and they all come to do something. Woods are for doing, like mountains and rivers are for doing. It's gardens that are for being. So they come to walk with ski-poles or dogs, to eat out of Tupperware on the ground, and to cycle. We stop at the cycle hire shop, where sturdy, bouncy, mountain machines are rented out; the serious bring their own and sit round talking nuts and spokes.

What the boys like is going downhill; downhill very fast. At the bottom small boys on smaller bikes practise being organ donors on smaller hills. The wardens talk about the accidents with a cheery bloodthirstiness, the way game rangers talk about lion attacks and hippo bites: 'Another one medevacked out yesterday. You know, nine times out of 10 it's a dad. They want to show off to their sons. We had one kid went down safely, Dad followed hell for leather, came to a jump, lost his nerve. Slammed on the brakes, fell on his head. Now he comes and watches in his wheelchair.'

We take a more sedate pedal around the family trail, where in strict size order dads, mums, kids and dogs chug along, shouting at each other to look, or look out. The forest accommodates all this with a handsome good grace: it puts up with relentless signposting, cycle paths, amenities, safety features and bollards, because this place is not what it seems. This isn't an invaded wilderness, it's not the careful and casual construct of time and rural practice. The hills are the slag of industry. At one time, the Forest of Dean hid dozens of coal mines and ironworks. It was more heavy industry than rural calm. The scars make for a picturesque landscape, but almost all of it is carved by man.

The very notion of a forest is not as straightforward as it may seem. Originally it meant open land that was kept by the Normans for hunting. Within its boundaries nobody could poach animal, vegetable or mineral. You couldn't plant crops or build anything. But over time, local people were given or sold the right to graze animals, collect firewood and other things. Kings handed out the goods of the forest to monasteries, and in this one, the right to collect sweet chestnuts. A man was fined a month's wages for shaking a chestnut tree – they were brought here by the Romans and flourished. The miners who helped Edward I to undermine the walls of Berwick were given the right to be free miners in perpetuity. Anyone born inside the forest is allowed to mine for coal, but few are, and fewer would want to dig for coal single-handedly.

The lanes are fringed with cudding, grubby sheep. 'Badgers' still have the right to free-graze them. The community here has a thick accent it nurtures for obscurity. They were fiercely against the proposed sell-off of forests to private ownership. The concessions to graze and dig seem to be ancient rights. In fact, they're the opposite. They are the crumbs of oligarchic ownership by Crown, Church and State. The idea that these forests are a people's place, a secret den from the time when all land was common, that in the cover of the trees there is still the commonwealth of old England, is the opposite of the fact that they are actually the remnants of feudalism, of heredity and hierarchy. They are here because most people and their occupations were excluded.

How we feel about woods and forests is irrational, and it may depend on how the forest features in our earliest memories, in fairy stories and mythology. The Romans hated them. The greatest disaster of their empire, the massacre in the Teutoburg forest in what is now Germany, made them places of mourning. Ever after in southern Europe, forests were full of monsters, or evil symbols of lawlessness and anarchy. In northern Europe, the forests and the trees are protective and rejuvenating, mystical, symbolic of rebirth and regeneration, fecundity and fruitfulness. But everyone agrees that forests hide things: legions, Red Riding Hood, bodies, lovers and bad sculpture.

Dean holds the largest collection of oaks in the nation. The trees are now mature and venerable. This place once supplied most of the timber for Nelson's fleet. The navy used colossal amounts of oak, and there was a concern that it was sinking faster than it was growing, so 200 years ago there was a great seeding of oak trees, and what you see around you is not an act of God but the fruit of military planning. Within 50 years of Trafalgar, battleships were being made of iron, so the trees were never needed. They reverted to their older, druidical role of looking mystical. The forest is not what it seems, and that is part of its allure. It hides another forest of conifers, planted for fence posts and chipboard. Around 50 per cent of the Forest of Dean is pine, but only when you climb one of the old slag heaps can you see it. The wardens dressed the paths with hardwoods, so they look light and Constable-ish, but behind them are dark alleys, the silent slums of conifer.

There's plenty of wildlife here: goshawks and peregrines, a herd of fallow deer, and wild boar. Their presence is noticeable everywhere, in wallows, scratching posts and churned-up cottage gardens. These big pigs can be the size of a Mini. They trip through the woods on ballet dancers' pointes, searching for Jack Russells to disembowel. The rangers spend a lot of time shooting them, which raises issues and ire with visitors and natives, who like to feed them and imagine that they, too, are refugees from an Arthurian England. In fact, someone unknown stopped a pantechnicon on the motorway, opened the back, and out spilt hundreds of confused and angry boars.

In a broad clearing there are picnic tables and holiday-sized litter bins, and stone altar slabs for tinfoil briquette barbecues, and a café for those who can't be fagged or forgot to make their own. Another souvenir shop offers hand-carved pixie homes and glossaries of local dialect. Outside in the sunlight a group of pensioners on their folding chairs drink wine and do quizzes. A group of girls are getting plastered, laughing and hugging in a rite of farewell. Fathers and sons throw balls, climb on stumps, prod sausages.

It is the constant pairing of fathers and sons in the forest that repeats and becomes especially touching. The dads teaching their boys to ride, catching them as they leap, carrying them to campfire suppers, kicking balls, bowling tricky leg breaks. These little men look up at their dads and see them somewhere else, somewhere new, not off to work or on the sofa. The woodland is soft and hard, sentimental and practical. It exudes anarchy and order. It has a bigger, more complex version of manliness than a city can offer. It allows the fathers to be gentle and strong. These boys and their dads beam at each other, ruffling hair.

And then a brass band turns up on bicycles and plays 'Swing Low, Sweet Chariot', because England are playing Wales, and half the listeners groan, but without rancour. The pleasure in being here is greater than the sum of the ice cream and the flat tuba and the bright sun. We stop at a pond of bulrushes. A babble of free-range eccentrics is out foraging in the manner of venerable herons, each carrying a butterfly net or a kitchen sieve attached to a broomstick. Some have rubber tubes in their mouths. They are the Gloucestershire Naturalists' Society, out on a field day. The hoses are called pooters, and they're for sucking up small insects. The Society are friendly but distracted. There's a moth man: 'It's a myth that they only come out at night – some do, of course, but not most. Not most at all.' There's a mollusc man, called in for slugs and snails; there are people for beetles and spiders – and within moments we find a toad in a rotting log, a small green frog, a pretty and unlikely beetle on a thistle, a lizard, three or four versions of spider, mites and springtails. It's hard not to assume that the wildlife is attracted to these benign, inquisitive folk rather than the other way around. They are Darwinian St Francises calling in the meek and uncounted to assure them that even the smallest and most insignificant shall be noticed and blessed.

Back in the bushes with the witches, who are part of the coven of Danu and Kerne. Kerne, or Herne, is the ancient pre-Roman hunter god who stalked the English woodland with his pack of dogs. He is a duplicitous deity, a frightening and protective poacher and game-keeper. He is also the green man that you see in the misericords and corbels of churches. The shy, angry, amused face of a man sprouting leaves.

The high priestess, Lisa, tells me that everything is energy. All of nature has the power, and it comes as two sorts: male and female. She shows me her wand, a willow twig with a spiral of honeysuckle: male and female, the eternal imperative of procreation, seed time and harvest, the driving, humming, snuffling need to breed. She takes us on a long, puffing walk to a magic well, St Anthony's, the meeting of two springs surrounded by dressed stones of a great age. The water is clear and cold. The witch says it's a good treatment for skin complaints.

A hundred yards away is an encampment of free campers; not gypsies or crusties, not alternative hedgerow greens but a semi-nomadic, feral group who slip in and out of the tarmacked world, outsiders who come to the forest to hide, to be free. There are a couple of girls, too young, too coquettishly direct, an old bull terrier, a brace of drunk men with smiling menace, and an old man with long, long white hair and a white beard that looked like the tendrils of the honeysuckle crawling from his mouth and nose and eyes. We walk back to the road and I realise I have picked up a beech twig like a wand, and I'm holding a sprig of beech nuts, three, attached in a trinity. I slip them into my pocket as some sort of amulet. The voices cackle and hoot through the branches.

In the early-evening light we climb to a famous Victorian view-point high above an oxbow bend in the river. Up here the peregrines nest on the flight paths of pigeons. This is what people see when they think of Britain, this rolling land.

Below us in the heat a pair of riders walk their horses into the river. A canoe drifts past. Out of sight, a pair of roe deer with this year's fawns step into the water meadow. The river curls round the wood. A pair of jays call. The forest lays itself out in the last soft, warm light like a lush and gorgeous nude, perfectly aware of its own allure and power, the curving, secret body reclining under the green mantle of trees.

September 2011

Hong Kong

I haven't been to Hong Kong for a decade. It's moved – I didn't recognise a thing. It's a sultry rebuff to old travel elitists who sniff that there's nothing left to discover. Turn your back on the world and it grows a whole new face. Hong Kong is God's Transformer. It's been twisted and turned into a new and improved temporary place in real time. You can feel it change under your feet. This city is sloughing its skin, the 'scrapers strive skyward like bamboo. The citizens rush and scurry because – who knows? – maybe your office or home has been built over or subsumed while you were having lunch. Maybe your kids have been replaced by better kids.

This fluidity, this sense of concrete and glass as malleable, sinuous, is exciting and disconcerting for someone who comes from the Old World, where cities change in geological time and altering the course of a bus lane or building a conservatory means lengthy consultations and inquiries and the default answer to all change is, well, better not. Conservation always trumps innovation.

In Hong Kong I wondered if I might not wake up to find that I'd been reclaimed for some new and improved purpose, gutted and truncated and rendered more user-friendly. The city is collectively, socially and philosophically metamorphosing. It hangs like a silkworm cocooned between the Empire and the People's Republic. After the handover from Britain to China, the territory was granted a waiting-room status. One country, two systems, Beijing said, gnomically.

Those who predicted that phalanxes of the People's Army would march in and hang shopkeepers from lamp posts have been proven wrong and disappointed. The army is here, the communists are here, but they're in plainclothes, probably plain designer clothes. You can take the Hong Kong dollar straight to the bank in Switzerland. As one resident pointed out, this is the biggest Chinese laundry in the world.

I'm here for the literary festival. A million Chinese people come to listen, take pictures and buy armloads of books. They are ravenous for everything: minerals, desirables, knowledge, fiction and romance. Hong Kong feels like being inside a hot, needy mouth; there is a peristaltic craving to swallow everything.

Hong Kong has shrugged off colonialism like an old school uniform. It isn't resentful or nostalgic for the past; the past is just irrelevant. Hong Kong has kept the bits that were useful for the journey – the second language, the business contacts, the trade and the reputation, the street names and the cenotaph – and used the rest as landfill. It's salutary and it's admirable.

One of the small things that has remained is an oddly elegiac mongrel cuisine. We are used to fusion food in the West. It is welcomed in a liberal cultural-cringe sort of way. We feel pleased that our stuffy, snobbish imperial sideboard dinner is open and welcoming to the hotter, brighter, sexier flavours of the developing world. We feel in a more inclusive way that fusion food is edible equality and global love. We're not so keen on swallowing the hegemony that goes the other way. Europeans still go to Thai restaurants and ask for the chopsticks because they want to be authentic. We don't like how much of the food we call Indian is Anglo-Indian or Portuguese or French-Indian. And in Hong Kong it would seem bizarrely contrary to seek out English food, particularly when the Cantonese set such a spectacularly good table.

I went out to breakfast in one of the last remaining *cha chaan tengs* – workmen's caffs – and here you can find what's left of an edible colonialism. Here is a soup with macaroni, a supine pasta that has been sent abroad and given short manners and a fork-friendly Western insouciance. Floating in the soup like a mad Ophelia was a fried egg and a slice of ham. The dish is Asian in design and concept – no one in England would eat soup for breakfast – but its ingredients were brought from the cold West. It's a strange, jolly approximation. The closest the two cuisines get to a natural meeting is congee and porridge, the one made with oats, the other with rice, but with mush in common. They're farinaceous, soothing, slow-release first-thing foods. The Chinese make it a heresy by adding savoury fish and oniony stuff; the Scots who came here to build bridges and hand down laws would've been yearning for brown sugar or syrup. I had mine with blood jelly – a big ask for a Western mouth first thing in the morning.

Perhaps the most congenial symbol of East and West was a hot drink called *yuanyang*, strong tea mixed with strong coffee, which sounds rather like a catering malfunction, but turned out to be surprisingly good, the Chinese black tannin curling smokily around the European caffeine. It was made with condensed milk. Condensed milk is one of the great gifts of Empire, perhaps its greatest gift. All over the world you'll still find people using sweetened, thick, tinned milk out of preference. In India and Africa, where there is plenty of fresh milk, it's still an old-fashioned luxury. In fact, it's an American invention, the great boom of its manufacture coinciding with the American Civil War. Throughout the world variations of desserts are made with it; in India there are boiled sweets, in England banoffee pie, in Latin America variations of dulce de leche. And in these sweet tins a sting, an element of nostalgia, and in this is the truth about the two-way traffic of fusion cooking. The one that comes from Western chefs travelling to Oriental destinations, picking up tips and ingredients, is a jolly holiday food that is both luscious and lotus-eating and always tastes like it was cooked wearing shorts.

The other, the expatriate or refugee approximations of home food, taste slightly of homesickness, of the damp of solitary tears, of absence, of loneliness, the sweetness of families a long way away and a familiar landscape that's only seen in photographs. It isn't as easily consumed, and in truth, condensed milk eaten in Hong Kong tastes very different from condensed milk eaten in Huddersfield.

September 2011

Shelter

There are many cities in this city. The Christmas city is not like the summer city. The tourists' city is very different from the commuters' city. There is a rich city and a poor city. There are those who live on top of it, and those who exist under it.

Sometimes, on a busy West End street, you catch sight of someone – a distressed girl sitting in a doorway, a man wearing a blanket, someone who is plainly not walking anywhere in particular, just moving, because the alternative is not moving – and, like drawing back a curtain, you soon realise that the streets you walk on are not the ones they walk on. The shop windows and the gusts of warmth from the doors, the smells from the cafés and the restaurants, have a different meaning for them.

We are each of us caught in the familiar runs of our particular place, and over time we imagine ours to be the real and authentic – the true – city. My city is over-endowed with restaurants, an embarrassment of complicated food. The smiles of maître d's, the bustle of waiters. But I know that, out there, there are many, many people who never eat in restaurants, and there are some who rarely get to eat at a table.

For as long as I've lived in London, there have been plans and promises to do something about the area around King's Cross. To get in the developers, the planners, the improvers, the decorators, the street-sweepers, but still it remains obstinately decrepit and deranged, cankered with the sores and blisters of negotiable sex and insistent drugs.

This is a threatening, dank and malevolent place, bathed in piss-yellow light, where plastic bags are flayed on barbed wire. Along the streets of corrugated warehouses you still get glimpses of Gustave Doré's other world and Gissing's cannibalistic metropolis.

After a nervous quest, our echoing footsteps find the door lit with a pale sign that promises 'Shelter from the Storm'. You wouldn't get here by accident. They don't do passing trade. Shelter from the Storm is a little slice of home for the homeless. It does what it says on the door.

The warmth and the light reach out and pull us in. The Blonde and I step into a room that was once industrial space, but is now a dining room, a living room, washroom and two dormitories for 18 men and 18 women for whom the city has no space or time.

It was started by Sheila Scott and Louie Salvoni. Sheila grew exasperated at her church's lack of practical commitment to the desperate need of the streets, so rolled up her sleeves and unrolled her formidable face. Louie says he just got angry. That there were so many lost and wasted people out there, in this hugely indulgent city.

It is a commonplace truism to talk of people like this as being extraordinary. They aren't. What they do is extraordinary. The act of day after day, week after week, every year, feeding and caring for the homeless is extraordinary.

What is special about them is their decent, funny, earthy ordinariness. Shelter from the Storm takes all who are sent to them by the social services, from hospitals, from churches and the police. They are the hands that reach out across the parapet.

There are no drugs here, and no drink, no violence, no sex, no acting out. There is a telly with the football on. A computer. There's hot water and soap, and there's safety, and respite. There's a warm bed and a couple of saggy sofas. There's company for the runaway lads and the trafficked girls, for the old, the lonely, the lovelorn, the unlucky and the lost. What they get here is safety and help, a hand with jobs and appointments, with doctors and lawyers, with all the defeating bureaucracy of nothingness. And they get dinner.

The Blonde said this wasn't at all what she'd been expecting. She thought it would be solitary men hugging cups of soup in corners, the hunched and mumbling, crust-sucking flotsam. An open kitchen dominates the room. There are round tables with bright cloths. The communion of eating together is central to what this place does. This may be the first time in a day that these souls have sat with a kind word, and a fork.

Dinner is prepared by volunteers. Today it's chicken and rice with a spicy tomato salsa, followed by plum crumble. It's all very good. Not very good for a soup kitchen, not good for free food, just very good, made with care, and gusto, and there's lots of it, piled hot and steamy. I sit down next to an old man with a gold tooth – he tells me he's a Baptist minister; he has a church, but nowhere to sleep – and a neat and quiet lady with a sad smile. She's lost her job, and her home. She was a cleaner. She came here from Ghana a long time back, following a man who didn't work out. She's buried her family. There's nobody left. To be African without a family is a peculiarly terrible cross. I talked to her about Accra, but the memory of her childhood overcomes her and, politely, with a whispering voice, her head drops, her hands cross neatly in her lap, and the tears trickle down her resolute African face. The gold-mouthed padre says, 'Trust God. Trust Him.' She nods and sobs.

Chicken and rice, I say, idiotically, that's a combination made in heaven. Chicken and rice could be the national dish of West Africa. She stares at her untouched plate, and whispers, 'Chicken and rice, made in heaven,' and picks up her fork, as if it were weighed down with the cares of her threadbare life, and slowly, reluctantly, begins to eat. We all eat together in silence, ruminating on the blessings of chicken and rice. I thank God for chicken and rice, says the hedge-row priest.

Now, I don't know a damn about the mysterious ways of God, but I suppose it's no coincidence that at the heart of all religions there is food. The sharing of food. The act of feeding someone is the most basic transubstantiation. To make them whole, and well, to feed their future, and the hope for the better tomorrow. After five minutes, she looks up and smiles. The sadness isn't gone, but it's not despair, and we talk and laugh about the great, strong, loud, hard-handed, bright, big women of Ghana.

Shelter from the Storm gets a lot of its food from supermarkets and, in particular, a great deal of help from Pret A Manger, which takes on the homeless and gives them jobs. Everyone leaves in the morning with a Pret sandwich for their lunch. You might want to remember that when buying yours. This dinner, with the guests of Shelter from the Storm, and Sheila and Louie, was one of the most memorable I had this year. Of course it was. I was reminded why all the other dinners are good, bad and indifferent, and that everyone in this city should be able to sit down and eat in company once a day.

It should be a basic citizen's right. We don't actually exist in different cities, we just choose to live selectively in the most expensive and beautifully appointed dining rooms. You still eat with the homeless, with the cleaning ladies and the tramp preachers, runaways and addict boys, and abused girls, the kicked-out, the kicking, and the kicked. We all sit at the same table. We just choose not to see it.

Shelter from the Storm could use some help. Not a lot. They're all volunteers. They get given stuff. They're good at asking. But they need a new van, and there are always expenses. Think about it.

This isn't about feeling guilty, it's about feeling good, and full, and being part of it.

December 2011

Botswana

'There's a porcupine down there,' says the skinny Bushman, staring into a large hole. He drops to the ground and wriggles forward. His bones undulate through his skin, baggy as an elephant's knee: shoulder blades slide together as he sidles his way into the earth. I wouldn't do that. There could be any number of things in the damp darkness – cooling snakes, scorpions, aardvarks with Freddy Krueger hands, warthogs with scimitar knives in their smiling mouths – and I wouldn't want to meet a porcupine in its dark parlour. The rest of us are dispatched to stand over other holes, holding leaf-bladed spears. Porcupines have been escaping Bushmen for thousands of years.

We watch the dark exits with muscle-knotting excitement. There's a muffled scuffling, then out of the earth comes the porcupine. He explodes pyrotechnically into the sunlight, scattering sentries, clattering in a blur of black-and-white spikes, and gallops into the bush, pursued by a clicking, howling, laughing band of Bushmen. My 18-year-old son stands aghast. Eyes wide as harvest moons, he shouts:

'Holy mother of all that's evil! That was hell spawn.'

'What did you think it was going to be?', I ask as we run.

'Well, sort of like a hedgehog.'

It was a satisfying meeting. Alasdair is a dear and charming boy, but, like his teenage contemporaries, is studiedly insouciant, with a knowingly underwhelmed disregard for the earth and all it has to offer.

The porcupine doesn't go far, down another warren of holes. Again, we camp up top with spears, taking turns to mine a shaft into the deep chamber. It's very medieval. Flora, my bookish and sedentary daughter, has discovered an unlikely blood lust. She crouches, fearless, an alabaster Amazon, fisted spear cocked at her shoulder, unblinking eyes slitted in murderous anticipation. Two, three hours we wait, until the porcupine is mortally stabbed underground and hauled up to be marvelled at and plucked over. Flora squats with the women, pulling out the spines. The skin, thick with a layer of muscle, is thrown on the embers of a fire. It bubbles and wrinkles, and we sit and chew hot strips of unctuous crackling, smoky and piggy, our faces streaked with red earth, gore, sweat and sticky fat.

Alasdair sits in a huddle of hunters, rolling them cigarettes. They watch his dexterity and try to copy him, chuckling and sucking in great gusts of smoke, slapping their thighs. Bushmen have an ardent, hacking love for tobacco. Who would have guessed that this prohibited habit, which back home has got him gated, punished, shouted and lectured at, threatened and sent to the bottom of the garden, would turn out to be the one really useful and enviable skill we could bring to the oldest people on earth, in the furthest reach of the Kalahari Desert? Ali catches my eye and beams.

I'd been promising the children I'd take them to Africa for years. Ever since they sat in my bed with damp hair, watching nature programmes and saying: 'Daddy, have you seen a lion? Will you take us one day?' And I'd say: 'Yes, of course.' But then, as all parents discover, promises are timeless, but the days to redeem them grow short. And here they are, 18 and 20 all of a sudden, and they're not going to want to go on holidays with me much longer; this seemed like the last chance to make good on the pledge.

I could have chosen one of the many comfortable safaris on offer, but I decided instead that we'd go fly camping in Botswana – 70 per cent desert, but also with one of the largest wetlands on the continent. Fly camping because it has the essential element of serendipity, tricky and challenging chance. Each day, you begin with a rough plan and crossed fingers, but what happens between dawn and dinner is down to caprice and fortune. You need a good guide, and we're here with Ralph Bousfield, one of the best in Africa.

We get to the Makgadikgadi salt pans on planes of decreasing size: a big one from London to Jo'burg, a medium one from Jo'burg to Gaborone, a smaller one from Gaborone to Maun, then a tiny, bouncy toy one that dodges the spiralling vultures and storks, and plummets onto an airstrip in the desert that serves San Camp – a spectacularly comfortable, Edwardian expedition caravanserai of white tents and long views. It is our point of departure into the desert.

The next morning, in the pale, hushed chill of daybreak, we meet the quad bikes that will take us across the flat pans. The sun will be ferocious; this is one of the most inhospitable places on earth. Half the year it's flooded, full of tiny shrimps and thousands of flamingos, but in the dry season nothing lives here – it's a flat, fawn-grey puff-pastry crust, a huge circle that stretches unbroken to the horizon. We set off in single file.

As the day heats up, the air begins to shimmy and undulate. Ostriches seem to walk in the vibrating sky; mirages surround us, lending the trip a dreamlike quality, like floating in space. The sky is huge, a vast blue bowl of light that dazzles to blindness, its straight edge a complete, unbroken circle. We ride on towards the air-sailing ostriches, on and on to the mouth of an extinct river. Its shores are littered with Stone Age pottery, shards of expertly worked bowls, charred from long, long-extinguished cooking fires.

We spend hours exploring, then look up to notice the sun dropping. We've a long way to go to camp; we've left it late. In Africa, the night comes up like thunder, a stampeding haste of shadows. The sky turns bruised rose-gold as the day dies. We hurry after the bleeding, luminous, final reflected glow, and get lost. Very quickly, things go from all right to all wrong. The bike behind me, driven by a guide, carrying all the water and all the petrol, disappears. With a pursed urgency, we travel on. Strung out in the great emptiness, following the pools of headlights in front, above us a sickle moon and the Southern Cross. A bike coughs and dies. We leave it behind and double up, my daughter sitting behind me.

My son has never driven anything before. The track becomes treacherous. I fill the darkness with the imaginary trees of an English beech wood.

Sometime after midnight, in the distance, there is a speck of light that flickers and disappears, then flickers again like a hermit's prayer. And, on a lonely island of 1,000-year-old baobab trees, are a fire, a table set for dinner, bedrolls on the desert floor, cool drinks, hot water, camp chairs and relieved smiles. We become garrulous; hair thick with dust and salt, knuckles burnt. The children laugh and shake their heads at what they've just done, their faces polished with surprise and disbelief, the way they used to look on Christmas mornings when there was still a Santa. We'd been on the move for 15 hours.

The Moremi Game Reserve is exceptionally green for the end of the dry season. While there are droughts in the east of Africa, down here there is an abundance of water and the roads are flooded. Ali has to walk up to his waist in front of our truck, moaning about snakes and hippos. Trees wave their branches like drowning men in impromptu lakes. Crocodiles lurk on their edges. We camp in a stand of mopane beside a river. At night, hippos graze outside the tent, chuckling and grunting; elephants pad delicately through the camp. Jackals cackle, lions cough – the noise that always starts you from the deepest sleep. Brutal and guttural, it travels miles without losing its power.

During the day, we watch game, see lionesses hunting wild dogs. They pass so close that Flora has to pull in her hand not to brush a sandy, fawn head with those murderous yellow eyes. Then we're on again, to the Okavango, and camp under mosquito nets on an island of sausage trees, out of which a monkey pisses into Ali's bed. The Okavango is one of the most fecund and rewarding habitats in Africa, a network of marshes and waterways that wind between stands of rushes and papyrus. The water drains down from the highlands of Angola; it's clear, clean, cool and drinkable. Here, we can do what I like doing best, birdwatching. There are islands that ululate with squabbling egrets, storks and herons. There are kingfishers and fish eagles and beautiful bee-eaters. The children swim. But it is the time spent with the Bushmen that they really value.

Kai-Kai, the waterhole and small community where we stay with them, has been visited by the same clans of people for more than 30,000 years. (The Great Pyramid is 4,500 years old.) These are our most venerable, most distant cousins. We all come from the Bushmen, but they are nearing the end of their long journey, melting into the rest of Africa. Fewer and fewer come out here to live in the bush, to hunt and gather medicinal roots. One night, the children are taken shyly into the trance dance, a ritual of healing and visions, a rhythmic turn round the fire while the women clap and chant songs that have names like the song of the rain, or the song of the new flowers, but have no words, just noises. The hums and clicks and vocal glissandos are learnt but may be so ancient that they are pre-language.

The old Bushman sitting beside me watches the sparks from the fire scatter up into the night. The inky sky is wearing everything in its jewel box. The Milky Way and the panoply of the heavens vibrate. He points and says: 'Those are the campfires of my ancestors.' They look down and see the prick of light here. Earth and heaven mirror each other, the countless generations stretching back to the first men and the first fires, the first hummed songs. And tacked on, right at the end, are me and my kids.

January 2012

India

It bears repeating that if you're planning on visiting only one foreign country in this life, you should probably make it India. Unless, of course, you are reading this in India; then you might like to consider New Zealand. Bombay is a phenomenal city. You can see in it all those nineteenth-century descriptions of New York and London. It is the whirlpool of commerce and expectation, sucking in great shoals of people equally desperate and hopeful. All the contradictions of metropolises are here: the unfairness of a nation sloughing off its past to become something new. Bombay is like a slice through an ancient tree – all the rings of life are visible at once. You can see things that look medieval, you can trace empires and invasions. Its problems are all the corollary of metamorphosis; the traffic continues to be absurdly frustrating and suicidally rude, but the road signs warning against drink or unprotected sex are curiously polite. The streets can be deep in filth, yet the people picking their way through them are pristinely clean. Bombay is crass and calm, tasteless and civilised. The buildings are crumbling as the skyscrapers spring up behind them. Bombay is the most sophisticated chaos.

One of the nicest things about being here is that it's not there: it's not Europe. Its concerns are not European concerns. India doesn't have the heart-clutching fear that is the leitmotif of the old West at the moment. Instead, it has to cope with too much self-belief, an overdose of optimism. It has a can-do motivation in a can't-do country. A lot of people point out that India is a twenty-first-century aspiration driven by thirteenth-century infrastructure. The basic mechanics of getting through life, from the disposal of sewage to the delivery of babies, are terrifyingly ad hoc. You could make a list of all the things that India does on one hand, and a list of all the things it doesn't do on the other, and they would pretty much cancel each other out.

This is a country where visitors rarely go to the country. The vast rural heart of India is too poor and difficult to lend itself to casual sightseeing. If the engine of India is still agriculture, its direction is decided by the middle class, much of it by the urban middle class. Much is made of India's middle-classness. In the West there is a self-justifying belief in the innate goodness of the suburbs and that the real agent of betterment in this world is a growing middle-class family. The bigger your bourgeoisie, the better they work for all the things that make modern life comfortable. The middle class wants education and car parks and policemen and international culture, but they also want to go to bed early and they are essentially law-abiding, but most usefully they have a ravenous appetite for stuff. The middle classes consume with an envious alacrity.

Commentators in the West assume that 'middle class' means the same thing in Maharashtra as it does in Vermont. An Indian economist told me that anyone who has bought a white good – a fridge, a washing machine, a TV – counts as middle-class here, but what they do share with the West is debt. The difference is that India is still for the most part a handmade country, a crafted place where the cheapest ingredient in any project is likely to be labour. The middle class is more like an entrepreneur class – it's ducking and it's diving, rather than diligently plodding. Everyone has a card and a project. It's an interesting high-wire act being practised by hundreds of thousands of people every morning. Soon it'll be millions.

I was asked to come here to talk to my old friend Camellia Panjabi about food in India. Nowhere is as instantly recognisable on a plate as the subcontinent; the smells and the flavours of masala, the textures and the intensity and the heat. But food here is rooted in home and region. Indians are as passionate as Italians about the grub of their villages and their childhoods, but they are also newly aspirational. The urban class want Western food, or at least a sort of Westernised food.

There is a dividing line here between the traditional Indian and the modern, and it's olive oil. There is a fad, a fashion, an unquenchable demand for the oil of olives which is totally foreign to this continent and the food that goes with it. India cooks with ghee, the clarified butter that is sacred and a blessing, the anointing of India. The BBC, along with a local publisher, has just produced an Indian version of their entertaining magazine. Its proud editor showed me the first issue. There was a chocolate cake on the cover. Few things could be as un-Indian, as anti-Indian as a chocolate cake, but the new India has exactly the same impulses to eat foreign food and wear imported clothes and listen to international pop music as everyone else. But one of the truths of travelling, and one of the traps that travel writers must strive to avoid, is to value the fragility and the pristine nature of other people's cultures above their own. No one's life is any more valuable than or intrinsically superior to anyone else's and we should stifle the snobbish wince when an Indian insists on a pizza.

Camellia took me out for dinner and said she had a surprise. We sat in a car for 40 minutes, and got out on a stretch of urban highway. I looked around for the delicious little street stall or doorway of some regional diner, and instead saw the dreadfully familiar yellow arches of a McDonald's. 'Really, Camellia. I understand the irony, the joke, but I didn't come all this way to eat a Big Mac. I wouldn't eat one five minutes from my own home.' She led me inside and gave me a lecture. 'People want to share in the things they see from abroad. They want what's new and Western.'

So how does a company that sells hamburgers work in India,

where if you killed a cow they'd burn Ronald McDonald in the street? Here there are vegetarian burgers, chicken wraps, paneer and a local version of Coca-Cola. People come because it's clean, fast and authentically Western. It's also cheap, very cheap. The best-seller is an aloo tikki burger, a patty made of potato and peas with a hot sauce in a bun and I must say it was pretty good, in the sense that it was a lot better than any Big Mac I've ever eaten in the West. It is wholly Indian in invention, an adaptation of a street food. India took the look and made the content its own. If there is one thing India can't abide it's blandness in anything, in clothes, in films or in food. They want everything to be vivid, spicy, and when you are here, it's difficult to resist.

February 2012

Bhutan

If you're flying to Bhutan, sit on the left. You overtake eight of the ten highest mountains in the world on the left-hand side, and that on its own is worth the steep price of the ticket. Everest shines against the pale breath of the sky, oddly familiar among all the other cool fangs, like spotting a celebrity in a queue. The stratospheric wind blows a plume of snow off its peak, making an Elvis quiff.

Bhutan's international runway is said to be one of the most testing in the world. It can only be attempted in daylight. The mountains reach up to grab the wings, and an old Bhutanese woman sitting beside me presses her hands together and intones a bubbling, repetitive prayer. She has undone her seatbelt. There is something very Buddhist about that; trusting the oneness of everything, not the illusion of safety.

The first sight of Bhutan makes you gasp. This is the world's attic; there just isn't enough stuff to breathe. It's slimmers' air, with half the lung-fattening oxygen removed. It takes your breath away and gives it to a passing yak. Breathing is a constant concern. It's a surprise, after the unconcern of automatic, in-and-out, airy life at sea level. Now you've suddenly got manual lungs and have to lie down every so often to give yourself the kiss of life. The land runs ahead of you in a series of rugged vistas, mountains that operatically echo each other for hundreds of hyper-real miles. Tintinnabulating rivers tumble past stupas, monasteries and forts that all have a distinctive architectural vernacular: part half-timbered, Surrey-Jacobethan, part Chinese cinema. It's grand and funny, Shangri-la-bizarre. All the buildings, from barns to palaces, are tattooed with delicate images, mostly of huge, excited, ejaculatory penises with fecund, hairy bollocks. Under the lea of a mountain, hidden by pine trees, comes the sound of sing-song chanting. A group of men stand in a cluster beside a bank of earth, between an alley of coloured flags. They are wearing the ubiquitous national dress, the *goh*: an elegantly striped and lined tunic, tied with a belt, that comes to just below the knee; it looks deceptively simple, like a dressing gown. In fact, it's an infuriating piece of personal origami with a broad box pleat at the back and neat white cuffs, and you need three hands to get dressed. The look is finished off with knee socks and brogues, or trainers.

Each man holds a 6-foot bow made of two pieces of bamboo attached to a wooden handle. They cluster round a brightly painted wooden target the size of a small dog's tombstone. The bull's-eye is round like a grapefruit. The men chat and laugh and fiddle with their bows, they appear to be waiting for something. An assassin's arrow arcs out of the blue, hisses past, missing the target by a foot, and the men by inches. They look up with a mocking, surprised shout and wave their hands in gestures of hopelessness, howling and cawing practised insults. Some 150 yards away, over a narrow gully, another, similar group of men looks back. One has already nocked an arrow. He leans to one side, judges the distance, feels the breeze and lets fly. The bamboo arrow, fletched with pheasant feathers and bound with thread that marks its owner and is a ward against evil spirits, is tipped with a lethal, iron bodkin. It leaps from the arm and sings into the air, marking a shallow parabola. The men clustered around the target dance insouciantly, daring it with their bravado. The missile quivers, lithe and deadly. A man swivels out of the way at the last moment, and it thuds into the target. There's a high, ululating call and three men with bows step forward and do a victory dance, palms to heaven, stepping high, chanting.

Now the archers queue from this end. A wizened old man steps forward. Without apparent concern, he trusts his arrow to the blue. Then, apparently changing his mind, runs after it, willing it on, miming directions, then stamps his feet and turns away as the distant mockery drifts over like the tide. Then another bowman steps up to the dusty mark. Archery is Bhutan's national sport. Every weekend, all over the country, there are competitions like this between villages, between clubs and businesses and civil servants. The competitions begin very early in the morning and go on till sunset. The night before, the bows will have been blessed by monks, and the order of the team chosen by an astrologer who organises and propitiates the spirits and planets to their best advantage. Archery is half lethal golf with the boys and half missionary outreach. The bow is a common symbol in the Buddhist iconography of Bhutan. Gods and spirits hold bows, everything in this country has a spiritual dimension, a duality of meaning and function. Women traditionally don't take part in these contests, but they come with the children and cook lunch, chopping onions, tomatoes and chillies, boiling great pots of rice. They also perform as cheerleaders. In their long dresses, they stand in chorus lines next to the archers, and put them off with mocking chants and suggestive songs. Yet somewhere out of sight women have taken up the bow: a team of girls competing for a place at the Olympics. The blokes sit on the ground and eat with their fingers, and drink the thickly fermented local Red Panda beer, and a lethal local whisky, from plastic bottles. They assure me that they all shoot much straighter a little drunk. Except that none of them is a little drunk: they're all grandiloquently plastered, though still uncannily accurate. The women sit in the shade and laugh at the men. The children make toy bows and grass arrows; the men shout and dance their victory jigs, and catch a nap. When they hit a target, they take a bright streamer to tuck into their belts. I never could tell who was on which team, because although they're competitive, and they're armed, the game is without any apparent rancour or animosity. Being for your team doesn't necessarily mean being against anyone else's.

Bhutan is a kingdom of 700,000 repeating souls at the eastern end of the Himalayas. It is a democratic theocracy. It has a red-and-yellow, diagonally bisected flag with a dragon on it, like a fiercer Wales. The colours represent the shared responsibility of Church and State; the illusory, covetable world, and the true, invisible world of empty perfection. Crucially, covetable Bhutan sits like an enigmatic smile between the Bric giants, China and India. They call Paro the rice bowl of Bhutan: a swatch of neat corduroy patches stitched up a long, wide valley, each little stepped allotment separated from its neighbour by a grassy ha-ha, and decorated with precious piles of cow dung, like moles' tenements. Flags flutter from bamboo poles, there are forests of flags. Along rivers, up mountains, wherever there might be animist spirits or local deities to be placated, or the dead to be remembered, the flags will ripple like the reincarnation of venerable laundry. This country is a convention of bunting, every rag a prayer. The wind tugs and frets them until they shred, and sends the incantations away on the gusts, whispers and whinnies of the wind as pleas to heaven. Bhutan has only recently stepped gingerly onto the motorway of international life. It kept Indian slaves until the 1950s, joining the United Nations in 1971, and still only has three resident embassies. Strategically this tiny country is vital to its neighbour in the south as a buffer with China. The Indians pay a lot to keep Bhutan onside. The nation began to emerge in the seventh century, when monks looking for solitude built monasteries here. It is now a member of that elite club of the eternally free: along with Nepal, Liberia, Turkey and Sweden, Bhutan has never been successfully invaded or colonised by anyone else. It fought long and vicious wars against Tibet, and a brief, uneven scuffle with Britain, which it lost, but remained independent. This freedom has lent the Bhutanese a shy and polite self-confidence, a stubborn belief in the

Bhutanese way of being and a solid toughness. It's like Norway in a frock.

Bhutan was a closed country until 1975, when it decided to admit pale people into the airport of reincarnation. Today, it charges us a premium of $250 a day just to be short of breath, thereby keeping out anyone young enough to want enlightenment or to smoke the dope that is said to grow wild or to hike in the mountains. Instead they've turned the place into a sort of Saga adventure holiday for the rich and sedentary, the symbolic destination for fourth-time-round honeymooners. There is no expatriate community here worth mentioning. Only a mere handful of Westerners are given permission to live in Bhutan. One of them is Michael Rutland OBE, the Honorary Consul, a physics teacher who found his way out here decades ago after a chance meeting at an Oxford party. He became tutor to the present king's father, like *The King and I*, but without the singing. He is part Graham Greene, part Deborah Kerr. He is also the best and rarest type of Englishman abroad, a chap who's gone completely native, wearing a goh (which his man ties for him). But it only goes to highlight his marvellously old-fashioned, intelligent, inquisitive, amused and unflappable Blightyness. He is something of a fond legend in Bhutan, adopting a local son and travelling to see us with a servant and his bright grandson, who calls him 'big daddy'. We meet for dinner in a hotel. He walks in and abases himself before a passing reborn Buddhist sage, collapses into a chair and orders a large gin and tonic, explaining that the royal family, the Wangchuck dynasty, was introduced at the beginning of the twentieth century with the encouragement of the British, who always like the stability of royalty, to rationalise the state's complicated power structure. The present young king has just married in an elaborately beautiful service. Royal weddings are invariably deemed fairy tales, but this one was really like a bedtime story; sprinkled with magic, not just snobbery and attitude and etiquette. The new queen is easily the most beautiful princess in the world.

The fourth king, the one Michael taught, decreed that Bhutan should be a democracy. The people were rather against it but he persisted, so they asked him who they should vote for. He said it didn't work that way. The king went on to demand that there be a free press, so they asked him what he'd like them to write, and he pointed out that it didn't really work that way either, and Michael tells me it's taken a few years, but they are far less deferential than they used to be. After dinner he leans across the table and says: 'I think there may have been a misunderstanding. I am not the British Honorary Consul to Bhutan, I am the Bhutanese Honorary Consul to Britain.'

The king also brought in television, which everyone loved, and didn't have to be told what to watch. They liked Indian movies and Indian cricket. The constant worry for Bhutan is not that it will be raped by the stuff of the twenty-first century, but voluntarily impregnated by India's bright and cacophonous culture that happily overwhelms its subtler, more delicate neighbours. But Bhutan now makes its own TV, and the audience seems to prefer their more parochial dramas of legend and romance. Football is growing in popularity, challenging archery. Michael has arranged for us to meet the heir apparent, or the heir presumptive. Anyway, the new young king's younger brother, who is patron of the Olympic Committee and particularly concerned with the plight of his archers. We meet at the archery training ground in the capital. There is a low wooden hut that has dormitories for the potential team. Everyone is smiley and shy and on edge, tugging at sleeves and checking their box pleats the way I expect they are everywhere before a royal visit. The young prince arrives with a retinue of Falstaffs and door openers, and an official photographer. He is a strikingly handsome young man, just down from Oxford, where he says he had a marvellous time. There is gossip that says it was a really, really marvellous time. He exchanges bows and puts everyone at their ease with crustless small talk, and we are ushered, in a confusing order of precedence, into a room with a long table and chairs down each side. I sit in the middle on one side, the prince opposite me. Everyone else files in around us. It feels like the official delegations for a peace treaty. I ask starchy, 1950s BBC questions, and the prince returns beautifully folded and politely delivered answers of such perfumed blandness that they evaporate before reaching the memory. Everyone watches with broad, blank smiles, like a dull tennis match. He bards his speech with rather touching, arcane public-school slang, as if conjuring happy memories of punting on the Isis.

Outside, chilly lady archers, who look strangely Victorian in their long frocks, show us how it should be done, sending their arrows thudding into Western targets. Bhutan's only qualifier for the Olympics is a woman – 28-year-old Sherab Zam – and their most successful archer is the woman who is now training the team. Yet the great sexist irony is that they are excluded from any of their own national contests and aren't allowed to compete against men. All men present nod in admiration of the women, but our guide, a keen archer himself, tells me that a woman touching your bow would bring bad luck. He hangs a small red wooden penis off his to reinforce its fortuitous masculinity.

The Falstaffs in the prince's retinue explain that as Bhutanese competitors shoot twice as far as their modern Olympic rivals, at a target that is one-third the size, the scale of close-up archery, its childish ease, is too confusing for their men, who failed to qualify for London 2012. There is also the kit: modern American bows are expensive and, though lots of Bhutanese are taking it up, it's still very different. You can't stand provocatively in front of the targets, and these kids hoping to go to London don't have enough carbon arrows to practise with. They are all charming and gauche, completely lacking in any of the psychological bravado and jargon, or the extreme physical conditioning we associate with modern athletes. They don't boast and preen, they don't flex and project. Rather than looking like elite archery, these ugly plastic bows and the garish pop-art targets look like some coarse kids' version of the bamboo game. Bhutan struggles with replacing both the spiritual and practical problems of a bamboo life with a modern plastic one.

The king who forced in democracy also laid down a question which has the most fundamental consequences for all modern nations. He decreed that instead of measuring a country by its GDP, they should weigh themselves against gross national happiness. This was noticed briefly around the bourses and boardrooms of the First World and met with a patronising chuckle. At best, they said, it was a cute, hippie, tourist slogan, and most likely the result of not getting enough oxygen. But over the years it has turned out to be rather astute, and now Western think tanks and economists are beginning to take notice of these telling measures of the health of a nation that account many things above money.

The concept of happiness is not the fleeting feelgood of hitting the target or getting drunk with your mates, but a more Buddhist ideal of contentment. In the most recent survey, more than 7,000 Bhutanese were asked detailed questions on a range of issues, including their sense of community, the quality of their environment, education, food, health, occupation, expectations and culture. Out of this has come a psychological map. They found, for instance, that the happiest people live in the capital, but also the unhappiest; that the city had higher standards of living than the country, but the most vital communities were to be found in the fields. Men are happier than women, and to have a primary education or no education is likely to make you happier than to have a secondary education. And that the happiest people are the young and unmarried. Gross national happiness is specifically measured to combat a number of conditions: greed and avarice, the diminishing returns of materialism. The happiest professions were discovered to be monks and nuns. There are 14,000 monks in Bhutan; they are subsidised by the state, for the good of the state. Buddhism isn't prescriptive but is often censorious; it colours every aspect of life, but is never practical.

It gives everything an ethereal dimension.

Bhutan's national saint was an itinerant lama called Drukpa Kunley. He imparted something they call divine madness; he was constantly on a search for girls to ravish and beer to become stupefied on – a mystical cross between Russell Brand and St Paul. Most of his poetry is lengthy limerick and still not fit to be printed in a family newspaper. But the Bhutanese, who are by nature profoundly modest in dress and demeanour, adore him.

When I asked for his book of verses in a shop, the girls behind the till giggled and covered their faces with their hands. In his monastery you can get a blessing from a bright-red wooden penis. Drukpa Kunley is who they have to thank for all the enormous cocks on the walls, and the rite of passage that has Bhutanese boys going out 'night hunting' – that is, climbing stealthily into the beds of young girls to have sex without waking their parents. Everybody knows this goes on, everybody laughs about it. It is a sanctioned, adolescent naughtiness.

Sex isn't wrapped in shame or honour here. Monks are celibate, and abstinence is a high calling. But the monasteries are full of sex on the walls, and mystical carnal unions are at the heart of theology. The monasteries are of a profound beauty, the monks in deep-red robes blow horns and chime cymbals. There is a constant chanting and the smell of butter candles. On the altars are offerings of water, because water has no monetary value, and the rich man's gift is worth as much as the poor man's. But there are also packets of crisps and biscuits, because even monks like to snack. Everywhere is crowded with psychedelic revelation and metaphor. The walls vibrate with the intensity of stampeding hallucinations. Eyes bulge, mouths scream, hands grasp, animals pounce, bodies fall and rise.

In the glowing other world, there is an immensely complicated cast of ghosts and holy men, familiars and all their various incarnations. Their stories live in parallel with ours; statues of gods on plinths dance with manic faces, and under their huge skirts I notice a snake, which looks suspiciously like Kaa from *The Jungle Book*, wrapped around the deities' large, golden balls. Nothing is what it seems, everything is a riddle, many things are a joke, an allegory, a simile, clues to the incessantly spinning complexity of life that you have to escape. Among the constant clamour of images there is the still, small truth that goodness, charity, acceptance and stillness are the ladders past the snakes that lead to the spark of the divine that is within all of us, that, once found, will release us into the void.

There are prayer wheels everywhere; you spin them as you walk past. Thousands of prayers are cast thousands of times into the air. I came across a monastic shed that contained three huge drums turned by cogs and handles, tended and spun by an ancient crone, a sweating man and a running child. They were a factory of prayer, churning out countless millions of incantations for enlightenment. In the West this would be a perfect Escher-like allegory of pointlessness, a self-defeating occupation that creates nothing and consumes nothing but time and energy. But here in Bhutan it is as vital as a power station. I spun the wheel and offered a prayer for the singular archer, and that I might become the spiritual pizza: one with everything.

As sport becomes ever more about science, genetics, money and marketing, it is salutary to include those who still do it for the pleasure of the game. The Olympics are supposed to be our community, all of us. The world's sports day. Nobody should be excluded, and whatever the sponsors and the advertisers pump out, it's not about excellence and gold, it's about being here, and everyone else being here, too. The bamboo archery, with handmade, God-blessed kit, is closer to the ancient Greek ideal of sport that is the prowess and celebration of community life: hunting, fighting, balance, elegance and the stamina of manual work.

Bhutan's flag and its place in the fellowship of sovereign states will be carried by a woman archer who represents her nation when, back home, she couldn't represent her village. The Bhutanese archers may not have a prayer in the high-tech world, but, as they would be the first to point out, that's really not the point. In truth, it's the rest of us who don't have anything like enough prayers.

May 2012

Canal du Midi

Of all of Jeremy Clarkson's ruddy, intransigently stubborn, pouty, Yorkshire-contrarian beliefs, hunches and prejudices, perhaps the most obtuse and unbelievably counter-intuitive is his deep, soulful love for the French.

You would lay good money on the fact that Jeremy would be an arch frog-botherer, that he'd have a Falstaffian loathing for the cringing, beret-wearing, philosophy-spouting, bike-pedalling, arrogant French. He'd be mocking their Napoleon complexes and flicking Agincourt V-signs from the Eurostar. But *non, mon brave*. He admires the French above all of God's creation. He says he likes their attitude, their style of life, their priorities, their dress sense, their undress sense, their flirtatious insouciance, the way they smell, the way they eat small birds under napkins, and the way they drink their wine. But mostly what he adores about the French is that they have never heard of Jeremy Clarkson. Jeremy's love of the French is unrequited. And that's the way he likes it. He can wander around without people stopping him to share a photo, or ask why he doesn't like Peugeots, or just to shout: *'Mon dieu, mon dieu, zut alors, c'est mo-torbouche!'*

He is explaining all this to me in the garden of a restaurant in Carcassonne, while we're having our photograph taken. 'Look around you and sigh,' he says expansively, waving his glass at the fig trees, the battlements and the remains of the cassoulet. A passing

Frenchman pauses to watch and asks if this is someone famous. He looks again and suddenly recognises the big fella. *'Mais bien sûr! Eet ees Tom Jones.'*

I, on the other hand, take a more orthodox view of the French. Like you, I think they are ridiculous, self-absorbed, cultural prigs who are breathtakingly selfish and dismissive, and suffer an inferiority complex that they cover up with bombast, boasting, Olympic sulking and baroque mendacity. In France, telling the truth is the sign of a boorish lack of intelligence and imagination.

So, here we are in the Midi. Jeremy – or Tom, as I shall now always know him – has come to show me why I should love them, while I trust that a weekend will convince him they are as adorable as their pop music. Carcassonne is a good place to start. Jeremy points to its ancient beauty; the old roses draped across pale stone, the gravel, that particular hoity *élan* with which the French move through the world, the over-coiffed ladies with too many rings on their lardy fingers, the young lovers with their wandering hands. The sky is pale blue, there are sparrows, and it's beguiling. But it's French, so not what it appears.

There is, as they say, beneath the paint and the perfume, the scent of *merde*. This crenellated hill town where they shot the film *Robin Hood* is a lie. It's a modern tourist's recreation. The French destroyed the original themselves. This bit of the country was host to one of the worst pogroms in Europe – one of the few times a power has managed to exterminate an entire religion. The Cathars were a Christian sect notable for their pacifism and abstinence. French Catholics saw this as an unforgivable heresy, and set about killing all of them. The cardinal in charge of the cleansing was asked how the besieging soldiers should tell the difference between a heretic and a Catholic. He replied: 'Kill them all. God will know his own.' The French are surprisingly bad at history, although it's perhaps not so surprising when you consider how often they come second in it. Unable to beat anyone else in Europe, the French regularly turn round to beat each other. The Cathars, the Huguenots, the Terror, Vichy, Algeria. There is a torture museum in Carcassonne, a lot of tableaux of nylon-wigged shop dummies being eviscerated, hanged, stretched and intimately ravaged, in a display that manages to be tackily sadistic and embarrassingly erotic. We are to take a boat down the Canal du Midi. Tom says he's wanted to do this all his life. I will, he says, 'be rendered speechless by the unfolding diorama of bosky French perfection'. Or words to that effect. We tip up at a hot marina, full of white plastic pleasure boats that look like bathroom fittings on steroids. We are shown the ropes by a friendly and efficient Cornishman, who sailed through here and decided to stay. Tom tells him to ignore me, because I won't understand anything, and then says he doesn't need to be told anything because he already understands everything, but is there a TV for the grand prix? There is.

We cast off, or slip anchor, or whatever the nautical term for 'mirror, indicate, move' is. The boat is really an idiot-proof wet dodgem with two cabins, dodgy plumbing and lots of rope. We fill the fridge with rosé and salami and olives, and Tom Pugwash gets in the captain's chair with a pint of wine, 40 tabs, a plate of sausage, and open water ahead of him. I must say, I've never seen him so happy. I suggest he puts on suncream, because his bald patch is turning the colour of a Zouave's trousers. 'Do I look like a homosexual?' he shouts gaily. No, not even a Frenchman could mistake Clarkson for a practitioner of *le vice anglais*.

The boat is very slow. But too soon, we approach a series of locks and a happily lethargic Pugwash turns into Captain Bligh, bellowing at me to do things with ropes and bollards while explaining the principles of lockishness. I'm not comfortable doing *matelot* stuff, I come over all Nelson when confronted with knots. But Tom howls and gesticulates, the boat jostles and butts the groyne. Locks may be triumphs of Archimedean engineering, but they're a terrible bore. Why can't there be a ramp, or a lift? The French lock-keepers all have jobs for life, and behave like it. They also have pleasant cottages and little businesses on the side, selling gardening gloves to soft-handed English people with third-degree rope burns. They take an hour and a half for lunch every day, from 12.30. It would be entirely possible to come on holiday to the Canal du Midi and spend all of it bobbing in a queue waiting for a Frenchman to finish his baguette and tup his neighbour's wife.

We stop off for lunch in tastefully picturesque little towns. French public holidays are arriving like locks at this time of year, and your froggy workman takes what they call 'the bridge' (*le pont*); that is, they make an extra holiday out of the loose days between holidays. So pretty much the only people who are open for business are English. And jolly good they are at it too; the best food we ate here was made by a couple from the Midlands. The excellence of French bourgeois cooking is now as rare as Cathars.

One evening we sat outside a café in a typically French square, where a French pop group was tuning up. At the other tables, families drank wine and ate a late dinner of steak and *frites*. 'Look at this, just look at this,' says Tom. 'You can't pretend you don't want to live here for ever and ever.' We'd already been beaten to it. The locals all turned out to be from Rotherham, and waved at Jeremy and took pictures and asked what he thought of Peugeots. Apparently, most of the town is now owned by expats, happy to exploit the locals' sophisticated reluctance to work. The band struck up 'Smoke on the Water'. Tom beamed and played air guitar.

There is no denying the canal is beautiful. Now bereft of practical purpose, it has settled into being a metaphor, a parable. Pootling down it past the arching beams of the plane trees is possibly the most relaxing thing I've ever done. There is something about the glossy water, the slow perambulation, the rhythm of the passing trees, the birds singing, the dappling, piebald light. You could feel the care fall away, your shoulders slump, the brain cease to race. It is, I expect, what dying's like. When you hear the faint voices calling, 'Go towards the light, granddad, don't fight it,' I expect this is what you'll see. I hope death comes to us like floating down the Canal du Midi. Through the tree trunks you could see the fields, running to the hills in the distance. They are thistle-bound and choked with weed. It looks so peaceful because it's moribund, comatose. France, with its huge state, its insincere smile, its polished manners, is rotting like a pear from the inside out.

There is one more thing we have to do. Jeremy wants to play a game of pétanque. We find a gravel pitch and he says: 'Now, I've got to tell you, I'm very good at this.' Jeremy is very, very competitive. Over the years, he and I have played golf in Cheshire, raced Ski-Doos in Iceland, jet skis in Barbados, fired Kalashnikovs in Basra and raced battle tanks in Baghdad. I've won every time. Except for golf, which was abandoned due to helpless laughter. Boules was Jeremy's game, on his adopted home pitch, and despite appalling gamesmanship and outright fouling, it was Agincourt and Waterloo all over again. Tom Jones, *nul points*.

July 2012

The Mekong

Always the same, always different, always passing, always present. Rivers are the original riddle. The first limpid byways of our species, the means of trade and conquest, of inquisitiveness and mystery. You might fancifully speculate that rivers were the first inspiration for narrative. They are explicitly unrolling stories. They have beginnings, middles and ends. For a travel writer there is nothing finer than a river. They write themselves. I would like the final quarter of my peripatetic life to float down as many of the world's great rivers as possible, watching the narrative drift past.

The Mekong is one of the great rivers. It starts at the terminus in the Himalayas, a snowball's throw from the Yangtze and the Ganges. They are all formed by the Buddhist meetings of the great ice blanket at the top of the world. I did a small section from Phnom Penh in Cambodia to Ho Chi Minh in Vietnam. By the time it's got here, the river is an expansive, abundant, wide-girthed, postprandial anecdotage. It is too broad for bridges. It rolls thickly out of the city and through the flat scrub and light industry.

I notice three principal things about Cambodia on the way down: first, there are enough English public schoolboys drunk in the street at 11 o'clock in the morning to constitute a cruel and unusual torture. There are no birds and there are no old people. Forty years ago the Khmer Rouge disposed of half the population. They consequently have half the number of elderly you'd expect. The other half nearly starved in the fields and ate all the birds. The surviving birds, unlike the surviving Cambodians, had a choice and flew away, and apparently don't consider it safe to return yet.

The scale and consequence of this most hellishly awful social experiment of the last century is everywhere in absence and silence. If everyone has lost family and everybody over 50 has a horror story, and everybody's history is a logjam of corpses, then it doesn't minimise the mourning but it makes it unexceptional. The killing fields and the torture prisons were visited by tourists. We are the ones for whom the tragedy is a catharsis, not the Cambodians.

The river runs on blameless, bearing everything, washing everything. Phnom Penh is an unassumingly charming city with an old, worn beauty. There are streets of noisy bars surrounded by dinky dark alleys with sleeping rickshaw drivers. On down the river we stop at a sandbar to swim and I pick up bones, brown and hardened. They are crocodilian – the spine, with its distinctive dimple, from huge crocodiles that haven't lived on this stretch of the river for generations. It is one of the most biologically diverse waterways in the world, with hundreds of species of fish, amphibians and reptiles. There is the Irrawaddy dolphin and the giant catfish that buries itself in mud and can swallow children whole. The riverside markets are full of spectacular, odd fish and eels and bundles of live frogs tied together like Valentine's bouquets for hopeful princesses.

When you cross the border into Vietnam everything changes. For a start there are birds – more birds than you can shake a wok at. The river is full of people. Vietnam is full of people – punting, rowing, fishing, selling, sleeping, washing, splashing. There are floating markets and the banks are bosky with tenements of tin huts precariously balanced on copses of sticks. The edges of the river are floating fields of water hyacinth and morning glory. There are gaggles of gossiping white ducks, floating houses that have fish farms in their basements, ancient couples chance their arms with gossamer nets flung from canoes skinny as wooden knives. On the shore cantilevered arms hold purse nets that are dunked and retrieved for dinner.

The river here bubbles with multiple life. The farms attract insects and amphibians which feed the birds and the fish, which in turn add nutrients for the plants. The river is a virtuous organic circle of mutual consumption. On the water's edge there are neat trays of freshly skinned rice rats ready for the fire. Barges gently chunter past, piled high with rice husks that'll be used for fuel in the kilns which make brick from the river mud. Palms will be woven into fish baskets and hats. Everyone waves. It's like a communist version of the *National Geographic*.

Vietnam is on a mission. It has been on a lot of missions, but since Clinton finally lifted America's embargo, Vietnam has grown its economy 10 per cent a year. It's grown its population, it's literate, it's ambitious and it has an appetite.

I was last in Saigon, or Ho Chi Minh, 12 years ago. It ran on pedal power. Now every pushbike is a motorcycle. No longer does the two-wheel traffic eddy round pedestrians like a clever magic trick. The city has grown another 50 floors with big Chinese skyscrapers and has that pan-Asian look of cash-and-grab. This too is a city that is burying the past under the present as fast as it can. The war museum exhibits look rusty and worn-out. Again, only gap-year tourists take the time to visit the old stories of the 1960s. And I learn, with some astonishment, that General Giap is still alive. He is now 101 – the most successful general of the twentieth century, which was surely the golden age for generals. He fought the Japanese successfully, then the French, winning the spectacular Battle of Dien Bien Phu that the French had set up because they were so certain that a rag-tag army of rice farmers could never beat the Foreign Legion. But they were soundly defeated and left Vietnam to the Americans the next day. General Giap went on to defeat them in turn and he's still going, having outlived every other general he ever fought.

I met a man who distributes film in Vietnam. I asked how they liked all those American war films about them. He smiled. 'No one watches them. We've been at war for a thousand years; no one wants to remember that stuff. We only want to be entertained and make money.' No one does capitalism like really committed and driven communists with an itch for a bigger watch. So what is the most popular movie here? 'Well,' he said, 'we really like *Kung Fu Panda*.'

And the river rolls on to the sea.

June 2013

Humberside

I'm Adrian, I'm an alcoholic. I haven't drunk alcohol since I was 30 – 28 years ago. Drunks court trouble: social, financial, physical, emotional and magistrate.

I was arrested just the once. I was stopped lots of times, shouted at, moved on, warned, searched on sus, pockets checked – 'I'm not going to find anything sharp in here, am I, sonny?' 'Only my wit, constable.' I was nicked for being drunk in public, which was bad luck because I hadn't been sober in public for a decade. I'd called the police, that's how drunk I was; or rather, I told the barman to call them on my behalf – either that or unlock the door – so I was arrested for being drunk. Actually, I think I was really arrested for calling a policeman 'darling'. They did the bar for having drinks on the table after hours and me for drinking too much of it.

The constable walked me down Earl's Court Road to the police station. I asked if he was going to handcuff me. 'No. You're not a runner.' I was pushed into a cell that was already full. We were an Ealing Comedy cast of drunks: a tramp, a businessman who'd passed out on the Tube, a Scotsman off the oil rig who'd been on a three-day bender, and a hippie who said he was actually stoned, but couldn't tell the police that.

I lay on the floor with my coat as a pillow. The light stayed on all night. In the morning, a piece of toast was thrown at my head. The sergeant said I could have a drink from the standpipe. We were taken to the Magistrates' Court, where we waited in a small Victorian cell for them to deal with the night's prostitutes. Even moral turpitude has manners: ladies first. As I waited to go into the dock, the policeman who'd arrested me whispered: 'Say you're sorry. They like that.' So I said I was sorry and unused to strong drink, and was fined £15. We were all stamped with justice in half an hour.

I was impressed at how the magistrate arranged the fine to suit our circumstances: the businessman got the most, the Scotsman, then me, then the stoned lad got a tenner and the tramp wasn't fined but held for a medical check-up. It was the class system at work, when any Englishman can glance at his countrymen and know what they should be fined.

We were tipped out into the street at opening time and, naturally, made for the nearest pub for a breakfast pint. At the other end of the bar were the policemen who'd arrested us. There was a curt raising of glasses and a nod. Now when I fill in forms that inquire about criminal records, I say 'yes'. It was a very Anglo-Saxon experience: none of us complained that it was unfair or a waste of time; it was simply part of the warp and weft of our island life. A night in the cells seemed a sort of birthright, part musical joke, part Rotary Club morality. We were, in that peculiarly circular English expression, no better than we should be. I only tell you this to show I am not a disinterested party in this story of drunk England.

Drink is a problem, it is our problem, the lubrication of our national character, and it appears to be getting worse. The after-dark centres of market towns and cities are given over to avid drunkenness, a zombie invasion, and drink is taking a greater toll on our health – particularly that of the young and, of them, particularly women. Liver damage is rising exponentially among the under-thirties, the price of alcohol has never been lower, and the amount of time you have to work to afford a bottle of vodka is shorter than it's ever been. Sober voices are calling for something to be done, among them the Association of Chief Police Officers and the prime minister, who say we need a return to drunk tanks – not that any-one can remember what a drunk tank is. So, I spend a night out in the north-east to see what they are talking about.

Matthew Grove, the Commissioner for Humberside Police, is an-other of these voices. On his patch, Grimsby: not as nice as it sounds. From London it takes longer to get there than to fly to Moscow. Somewhere north of Doncaster, everything turns to black and white and fades to mono. Grimsby is on the road to nowhere. If you have ever wondered who lost the cod wars with Iceland, the answer is Grimsby. It didn't just lose, it was routed. This was once the liveliest, gutsiest fishing port in Europe. Now it does a bit of processing when the Icelanders pass on stuff they're too busy to handle. It suffers all the dull litany of deprivation: high youth unemployment, lack of investment, worn-out infrastructure, underachievement, bad edu-cation, and is one of the least diverse and pasty white pockets of England. There is plenty of grubby petty crime and domestic abuse, but apart from that it's lovely, as is Cleethorpes next door.

Cleethorpes: that isn't as nice as it sounds, either. A chilly holiday resort – the tourists have all gone the same way as the fish. Grove meets me off the train with his press secretary. They're firm-handshake men. Famously, Grove defeated John Prescott on his home ground to get the Commissioner job. He is a man I expect would describe himself as direct, no-nonsense, a people person. He thinks he's a leader of men, a natural doer. Every sentence comes with an implied exclamation and a smiley face. He is the sort of man perennially drawn to local politics, a civic bull in search of municipal china shops.

He drives us through the dark and silent streets of Cleethorpes early in the evening. They're horror-film empty, nothing stirs in hunched and grubby semi-detached streets that emanate a forbid-ding depression. Grove talks in capital letters about the need to claim back the night, how decent people are scared to go out after dark. He resents the squalor, mess, rudeness and implicit violence of the drinking culture. It's an insult to a decent community! Far too much police time and effort are being put into cleaning up after people who can't hold their drink. So he's posited the idea of a drunk tank, which sounds solid and exclamatory.

What actually is a drunk tank? The details are still sketchy: a place, perhaps a converted container, where the inebriated, the hopeless, could be taken to sober up, possibly copulate and then be fined, as with a traffic offence, without taking up magistrates' time or causing trouble. Who would do the locking-up, I ask. G4S can't arrest people; the police would still have to do the detaining, and the drunks have got to be offered some sort of medical help.

'Well, all that can be worked out,' he says with the airy dismissiveness of the big blue-sky thinker. 'It's just a suggestion. But something must be done!' We get to the police station, a forbidding compound surrounded by a tall fence and electric gates and arc lights and clusters of CCTV. There's no blue light or obvious public entrance. 'If I want to report my cat's missing, where do I go?' I ask. 'Oh, I think there is a public entrance somewhere, but it's probably not open now. This isn't a very nice area, you know.' So they had to lock up the cops in case they get robbed? Inside I'm shown a call centre, which is not as exciting as it sounds, and have a briefing with the Police and Associated Forces Outreach Organising Public Safety Confederation, or something or other, that comprises real cops, auxiliary hobby cops, the fire brigade, the drug squad (but they've lost their dog) and the council licensing authority.

We're briefed by a lady who addresses us all as 'people' and apparently learnt her public-speaking skills from watching American police dramas. Everyone looks bored and shifty. A girl from the council winks at me, not because she wants to check my basement access, but because she wants me to know that this is being concocted for my benefit. The Commissioner looks pleased and motivated, the police watch him with weary stone faces – the way circus animals watch the man holding a chair. So we walk out into the chilly sodium night. A policeman looks up and says: 'Full moon. It's going to be a rough night. It's always worse when it's a full moon, coppers know that. And the last Friday of the month: payday. That's bad. And heat: you don't want it to be too hot.' Then it begins to drizzle. 'Ah, that's better. Rain, it's like having an extra police-man on the beat, is rain. The copper's friend.' I had no idea policing was so like gardening: rain at night, copper's delight; full moon in sight, Old Bill's blight.

Cleethorpes' strip of bacchanalian sin is a sorry and insipid little thing. It's not Las Vegas, it's not even lost property: a meagre high street that is, like most high streets in provincial towns, gasping for trade. The shops are given over for charity and hairdressing. (Why are there so many hairdressers in the world?) There are payday-loan shops and dozens of fast-food caffs, pubs and cavernous clubs. At 10 o'clock the streets are busy with men who have plainly been drinking since knocking off work. It doesn't kick off until about 12. The young stay at home, preloading on cheap supermarket beer and own-brand vodka, telling stories, watching telly, Facebooking, texting, orchestrating the night. They turn up lively, with the edges sanded off.

We're joined by Martin Vickers MP, a local man and a Tory. I ask what he thinks of drunk tanks. 'It's an interesting idea,' he says, in the way politicians do when people suggest funding research into extraterrestrial rectal probes. We stand outside a club, looking like a Victorian Methodist fact-finding tour. A policeman with a lot of braid asks if we'd like a uniformed escort. We all say 'No', emphat-ically and too quickly. The youth begin to fill the high street: loud, bouncy and effortfully up for it, or for something. The girls are in tiny frocks with plunging cleavages and gaping backs, chubby car-mine toes squashed into perpendicular platforms. The shoes are enormous, vertiginous, plinths of self-proclamation. Tattoos dodge down spines, across builders' buttocks, and slide off cleavages. The girls tug at themselves, pulling down hems, cantilevering bras.

They're loud and confident and brilliantly vital. The MP regards them askance, not in shock or surprise, but with a sort of paternal concern. They frighten me.

The boys have all made an inverse effort: they wear jeans, T-shirts and trainers, the uniform of active insouciance. Only the carefully gelled hair gives away some personal insecurity. Everyone is pissed, stoned or both. I've been led to expect a Hogarthian melee of violence and vomit: girls squatting in gutters, lads jumping on heads, comatose sex against wheelie bins, screaming rows, hair-pulling, bottling, blood and puke. Actually, it's all rather good-natured. Every bar and club has three or four bouncers: tough, calm ex-servicemen, mostly, all licensed, all wearing badges of office, implacable as they go through the dull ticket collection of checking fake IDs.

A boy hasn't got his. He feebly exhorts, wheedles, then begs. It would be easier for a camel to get through the eye of a needle. He nods in surrender and trudges away. His mates call blessings after him. Head down, he is the saddest kid in town. One of the few obviously foreign men, in a suit, comes up and asks who I am. I tell him I'm a journalist.

'Oh, that explains it. This is my club,' he says as girls say hello and boys pat his shoulder. He is clearly the man to know. 'I wondered why the extra police were out. It's not normally like this. I wish you were here every week. My staff have to take care of the street, look after the incapable ones, break up squabbles. It shouldn't be their job. You write that.'

'How's business?' I ask.

'OK, up and down. It's quiet tonight. My margins are down to the bone. We're being killed by supermarket booze.'

His drinks are a couple of quid a shot for some childish-looking coloured cocktail or £6 for a bucket and half a dozen straws. Inside the music is thuddy and ear-splitting, primary-coloured lights streak and syncopate. There's not much sophistication or glamour here. It's a functional space for the kids to make their own, like a school dance. They show off their bedroom-mirror moves in little votive coveys, as if imploring a good harvest, or a boyfriend, or an end to world hunger.

Anthems bang out of the speakers and suddenly the whole room is miming the same words, with exaggerated operatic movements. Confessing love to each other histrionically, couples fall onto each other's faces with sweaty, open-mouthed snogs. They touch all the time, like bees communicating simple pheromone truths: I'm here, you're here, we've known each other all our lives, we grew up here, we belong here, this is our Saturday night.

As the night tips over into the next day, the dancing becomes more incoherent, the snogs reduced to general face-licking. Outside the police arrest a drug dealer, a sorry-looking boy who's staring down a whole new life path. There is a fight between two girls and a chorus of supporters. It's broken up by bouncers, who hug the combatants like amorous bears, while the mascara-striped faces screech invective and vicious promises. Kids mill in the streets, smoking and telling stories of the evening: who with whom? Where? Who knew? Who's going to tell? Who cares? It's the elaborate narrative web of belonging and community that weaves the tapestry of your life from nappy to shroud. Most people are now really, really drunk: glassy-eyed, staggering, lamp-post-butting, hedge-vomiting drunk. The kebab, pizza and chicken shops are crammed with children shovelling glistening, greasy gobbets of meat and bread into their mouths. Chewing and laughing and shouting and singing and smoking, like a great choir of the orally juggling.

A girl comes up and hugs me because she says I look sad. I do look sad. Then an excited lad points and shouts: 'A scientist. Look! A scientist. Are you a scientist? Are you Doctor Who?'

The last nightclub on the strip is by the sea. It has a licence until 5 a.m. The manager worries. Nobody's in good shape now. We, three old men, stand and watch. I feel awkward, uncomfortable, I radiate a parsimonious sobriety. Grove asks rhetorically: 'Where's the sense of shame in society? No one feels guilt or responsibility. When we were young, if we were caught like that' – he points – 'we'd be ashamed. Your dad would make you ashamed. I want to bring back the sense of shame in our communities.'

We pack up and go back to the police station. The desk is quiet, the cells hold the drug dealer and another sorry boy who's been brought in for a domestic. He thumped his girlfriend. He doesn't look ashamed, he looks stoned and resigned and unsurprised.

At five in the morning, the emergency ward at the hospital is calm and efficient. There's only one person in the waiting room and the doctor says it's been a relatively normal night. Perhaps a third of the cubicles are occupied by drink-related injuries. 'We don't distinguish between causes,' he says. 'The only thing with drunks is, if they're passed out they have to be supervised. They can die. It's rare, but you lose the swallowing reflex and can inhale vomit, so they are put near the nurses' station. We stick a drip in them to rehydrate them, and they wake up without a hangover.' He smiles. 'All part of the service.' You couldn't do that in a drunk tank.

As the Commissioner drives me back to the train station in the dawn, he asks why we can't drink like the Continentals: a glass of wine with some tapas in a café, all ages together; a glass of beer, an aperitif, then the *passeggiata*, dressing up smartly. Why can't we change the culture? I look at him and keep my mouth shut. At the station a fox trots down the line, a drunk is sprawled over a bench. 'Why don't we drink like the Greeks or the Italians?'

Really? Because we have a choice, that's why. Because we're from the north, from the cold, from the drizzle, from the place where the moon drives us nuts. Who would want to drink like an Italian granny? Sip wine with a raised pinky, chew a carrot, when you could be out there with all your mates, people you fancy, people you don't, people you shag, people you want to. You can go mad, get totally muntered. You can let go. Why have a polite chat when you can have a legend? When you can weave a myth that will last you all week, that will stay with you for ever? Why would you want to ponce about in the grottoes of Dionysus when you can get trollied in the mead halls of Valhalla? This is who we are, this is what we do – or what I did.

I don't miss drink, ever. Being an alcoholic is not the same as being drunk. But I look at these kids in this thin, worn-out, under-privileged, unlovable corner of England and I think: how brilliant that they can still get out and manufacture this much enthusiasm, fun and mad entertainment, this much togetherness and commu-nity and hope out of so little, such meagre education, so few jobs and prospects. The drink, drugs and music are not just their culture, they're their achievement. I mention to the Commissioner that if he wanted to stop this carnage every weekend, all he would need to do was pull the licences and make the pubs and clubs close at 11 p.m., like when we were teenagers. 'Ah, well, yes, of course, but it isn't quite that simple,' he says. 'Why not?'

Well, I'll tell you why not. Because it's the kids' nights out that are keeping this town above water, solvent. Grimsby and Cleethorpes are living off the money the kids scrounge, earn, get given: the taxis, the fast-food joints, the watching police and the tooth-sucking, finger-wagging, slut-shaming Commissioner are all serviced and paid for by these inventive, funny children. If you want to shame someone, try pointing in the mirror. You should buy them all a drink, put up a statue to the inebriated kid, Cleethorpes' biggest benefactor.

December 2013

New York

———

One of the great pleasures of having children is the ability to use them as time machines to go back and make a traveller's oxymoronic visit for the first time, again. I took my seven-year-old twins to New York for the first time (for them, not for me, obviously) and I was excited, more excited than they were. I love New York; I might have mentioned that before. I lived there at the end of the 1970s and was very happy. It was a happy moment in my life and I wanted a revival.

The children were underwhelmed by the first sight of Manhattan as you cross over from Queens. I thought they might've been tired after the flight, so the next day I made them do it again, going over the Brooklyn Bridge to Williamsburg.

'Look, Daddy, there's the green lady with the burning stick.'

'It's a torch.'

'No, Daddy, it's a burning stick.'

'Well, it's an old-fashioned torch.'

'No, it's an old-fashioned burning stick. And she's holding an iPad.'

Then back over the Williamsburg Bridge, which has one of the most spectacular panoramas in the world. It was a spectacular day, the flat blue sky, the air polished to an obsessive shine. The light in Manhattan in spring and autumn has a hyper-real clarity. It bounces off the water on each side of the city like a photographer's reflector.

The children regarded the skyline with a passing boredom, more interested in the ghastly, intrusive, snot-covered screen in the back of the cab playing a loop of Broadway show tunes. We took them to a Broadway show.

'This is Times Square,' I said. '*The* Times Square.'

'Where?' asked my son.

'Here, we're here.'

'I can't see it.'

'We're in it.'

'Where is it?' he asked, with a rising panic. 'There isn't any square here.'

'No, it's actually not a square; it's a street.'

'Why don't they call it Times Street?'

'Well, because it's Broadway.'

'Why don't they call it Times Broadway?'

'Because it's Times Square. Look, we're on 42nd Street!'

'It's the same as 41st.'

'Yes, but it's *the* 42nd Street.'

'Can we go back to the hotel?' asked his sister.

'Yes, the hotel, please, Daddy. Can we go back to the hotel?'

Why do children love hotels so much? The Lowell is a very nice hotel; it's one of my favourite hotels in the world, but mostly because it's in New York. I come to The Lowell because it's in New York. I wouldn't go to The Lowell if it was in Cleveland. My children would happily holiday in The Lowell if it was in Gdansk. Pushing the lift buttons was a high point that they could reminisce over for hours.

We went to Central Park Zoo, which I never liked much. There was a poster that had a picture of a polar bear and said sadly the polar bear had died. I remember that polar bear. It had all the symptoms of anxiety and depression: rocking, pacing, trying to hail cabs at five o'clock. It was a source of shame and embarrassment for ecologically sound New Yorkers and finally the city gave the thing antidepressants, so it had the blank, dry-mouth look of every other

Upper East Side lady in a fur coat.

'Oh, can we see it, Daddy?'

'It's dead.'

'Yes, but can we see it?'

'No, they don't keep the dead ones.'

'Where do they put them?'

'They feed them to the live ones.'

We walked across the park to the Natural History Museum with the dioramas of dead animals in the most beautifully painted sets. It is possibly my favourite museum exhibit in the world.

'Oh, look,' said my daughter. 'There's the man who came alive.'

'That's the statue of Teddy Roosevelt,' I said, 'the American president.'

'No, he's the man who comes alive in the museum with the dinosaur.'

'OK. Do you want to see a whale eating a giant squid?'

'Are they alive?'

'No, they're dead.'

'Oh, I only want to see a live whale eating a live squid,' said the boy.

'You're doing this on purpose now, aren't you? Being contrary. Every time something is alive you want it dead and whenever it's dead you want it revitalised.'

'Can we go back to the hotel, Daddy?'

As we drove out to the airport, I asked what was the best thing about New York. 'Breakfast,' they said in unison. 'Pancakes and bacon, muffins and doughnuts, and the TV in taxis.'

I realised that what I found frustrating showing the kids my New York was the realisation that they didn't see it. They couldn't see it because it's not there any more. I walk around the city I've loved for 40 years, I tread the old trails with a white stick; I still see and feel the things I saw and felt in my twenties.

I look up at the incredible skyline of hope and aspiration whose reach ever exceeds its grasp. That concrete and grass forest of fingers pointing onwards and upwards into the great blue dome, the statues in Central Park, steam from the sidewalks – they're all from a Gotham that really isn't here any more. I discount things that don't confirm my historic knowledge of this place, except for one, the new Freedom Tower, in place of the Twin Towers. It's a tooth designed by a committee. If they had asked me, I would have put in a gold one with a diamond like a jazz singer's smile, but instead they've replaced it with this frail, twisted thing from the Dubai school of skyline orthodontics.

We went from New York to the Caribbean, to Mustique, a strange island owned by a company which itself is owned by absentee holiday home-owners. It's odd and manicured, and labelled 'a plutocrats' utopia'. I keep telling myself it wouldn't seem so uncomfortable if it were a gated community in Florida or Spain and, despite my reservations, I have a really wonderful time because the children show me their beach. I'm buffeted by the sea until my skin is made entirely of pink turtle scrotum. I can't imagine spending 10 minutes on a beach without children, and I realise I've got this thing the wrong way round. I shouldn't be looking for my world through their eyes; I should be allowing my eyes to look into their world. Forget everything I wrote in this article.

June 2014

Scotland

The bridge at Coldstream is a braw and sonsy thing, spanning the swan-bobbing Tweed that slowly, elegantly and expensively patrols the border, where Englishmen pay Scotsmen to row them up and down, where they flagellate the water, stalking salmon they put back. It is from here that Robbie Burns crossed over so he could set foot in England. Then, looking back, became so homesick with awe and love that he threw off his hat and quoted himself: 'O Scotia, my dear, my native soil!'

The sun dapples the Scottish bank, which is wooded and bosky with daffodils and wild garlic and benches where you can sit and enjoy the schadenfreude of the view of England, which is cloudy and consists of a scrubby electricity substation and the road south. Bridges tend to go one way or the other, and this one goes from Scotland to England. It has carried away so much, so many Scots, so much hope and ingenuity, aspiration and muscle. Along with the first regiment of the English army, the Coldstream Guards, and the army of James IV that, just a couple of miles down the way, suffered the cataclysmically dearest of defeats in all of the many desperate fights between England and Scotland: at Flodden, where the flowers of the forest were cut down and are remembered in one of the most haunting bagpipe laments.

Someone said that Scotland doesn't have history, it just has a longer memory for current events. Before talking about whether this uneven union should be split, it's instructive to understand what forged it in the first place.

In the 1690s, the Darien scheme was Scotland's attempt to bypass its cap-in-hand dependence on trade through and with England, by forming its own colony at Darien, on the isthmus between the Atlantic and the Pacific in what is now Panama. It was to be called Caledonia. Scots individually and collectively invested a quarter of the nation's entire wealth in the project, which was an unmitigated disaster. Mismanaged, purloined and frittered by adventurers, romantics, crooks, murderers and the wholly inept – the usual quorum of a Scots lounge bar.

It was effectively thwarted by the English, who bullied and threatened European banks into withdrawing support, the East India Company who, fearing for its monopoly in trade, sued and King William who, having never bothered to visit his kingdom of Scotland, made sure that no neighbouring colonies offered help because he didn't want to upset the Spanish. Scotland was very effectively bankrupted and England – ever helpful – came up with a plan: amalgamation, rationalisation, a one-nation takeover. They got it through the Scottish parliament with bribery. The Duke of Hamilton, an implacable anti-unionist, dramatically changed sides for cash. Others had their Darien debt repaid and members of the Scottish parliament would sell their country for as little as a fiver. As Burns had it, Scotland was 'bought and sold for English gold/Such a parcel of rogues in a nation!'

The English, while offering gold with one hand, waved the cudgel with the other and passed the Alien Act, making any Scot not in the army or on business an illegal immigrant. London threatened tariffs on Scottish exports. So the vote was passed. As Daniel Defoe, an English spy, said, for every one Scot in favour of union, 99 were against. There had been hundreds of petitions agin it from every corner of the country, and not a single one in favour. There were riots in Edinburgh and Glasgow, martial law was imposed.

In the new parliament at Westminster, Scotland got 45 MPs out of 558 and 16 seats in the Lords out of 212. Individual Scots might find a voice, an advancement, and disproportionately, one at a time, they did, but the country would be drowned out. As the ancient Caledonian parliament voted itself out of existence, the Earl of Seaford, with a heavy heart, noted that it was the end of an auld sang. And at St Giles Cathedral, the national church of Scotland, where Knox had preached, the bells rang out. The tune was 'Why Should I Be So Sad on My Wedding Day'?

Not many Scots, and even fewer English, know this story, the inglorious nuptials of the Union. But you don't have to remember history to be affected by it. This act and all the bullying and per-fidy, venality, weakness and snobbery that went before it has made the relationship between the two countries what it is. The informed view of Big Ben seen from Ben Nevis was never a love match, nor the uniting of mutually benefiting equals. It's the English who roll their eyes at the raking-up of the past and say, 'Oh, get over it, move on. Stop being a victim,' which is what wife-beaters always say to their victims.

What is so surprising about crossing the Coldstream Bridge is that within 100 yards you know you are in another country. The dis-tinction between Scotland and England remains clear and marked as the Scottish lilt becomes a Northumbrian twang. You can move from Venice into Italy without ever noticing that these were once different nations, or travel through Germany's city states and prin-cipalities without any sense of crossing borders, though this is a country half the age of Great Britain.

Still, despite 400 years of patronage and propaganda, Scotland isn't the heathery extension of England. It remains stubbornly and grimly, often amusingly, a different place. Its humour, its character, its stories, its expectations, how it gets married and celebrates, how it gets buried and sees in the New Year, what it sings about and fights about, are all markedly, noticeably, fiercely different. Indeed, this quiet river divides two of the most distinctively separate nations in Europe.

Along the empty high street of Coldstream, most of the shopkeepers say they will be voting for the union. It's better for business. 'And anyway,' says an antique dealer, 'we're Borderers. This is neither Scotland nor England, it's reavers' country. We have more in common historically with Hexham and Alnwick than Glasgow or London.'

Travelling along the winding border, it is difficult to see that anything even a little bit important might be in the offing. Some Scots have pointed out that this is an independence struggle in which no one has been killed. Perhaps it would be more to the point to say that no one has thought it important enough to die for. It is also one in which no one has bothered to pick up a spray can. There is no independence graffiti, no posters of born-again defiance. The occasional saltire flutters for the benefit of the tourists.

Berwick, where the river meets the sea, is a small, pretty market town surrounded by an enormous, bombastic battlement, like an Elizabethan Camp Bastion. This was once the second-largest town in Scotland. Its football team, though geographically in England, still plays in the Scottish league. It was annexed by Edward I as a base for punitive invasions of the north and to deny the Scots a southern trading port looking east. It feels like a frontier town. In the local pub, most of the people I ask say they wouldn't mind independence, that it would be good for the border. There is always money to be made out of differences in tax and VAT, the possibilities for smuggling and laundering. Which side of the border? I ask. 'Oh the English side, obviously.'

The arguments about independence are all small change. How much will this cost me? Is my pension safe? How will house prices be affected? It is as if being a nation is such a daunting enterprise that we would rather concentrate on the esoteric detail. In fact, most people say they don't know or won't vote.

A mother pushing a pram says: 'It's such a big thing, so complicated, so many risks, I don't feel I can decide.' A man – possibly the pram father – adds: 'Seriously, someone should just make a decision. Someone who knows what's best.' And then adds: 'But if we were being invaded by the English, I'd be the first with a blue face and a Molotov cocktail.'

There is a constant hum of doubt, not in Scotland's ability to be Scotland, but in the Scots' ability to make the right decision on behalf of Scotland. Scots history is a long succession of people jumping to their feet, waving their banner and making exactly the wrong decision, usually for precisely the right reason. Scotland's motto is 'romantic but wrong'. The nation's long reputation for pessimism is, as one bar blether put it, just miserable realism.

'How different would my country be,' a man delivering parcels asks, 'when I wake up on the day after independence? What would have changed? My job? My kids' school? The shops? The things I buy in the shops? The TV? The neighbours? The weather? It would all be exactly the same, except we'd be smaller, and I'd have the mither of all hangovers.'

We drive up the coast road to Edinburgh, the city that has been capital of an independent country for longer than it has played second fiddle to London. It is by a considerable vista the most beautiful city in Britain and, contrarily, the most English city in Scotland. It sits politely but awkwardly at arm's length from the rest of the nation. The New Town is stamped on every corner with the names of fat, chinless Hanoverians; a reminder that Bonnie Prince Charlie's romantic-but-wrong tartan flounce for power wasn't on behalf of independence, it was for the throne of England. If his army hadn't turned back at Derby, Scotland would have never seen him again, like all the other Stuart kings.

The only monarch to visit Scotland between 1603, when James VI took the low road as fast as his little mincing legs would carry him to be James I of England, and 1822, when George IV turned up in a puce kilt and pink tights, was Charles II, who arrived running away from Oliver Cromwell. George only came because Walter Scott had invented the modern novel and, along with a fake Scottish Homer, Ossian, had made the noble savages in skirts romantic and fashionable.

Edinburgh is my city. I was born in the old Royal Infirmary where Burke and Hare, the bodysnatchers, sold their cadavers to help make this a world centre of medical research. We lived in Northumberland Street, in the new town, surrounded by stuffed heads, Indian brass, gothic mahogany, burgundy velvet and my grandmother's piano. I was baptised on Princes Street, where my parents had been married: my dad just out of university, my mother an ingenue star of the Scottish theatre. But before I had a chance to pick up the sing-song accent of polite dissent, we moved to London. Andrew Neil, who brought me into *The Sunday Times* and who used to send me back to do Scottish stories, would say that he was a real Scot and I was a reel Scot.

My social links to the country are few, but they're fierce and they're blood. This is the place where I feel the choke and the pulse of my creation myth. My first memories of the seaside are North Berwick, the first food I remember is warm breakfast rolls with my grandmother's porridge and Scots tea, which is a finer drink than any concoction you can brew south of Ecclefechan. I'm just Scots enough to make me immune from ever being English, but not so much that I can't also feel equally European. The English grab at canapés of Scottishness, or Scotchness as they say, corners of bright culture to intimate some shared collective togetherness: 'Auld Lang Syne', a dram, the myth of stubborn bellicosity and mordant wit.

Last Burns night, I had dinner at Brown's Hotel in London, where the broadcaster Hardeep Singh Kohli, in a kilt and a turban, delivered the address to the haggis, demanding it vote Yes in the referendum. I had to deliver Burns's Selkirk Grace because nobody else at the table knew it. The piper was off to serenade other pluck steaming puddings. It's a rich night for pipers; the rest of the year it's mostly funerals. And then on to a ceilidh at Hammersmith Town Hall, where the moves for the reels and country dancers were called out across the loudspeakers for a jolly international crowd of drunk students and immigrant workers. It was like a series of musical bonding games for an international get-together of travel reps.

Scottish culture has always been equally romanticised and mocked south of the border. An awful lot of it was invented specifically to ingratiate the English, to facilitate acceptance, generate goodwill, to dispel fear and draw in revenue: shortbread, tartan, meanness and funnymen from Harry Lauder to Rab C. Nesbitt.

Scots are conflicted over all the bagpipes and sword-dancing, eagle feathers and badger-faced culture. So much of it was made up to sell tea towels and Dundee cake. It's humiliating and infuriating. You won't see many kilts today at SNP meetings. The Edinburgh Tattoo is our version of the *Black and White Minstrel Show*. All Scots find themselves hung between the real and the reel, moved to tears by Runrig, overjoyed when anyone beats the English at anything.

This United Kingdom was never ever a marriage of equals, not socially, economically, or of opportunity, but it was of intellect. Edinburgh became a city of eminent culture and civility. Out of the patronised, mocked and ignored darkness of the north came the golden Enlightenment. Adam Smith, David Hume, Allan Ramsay and the Adam brothers met at The Select Club. The breadth of their interests, from economics and philosophy to art, design and architecture, is astonishing for a country ignored and starved by its fatter half, who looked east and west but never north. And the first thing they collectively did was take elocution lessons to lose their embarrassing Scottish accents. And that is the authentic cringe of the city of my birth; simultaneously you are a cut above and not quite enough. It is no accident that *Dr Jekyll and Mr Hyde* was written here.

The debate on independence is ferocious, personal, but delicately polite, like a lost sequel to *The Prime of Miss Jean Brodie*. I have a lunch in The New Club, an old establishment Tory eyrie for lawyers, politicians and journalists, with an exterior that looks like Poundland and an interior that looks like St James's. These are mostly unionists, believers, and there is a panic. Their 'Better Together' slogan is widely seen as meaning 'too frail, stupid, poor and insignificant to make it on your own'. The Scots have taken agin it. It triggers a nationally contrary cussedness and there is one huge problem: no one can come and talk about the union from the union. The prime minister of the collective nation knows he has to keep his mouth tight shut, even if he is a Cameron, because anything the Tories say up here is like pissing in the soup. The campaign is being fronted by Alistair Darling with the help of Gordon Brown. And though a pair of recognisable Scottish types – dour, dry, crabbit denizens of the kirk and the school room, offering hellfire, hard work, hardship and selfless self-restraint and judgment – it is not a look that most Scots warm to.

The Aye campaign may have had the best tunes, but the words to go with them are miserable, little and unappealing. Both sides argue over pennies like a couple of old misers. The referendum has shown that Scottish politics is quite unlike English. This is a united kingdom disunited by a venerable old political system. There will never be a Tory government in Scotland. The Labour Party is a separate animal up here. Half of them secretly see a redder socialist future in devolution. Scotland can vote, but it will never see itself adequately represented. All too often it is governed by politicians who have no resonance or traction in this country.

The democratic problem is not the epicurean debating point of the West Lothian Question, but how can you have a whole nation whose views never get listened to or acted on? But then the thought of Scottish politics is enough to make some vote for the union as the lesser of two evils. I spoke to rural workers in the Highlands, all of whom said they would rather stick with London because they mistrust Glasgow.

The tight political pleats of the central belt aren't exactly corrupt, but they're small, close, clubbable, inward-looking, sweaty and vicious. There is an old 1970s collective socialism about the centralised bureaucracy that favours the urban and industrial over the rural. 'We're better off under Brussels,' said a forester from the west coast. 'Europe has been good to us, built roads, handed out grants. If we get independence, the SNP will be like the MacANC – we'll have a Nelson Salmond statue in every village, and it'll be handouts for the faithful and a reckoning for the traitors.'

Outside the eccentric new parliament building that cost a ridiculous fortune, just along from the new tram system, which cost an even more ludicrous fortune, neither of which inspires a belief in Scotland's ability to be trusted with its own chequebook, I meet Blair Jenkins, the journalist who is running the publicity for the Yes campaign. He says: 'You know, there is a particular Scottish mentality. We'll run towards a fight, there is a sense that we can endure anything and it would only take a small turn of the dial, just a little look up, and we could turn that enduring into achieving. We could achieve anything.'

Scotland has seen its kith and kin achieve amazing stuff. You can get tea towels on the Royal Mile with lists of home-grown inventions, discoveries and creations, but the common denominator in them all is that they were Scots, and they left. The biggest donors to the campaigns do not live in Scotland. It would be a brilliant thing if the country could move the dial and do something for itself that was amazing, and not for London.

I should come clean and declare that if I had a vote, I would vote for independence in a heartbeat, and if Scots take what is theirs I'll be the first in the queue for a passport. But like all expats I do not have a vote, and our view looking back is more tweedy and heathery and smells more of shortbread than that of people who have to live there. I do know that making a nation is more than just your pension and your water rates, your fear about a currency and whether or not you'll be able to get the BBC. A country isn't just for life, it's for all the lives to come, and the final lesson from history is not actually Scots, but from just over the way.

Ireland had a far more fraught and aggressive struggle for independence. They did not have oil and they don't even have a fishing fleet, they've got second-rate whiskey and tweed and, finally, they gained a grudging and penurious independence without the EU, with a currency that was tied to the pound, and they immediately fell into a vicious civil war and then a depression. The new Eire had precious little goodwill from London or the Continent. The Republic will be 100 years old in eight years, and if they had a referendum and were asked 'Look, you've had a century of this, wouldn't you rather come back and be part of the UK again?' do you imagine there would be a single vote for yes? Because whatever happens, it is always better to be yourself.

And when you ask, 'Will it be different the morning after?' well, everything will be different and how fabulously exciting will that be? And if you have a vote, how will you be able to turn to your grandchildren in years to come and say: 'Well, I did have the chance to right an old wrong, but actually I couldn't be bothered. I was a bit scared.'

August 2014

Dhaka

Dhaka – ninth-largest city in the world, 15.4 million souls, 400,000 bicycle rickshaws, two million tonnes of solid human waste a year. Dhaka – named after a tree, famous for mosques and thin cotton. That's Muslims and muslins. I have a thing for big, smelly teenage cities like this – messy, growing-pained, energetic cities.

Tasteful travellers are encouraged to visit and tarry in moribund, comatose, life-support, dozing places with their futures all behind them, and well-labelled burgs that sentimentalise the dead and are inhabited by curators and waiters and tour guides. And I love them, too, but after a couple of days in Bruges or Ulm or Lecce I have to check my pulse that I'm not becoming an aesthetic zombie. And you have to wonder, what did they do in these places for the 400 years before they gained the honorific 'historic and memorable' as a week-end break, and five stars on TripAdvisor? When they were just failed and smelly with urban dementia before the tourists turned up, what were they like then? At least the Cambodians had the good sense to get out of Angkor Wat when it ran out of juice and ideas.

I like cities that are there to serve people rather than the other way around, and Dhaka is certainly that. I was there for two days and I'd like to be able to tell you some interesting things to see, a couple of places to eat, a not-to-be-missed local specialty, but I can't. Not because there aren't any – I'm sure there are – but because I spent two days in traffic jams. Fifteen million people, 400,000 bicycle rickshaws, and they were all ahead of me.

If you really want to be a traveller, as opposed to a tourist, then you have to know your developing-world traffic jams. Obviously, I mean traveller in the static sense of the word. It is the truth of almost all growing cities now that the time allotted to getting anywhere is twice that of the time spent doing whatever it is you have to do when you eventually do get there.

I have an autophilic friend who says he always believed that motoring would be governed in a Darwinian fashion, would be driven by natural selection. There was no point to traffic management because the imperative of cars is to behave like cars. They would overwhelm everything until the point when they could no longer behave like cars and it would be quicker to walk or take the Tube or move to the country, and then cars would die back until they once again became more efficient than bicycles.

But then he got caught in Kampala traffic. Kampala's roads make glaciers look sprightly and, after a couple of static hours, he abandoned his car and went and had lunch in an adjacent restaurant. He came back two hours later and found his car and everybody else's car where he had left them. No one had moved. It was there, he said, that he realised there was something else happening that was overriding the common sense of time and distance management.

People now sit in Chinese traffic jams for days, have babies in them, go to school in them, get married, have affairs, break up in traffic jams. I was once told that to get to the airport in Dar es Salaam from my hotel could mean doubling the length of my flight, depending on what time the plane took off.

Traffic jams in the developing world are not symptoms of infrastructure collapse and Third World hopelessness; they are positive signs of economic boom and an expanding economy. Contrarily, stasis is what progress looks like. I'm convinced that the quite extraordinary rise in mobile phone use in the Third World is mostly down to people needing something to do while waiting for the bus.

You have to learn to sit in traffic and enjoy the not-getting-there. They say it's the journey that's more important than the destination. Well, sometimes it's not even the journey – it's the anticipation of a journey.

A traffic jam teaches you to reel your head in from expectations. Jams are essentially Buddhist, a deposit box for the karma bank. And, I must say, the traffic jam in Dhaka was marvellous once I stopped worrying about getting anywhere. Out of the window the city teemed. There are thousands of people who use the traffic as a natural resource, as their office, their field to be harvested – the pedlars with armfuls of stuff you never knew you wanted until you were in a traffic jam: plastic Chinese warships, *Asian Vanity Fair*, a set of spark plugs. I had a competition for the most optimistic item I was offered through the window, and for a time I thought it was bound to be the set of tin saucepans and a bottle of drain cleaner until a bright boy tried to flog me a five-foot standard lamp with a ruched-silk shade.

Then there are the beggars going for captive marks. Nothing high-lights the incapacity, the static hopelessness of a developing traffic jam like the desperately needy holding a child up to the window. They play an endurance game: how long can you hold out against the arrhythmic tap, tap, tap and the view of the bottom of human-ity three inches from your face? How long before the guilt and the steepling irritation and embarrassment force you to crack the win-dow a centimetre (not to lose the air-con), and post a scummy, sticky banknote? If anyone asks what the gap between the haves and the have-nots is, that's it – the crack at the top of the window.

In Dhaka the tuk-tuks are caged in with rigid cross-hatched wire; it makes the people inside look like chickens going to mar-ket. It's there because the jams became a dramatic opportunity for bag-snatchers and pedestrian muggers. It's an interesting cultural difference that in Pakistan the tuk-tuks are seen to be safer because they're open-sided, hence you can leap out and run away.

The view from a Dhaka traffic jam is engrossing – the endless flow as this ginormous city bustles about its business. Bangladesh is a place where the profit of a day is measured in wafer-thin increments, in tiny gaps in the window. In the First World we would think most of this wasn't worth getting out of bed for; people hustle for a tiny corner of economic good news. The bicycle rickshaw drivers are quite literally the engines of their own destiny and a perfect medieval illumination of capitalism at work. The two days I spent in a traffic jam in Dhaka were two of the most provoking and memorable and inspired I've spent all year.

August 2014

Trieste

——

Largest war grave of the Great War – where would that be? The Somme? Vimy Ridge? Passchendaele? Perhaps Russia or Gallipoli? It depends on your national sensitivity, the place that you turn your bowed head towards for the two-minute remembrance. The thing with world wars is that they are still a collection of different wars to different countries.

Unless your grandparents were Italian or Austrian, you're unlikely to get this right. The answer is Redipuglia. No one else has heard of it either. It marks a quiet end of the least-remembered theatre of the first war between the Austrian Empire and the newly formed nation of Italy. In particular, it is the field of the Battle of Caporetto, a name that still has dread inflection in Italy and became a byword for any disaster of uncountable size.

In September 1917, the Germans decided that the faltering Austrian front was worth shoring up. So they sent six German divisions and a general to Caporetto because there was a good road there and a plain that was suitable for gas. They covered the Italian front line in chlorine. The Italians died or ran. The Germans advanced in a new way – fast, mobile, relentlessly aggressive. It was the opening bout for stormtroopers, and a young Erwin Rommel discovered the efficacy of speed against a static enemy. The Italians were pushed back 60 miles. The Austrians finally ran out of logistical support. A year later they lost the war and the Habsburg Empire finally expired.

All battles are like all beaches: they sound and they look the same in retrospect. An emphatic, exclamatory litany of the mundane, with figures for emotional content. The telling of them diminishes the experience of them, which may be why soldiers rarely try.

The monument is stark, imposing. A line of steps as wide as a football pitch rises up into the distance. On the horizon, at the summit, you can barely make out three crosses. This is the Calvary of the Italian army. Its size and solemnity and silence deafen you. It's implacable. Its shiny grief rises up the steps on which are written one word, over and over: PRESENTE, PRESENTE, PRESENTE, in capital letters. It is the soldiers' answer to the roll call.

Under this ziggurat, 110,000 Italian soldiers lie. They are, of course, both present and not present. Dead, but here. Always with us. Responses are caught in stone like a fossil of an echo. Voices that were silenced a century ago. The repetition of the word becomes metronomic, hypnotic. You can't stop yourself reading and hearing it in the stillness. It is as powerful as any memorial I've seen.

I was there last week, not entirely by accident. I've been meaning to go and visit Trieste for years. An anomalous city that has suffered from the defining design fault of all cities: an inability to move. Not being able to get out of the way when history was having a temper tantrum has been the undoing of a lot of places. But Trieste has been in the way for more than its fair share of turbulent times.

It's managed to retain a commendable sense of calm, a fatalistic elegance. Trieste was the aim and the anchor of the Italian-Austrian war. And as this is the year of war tourism, I wanted to see the largest war grave, and the least-remembered of the theatres.

War tourism is a thing now, a retrospective, nostalgic thing. Northern France, the D-Day beaches, are thronged with people who search for some great-uncle who fought or fell to give the emotion a personal edge. The heyday of war tourism was the 1920s, when northern France was thronged with stoically bereft parents and wives looking for graves and some sort of personal peace. The well of unconscionable sadness left by the Great War is something that we still want to visit without having to experience.

It's all too easy to sneer at war tourism. Appending the word 'tourism' to any activity diminishes it, makes it ersatz, collective, prearranged. But the desire to make travelling more than a purely hedonistic or childishly pleasurable experience in search of warmth and food is a good thing, and the desire to understand the struggles of nations and the deaths of youths on their behalf must be important.

The mute lessons of the war graves, though, are not the simple story of lost youth, sacrifice, failed diplomacy and valour. You have to ask not just who is buried here, but who buried them. Very early in the First World War it was decided that no dead soldier would be repatriated. They would all be interred where they fell with their comrades. And there was a great outcry at this, from parents and families who wanted to bring loved ones home. But the building of large cemeteries, commemorative arches, crosses and the great stone lists of names was taken very seriously by all nations as propaganda. The beautifully kept graveyards are a constant tool for politicians to extract and stoke national pride and self-interest. Australians and New Zealanders understand this as well as any.

This great Golgotha memorial, on the border of Slovenia beside the trophy city of Trieste, wasn't actually built until 1938. It was ordained by Mussolini, who was again stoking the embers of Italian nationalism and expansion. Italy had already occupied Ethiopia, essentially destroying the efficacy of the League of Nations, which had itself been created out of the graves of the Great War to end all wars. And the year after it was consecrated, Italy annexed Albania. A move that seemed to offer an international amber light to the Anschluss of Germany with Austria, which could all be seen as the neat interlocking circles of a Venn diagram of European hegemony and ambition.

So while the motives of war tourists are admirable and mawkishly sentimental, the motives of those who raise grand and bellicose memorials over the bodies of their dead children should be visited with more than just a pinch of cynicism.

November 2014

Holland

___

The first foreign country I went to was Holland. I was nine. My grandfather had just died. I think the only time he went abroad was to fight the Kaiser. I just looked it up, 1963. It was the first year of the Beatles, *Lawrence of Arabia* and *Dr No*. Colonial Africa was sloughing off colonialism. Hands up: what did Nyasaland wake up calling itself? Well done if you managed to remember Malawi. Yugoslavia became a country. In England, the distinction between amateur and professional cricketers was finally dropped by the MCC, along with all the catches against Australia, who thrashed us. Russia announced it had a 100-megaton nuclear bomb; Martin Luther King had a dream; Nelson Mandela went on trial. It was a big year – the start of the contemporary age.

The 1960s really kicked off in '63, but I only remember this in retrospect. For me, 1963 was the year I went to Holland, the first year I ever went abroad. Except technically, it wasn't. Coming to England at six months old from Scotland was the first border I crossed, and actually the first foreign country any of us visit is the one we're born into. A trip that is so surprising, so unexpected, so spectacular, no one has ever been able to remember it. Compared with being born, all other journeys are pathetically mundane.

But Holland was a good place to begin abroad, a safe choice. The early 1960s were the start of packaged family holidays; travel got cheaper, the Continent was inviting. Tourism looked like it might

163

be an industry, not just a hobby or an escape. My parents chose the Low Countries because it was close and cheap. We went by boat from Harwich; it was the first time I'd been to sea. And also because we had a couple of Dutch au pairs. They were the first foreigners I got to know and they brought a jolly, bustling, down-to-earth Dutch sense of common sense, earthy humour, comfort, cosiness and liberality to our house. They introduced us to syrup waffle and Santa Claus with Black Pete.

And there was another reason for my father wanting to go back to Holland: he discovered that the grandparents of one of the girls had been killed in the Allied bombing raid on Rotterdam. She knew the date. My dad had been in the RAF and it was the day his squadron had attacked the city. The girl said that there was no animosity to the RAF in Holland; the Allies were fighting for Dutch freedom and it was a sad consequence of the war – people died. Lots and lots of people had died. I think my dad wanted to go and shake someone's hand.

Holland seemed suitably and satisfyingly familiar in a foreign enough way. The things that delight you abroad are those that are nearly the same as home, but different: the smell of houses, the sound of bells, another language heard in shops. I loved the sugar on bread with sprinkles, pickled herring, and the astonishing, elaborate riches of *rijsttafel* – an Indonesian feast, the gift of colonialism. We were taken to eat it by the son of the couple who died in the destruction of Rotterdam.

He was a high court judge. It was the most elaborate and surprising meal I had ever been offered. At home we were still living with the phantom shadow of rationing, and not talking about food as pleasure, but only as a wholesome bodily function, a gift, a privilege, and too often a penance and a punishment.

I recognised the Dutch were very like everyone else I knew, but they were also quite different in a way that was exciting, and I thought, even then, an improvement. To begin with, they were more open and comfortable with children than the English; they didn't refer to me as 'a little man' or spout a strange 'I'm talking to a child now' voice. They were more relaxed around each other, too – quite polite but not formal; gentler than the angular, flinty English, with their wall of resentments and damp pride.

So I've just been back to Scheveningen, on the outskirts of The Hague – Den Haag, the hedge – 50 years later. Not on holiday, but to talk to a UN convention on statelessness, which was interesting and infuriating and, as conventions tend to be, exhausting. (I don't really know what it is that's so tiring about listening to very good and knowledgeable people, but, contrarily, it's much harder than watching immoral, dim people.)

I skipped off for a sunny afternoon. The pleasure of Holland is all in the man-made environment. It is almost all a man-made environment. The Hague is a lovely city to walk through, a capital without airs or graces. The Binnenhof, the parliament and the civil service buildings are self-effacing, with far more charm than the grandeur of most European parliaments. Beside it is the newly refurbished Mauritshuis, a merchant's house that is a gallery. I'd never been to it before and, in general, I try to avoid galleries. I used to be an art critic and it put me off these creative zoos, where pictures go quietly mad and are made to compete with each other. The Mauritshuis is different – the art hangs among friends in a cultural nature reserve.

I knew this is where I would find the *Girl with a Pearl Earring*, and *The Lamentation of Christ* by Rogier van der Weyden, but I was quite unprepared for what a spectacularly coherent collection it is, and how much I would be moved by it. I had forgotten the great arty truth – that of all art, Dutch seventeenth- and eighteenth-century painting reproduces worst, although it is printed, anthologised and sent as a million postcards. Being in a room with a Vermeer, as opposed to seeing a picture of a Vermeer in a book, is like being in a room with a tiger or seeing one on television.

I'm not going to offer an ex-critic's art lesson here, but the Dutch

Golden Age, as it comes to us in painting, is such a gloriously humane moment in European culture: both austere and bawdy, serious, commercial, but also lazy and loquacious, rude and inquisitive, concerned with simplicity as well as comfort, and exquisite beauty. The portraits are of people who look straight at you from across the centuries, recognisable, convivial, human, miraculous.

I can't remember when I last left a gallery so bursting with the pleasure of being European, in the sense of being connected to a long European tradition that is, at its broadest and richest, unparalleled – a direct succession of 3,000 years of brilliance, wit and joy, and somewhere near the end, the Golden Age of Holland gathered to itself some of the most attractive European qualities.

Perhaps it was because I had been talking about the desperate tragedy of statelessness that I felt such empathy and deep gratitude to this merchant's house, and the vaunting, ululating pleasure of art when art does what art is supposed to do. Of all the facets of civilisation the plastic arts and music fulfil their mission more regularly and emphatically than anything else – more than science or politics, religion or knitwear, which are all memorable, mostly for their shortcomings and their failures. With art you still feel replete at being human and, in this case, speechlessly grateful to be part of the European tradition.

Perhaps it was something to do with the convention on statelessness, but my dad in the RAF, the fires of Rotterdam, the girls who helped bring me up, this modest, jolly city, the divine Mauritshuis – all seemed to be connected to each other, and to me, and I felt profoundly lucky. By the skin of my teeth, lucky.

December 2014

Colombia

If you're nervous about flying, buying a ticket to a mythical place that has already cost thousands of lives, the destruction of empires and civilisations might make you think twice. But then, El Dorado is what people have come here in search of for 600 years. It literally means 'The Golden One' and derives from the most powerful and, it turns out, misguided and pitifully cataclysmic myth of all of Mesoamerica: about a pre-Columbian king snappily called the Zipa, who would be covered in gold dust and dive into a lake, glittering like the setting sun. His capital was Muequetá, high in the Andes. The lake is still here, out of town, along with a salt cathedral.

But first there's the traffic. Bogotá suffers Gordian traffic jams, made bearable by the novel and quite flamboyant Cirque de Traffic Lights. As you stop, a man on a unicycle unsteadily pedals out. He juggles unsuccessfully, while a chubby girl with a comedy hat and clown's make-up does callisthenic dancing with silk streamers like a one-woman North Korean dictator's birthday celebration, and another child will tap on your window for change.

This is part of a general drive to lift the city, give everyone a role and bring culture to the street. Drivers grin and mostly offer a few coins. It's the most inventive traffic calmer I've seen in any city. Bogotá has decided that everyone and everything must have culture and self-expression: its mission, art growing from the cracks in the pavement. Barely five years ago, the only people who'd visit this place with a sense of expectation or excitement were drug mules or kidnap negotiators. Bogotá had a hard-fought reputation for being one of the most dangerous cities in the world. Colombia was known only for drugs and terrorism, the Siamese twins of misery, the world's biggest cocaine producer and the world's most consistently intractable old-school communist revolutionaries with the best terrorist name, the FARC.

When drugs met Trotskyist dogma there was a perfect storm of nihilism. But then something happened that wasn't politics or common sense or revolution. No one knows quite what it was, but a sense of exhaustion with the misery set in and the FARC announced a unilateral ceasefire, and the government is about to make a serious peace offer. Politics have become softer, more malleable, and at the same time the drugs seem to have gone limp and legit.

A conflict negotiator (a job description that's as ubiquitous here as hedge-fund manager in London) said the coca is still grown but the business model has changed. A generation ago, drug gangs and gangsters saw themselves as mafia or wanted to be Scarface: it was bling and hookers and drive-by Uzis, and headless bodies left in ornamental fish ponds as a warning. Pablo Escobar ended up as a bullet cushion on the roof of a favela in Medellín.

But today the drug lords have been to Harvard Business School and they see themselves not as dealers but brokers, and the business model isn't Al Pacino but Amazon, which is appropriate because they actually do have the Amazon. The fratricidal violence in Mexico today, they say with a knowing shrug, is what Colombia had a decade ago. So passé. Now that Colombia's carcinogenic problems are in remission, we can look at what else it has, and that comes with a shock.

This is the most biodiverse country in the world. It has a bewildering number of habitats: the mountains, the rainforests, pampas, wetlands, a great network of rivers, including the Amazon, two coasts – the Caribbean and the Pacific – and it has more species of birds than all of Europe and North America put together. A phenomenal number of things grow here. This is some of the finest, fecund farmland on the globe. Some say, if a man with a wooden leg stands still for too long, he'll turn into a guava tree.

The Paloquemao market in the city is a jaw-dropping carnival of fruitarian wonder to anyone who's remotely interested in the riches that really do grow on trees. The sad, ghostly taste of our imported fruit is, here, transformed into a steepling cornucopia of astonishingly beautiful things. Half a dozen varieties of bananas and plantains and mangoes; limes, lemons, oranges, guavas, carambolas, kiwis, strawberries, dragonfruit, mangosteen, all the rare and exotic fruits of the east, and then the wonders of the rainforest: knobbly, finned and flared, bright and dowdy fruit, guyabano – which tastes a bit like a banana and a bit like a strawberry, but then again, a bit like a lime – lulo, nispero, tree tomato, sapote, curubu, sugar apple, guaba.

The smell that wafts through the narrow alleys of stalls is the scent of fairy tales, heady and brilliant, the bounty of Eden. There's meat, as well: any number of indigenous and effortful things to do with a pig, including a huddle of pigs' heads attached to neatly flayed skins, like lifelike glove puppets, or rugs of crackling. I stop at a little wooden shack in the heart of the market. Inside it, a fat chef manhandles the ladle through a thick, simmering cauldron. It smells so good, I sit down beside them and point at the bowl and then at my mouth, and smile. The market also deals in cut flowers, huge bundles of arum lilies, bunches of tulips, roses and orchids and strange wreaths of ruddy, fleshy, erotically promising rainforest blooms.

The two quickest guides to the nature and wellbeing of any city are its markets and its graffiti. Graffiti is a feature of Bogotá, encouraged by the municipality. The central motorway that bisects the town is a long gallery of political manga, paintings commemorating the dead and exalting political change, extolling healthy diets, making jokes, offering dystopian visions and caricatures and belly laughs. There are huge political murals and tiny stencilled graphic bons mots. The street art is itself a reason for visiting the city: an inside-out gallery of contemporary thought and social commentary, energetic, angry, licensed but not tamed. Given the space and the freedom, you see it as a beautiful addition to the practical infrastructure that is so often a sign of urban decay and neglect. Here it is rejuvenation, energy, commitment and joie de vivre.

Above Bogotá there is a church on a mountain that makes you lurch for breath it's so high. You reach it by funicular and the view of the city from above is spectacular: 8 million people, palely confused like a spilt sack of mosaic tesserae, stretching away. There are bits that have kept their colonial elegance and some places that look weirdly like commuter-belt Esher, built in an English Tudorbethan vernacular. There are parts that have a licence to run speakeasies and brothels, and others where it is probably not safe to wander around looking rich or gormless.

One of the consequences of years of terrorism and drug gangs meant that anyone who was a kidnap risk, and who could afford to, left Colombia. The diaspora went to America and Europe and a generation of children grew up cosmopolitan and educated abroad. Now they are returning and property prices in the most exclusive areas are as high as New York or Paris. The expats have brought back money and culture and avariciousness for smart shopping centres and chic atelier galleries selling contemporary art at international prices. I walked around one with a gentle, young curator who spoke the fluent, international art bollocks you hear in any Western city that has a Frieze or a Biennale.

Bogotá has managed to grow the delicate proof of a healthy social ecosystem: indigenous hipsters with beards, short trousers, fixie bikes and an obsession with coffee. Bringing barista OCD to Colombia is coals to Newcastle because they already have the most delicious coffee, but now you can talk about it for five minutes to a hirsute waiter with ironic tattoos.

Along with the return of middle-class Colombians, there is also the desperate influx of refugees. Colombia has the highest number of internally displaced people in the world. On the street corner, I stop to chat to four Michael Jacksons in full costume with a boom box. They take it in turns to moonwalk and jive in front of traffic at the lights. They're very good at it, they make it look fun, but it's tough.

Hotels are the bellwethers of a city's state of mind. Are they large concrete boxes with speed humps, guards with mirrors on sticks and lobbies full of UN aid executives, television crews and security advisers? Or are they bijou, low-lit, open-plan hostelries with chillaxing bars in the lobby and smiley girls in black frocks who make you think they've gone to a shop and said, 'Yes, this fits me perfectly, do you have it in a smaller size?' Bogotá is attracting the latter. There have been trendy new openings of the W and the deeply unfortunately baptised BOG Hotel, which are proof that it's safe to dive into the city again. The bedrooms have suggestive buttock cushions and the minibars are stocked with condoms. They're opulent, suggestible and effortfully sophisticated, but more importantly, they are not just wishful thinking. Someone has taken a long accountant's look at Bogotá and said: 'This is open for legitimate business, and après business shenanigans.'

In a square in the middle of the city, groups of old men stand talking in the slowly loquacious manner of chaps who have nowhere else to be. They're all dressed beautifully – nicely cut Sunday suits with flashy accents: a broad lapel, a jazzy check, a bit of a watch chain, two-tone shark-skin shoes, a straw fedora. They're tough men. Short, like most Colombians, with stubby, hard hands. If you hang around long enough one of them will saunter over and produce a small wrap of paper from a pocket and open it. They're not drug dealers, they're emerald miners, probably emerald poachers, and they will show you little intense shards of viridian-green precious stone, or beer-bottle glass. You decide.

Women like to be noticed. There is a sashaying fashion for prominent derrières. Like the great poop decks of sailing ships, they sway in the crowd, pressed into spinnaker skirts. The bars and restaurants are full of long, repressed flirtations and the daring of hope and plans and commitment. Many chefs and restaurateurs have come home, bringing a renaissance of indigenous cuisine mixed with other Latin American traditions and hyphenated with eastern and European kitchens: Colombian-Japanese, Colombian-Italian, and an awful lot of this season's food fad, Peruvian. The ingredients are so good that you'd have to be a seriously cack-handed cook to muck up dinner.

Bogotá is a city that feels like it's letting out a long sigh of relief, that's remembering old dance steps to half-forgotten tunes. The two most famous Colombians are Botero, the painter of fat people who once looked like naive social commentary and now just look like life paintings. And Gabriel García Márquez, who has a library built in his name. Although he spent most of his life in Mexico, they say he is quintessentially Colombian and the tourist board relentlessly pushes 'magical realism' as a slogan. Driving through a residential neighbourhood I see a man sitting on a child's swing swaying backwards and forwards, his back slumped, chin on chest, hands gripping the ropes. There is something intensely pitiful in this brief image. Then, when I walk in Bolívar Park, the big open space with its boating lake and cafés, where the city folk come to run and cycle and lie in the grass, reading and kissing, I notice again solitary men rocking on swings like bears in zoos, soothing the trauma with rhythmic movement.

There is, under the resilience and fashion, the eating and shopping, the dressing up, a low, keening melancholy. Everybody here has been affected by the years of strife, the murders, the kidnappings, the disappeared, the collateral damage, the loss. The sense of grief in the thin air adds a depth, a cello note, to the jollity. The thing about magic realism is you never know when the magic will evaporate and leave you with the very real reality.

The Gold Museum is Bogotá's greatest treasure, both in reality and magic. Here's the work of the pre-Columbian civilisation that made votive and decorative objects out of yellow gold. It is a singularly stunning collection, not least because of what it conjured up and what was lost. How delicate and mercurial the gold seems, so unaware of its terrifying power. Finally, you walk into a dark room. The lights slowly come on, illuminating a panorama of metal that glitters and glints and stares back an accusation and reflection of the riches of the new world, and you feel yourself sinking down and down, through a great magical lake surrounded by the offerings of the future and the drowned prayers of the past.

March 2015

Colorado

The mile-high city is what they call Denver on the tourist brochures and the posters – it sits in the lap of the Rocky Mountains. So it was with the serendipity of nominative determination that Colorado became the first state to legalise recreational use of marijuana in America – thus transferring the slogan onto a million hilarious hippie T-shirts. Two and a half years ago, Colorado voted for Amendment 64, a piece of legislation that approved the sale of weed, dope, pot, grass, wacky baccy purely for pleasure. I should admit an interest here. I don't smoke dope – I haven't rolled a Camberwell carrot for 30 years – but I used to. From the age of 15 I smoked a great deal. I'm a recovering addict and I'm particularly interested in a state the size of Scotland that holds up its hands and sells drugs for fun and profit.

That state has about 1,000 establishments selling or prescribing marijuana. It is estimated to have created tens of thousands of jobs, including a small brigade of civil servants employed by the marijuana department to regulate the businesses. Recreation, as opposed to medicinal drugs, is stoned by the state with a 21 per cent sales tax. Last year this made the city $12.5m. It turned out to be the equivalent of attracting a sizeable industry to the state. No one knows quite how much tourism the smoke inhales but, anecdotally, plenty. Denver is a big convention destination. All those middle managers and salesmen come to this safely laid-back town for a bong of UK Cheese or Warlock Haze.

Colorado's capital sprawls like a teenager's bedroom across the great parking lot plains at the edge of the Rockies. It's here because this is where the unstoppable railway from Chicago meets the immovable towering majesty of nature. To worship both, they built a station the size of a cathedral.

It's difficult to tell quite what difference the promise of unlimited narcotic consumption has made to the city because it's already stoned on fresh air and an absence of culture or conversation. Denver has always been karmically twinned with spliff. Walking through the downtown shopping precinct, you notice the folk are slow and zoned out, skinnier than most Americans. A shoeshine shouts out his services: 'Wear suede and never get laid!' There are lots of buff-looking beggars with pleading signs: 'I'm hoping for the kindness of strangers.' 'Pregnant. Any little helps.'

Euflora (smoking weed seems to stimulate the brain's pun cortex) is a blank shop front, one of 205 ganja retailers in the city. Last year there were just 19. They're not allowed to advertise or show their wares to the street, so in a basement a security guard with an aggressive utility belt asks for proof of identity. Foreign driving licences won't cut it. 'We don't believe in them.' The room itself is cool and white and as far away from being a pre-legislation head shop as it can manage.

There is no counterculture paraphernalia, no psychedelia, no promise of free love. There are pot plants though, but of the unsmokeable office type. Bongs, pipes, vapes are displayed in glass cases. The look they're going for is developing-world airport cosmetics counter. It is unthreatening and utterly without attitude or opinion. It is as bland as a shop can be while still having a till – almost embarrassed to be out of the closet.

They are less shy when it comes to the mark-up. Grass is $20 (£12.50) per gram, plus tax (pipes are from $2.50 to $50) – the average cost in Colorado is closer to $9 per gram. Samples are arranged on tables in glass jars with perforated lids so you can smell them.

Beside each is a card with a name – Candy Cush, Alien Dawg – and a description of its efficacious effects. 'An indica oozing with mango resin.' 'Smoke is dense and luscious. Mellows out in a peachy-smooth daydream.' This is a bourgeois attempt to imitate the 'sophistication' and imprecise eloquence of winespeak. Imagine taking a lungful and saying, on the strangulated in-gasp: 'I'm getting tones of oak and farmyard with an undercurrent of boiled sweets and Marianne Faithfull's armpit.'

I linger for an hour and watch half a dozen customers come in. They are all middle-aged, paunchy, balding, wrinkled, clicky-hipped. There isn't one of them that doesn't have some talisman of a former self: a greying ponytail, a bit of ethnic jewellery, a touch too much kohl. They are here for the smoke of remembrance, the s'mores of nostalgia. The very stoned boy behind the counter says that most of these customers are tourists. A couple in their fifties, professional, conservative, ask for advice for something to smoke after dinner. They both have badges. They're from out of town, here for a convention, and there's something about their discreet buttock-touching that implies they're having an office affair.

The boy recommends something mellow but with a sexy Hendrix euphoria, not too heavy but with a definite libido kick. They ask if he's got it in a ready-rolled joint but they're out of those, so they settle for a paper cone and the grass to see if they can remember how to do it themselves. The man adds an impulsive box of stoned-breath mints.

The boy tells me that 50 per cent of his sales are for MIPs – marijuana infused products – from mints to chocolates, cakes, oils, infusions, drops and brightly coloured sweets. Edibles are the fastest-growing market. You can even get yourself a mile-high massage using cannabis massage lotion, for $65 an hour and free parking.

It is widely acknowledged that the state has made vast amounts of money out of weed, but there are many dissenters. Pastor Bob

Enyart was one of the most vociferous anti-marijuana campaigners. He has a personal radio station and sounds like an evangelical Dirty Harry when he tells me: 'It's the most powerful transmitter allowed by government.'

His radio station is stuck away in a little office, in a locked-down parade of shops, in an anonymous suburb. His mum and stepdad are the engineers. Pastor Bob pontificates into the ether on the soul-sapping evil of dope. He's a personable, friendly man with a Rolf Harris beard and the merest twinkle of deific megalomania. He tells me about a schoolboy who smoked a joint and fatally stabbed himself 21 times. I suspect he only fatally stabbed himself once and had 20 other goes. Or of families who've had their children taken from them because of grass. 'Drugs are opening a manhole for moral and social degradation, and government conspiracy.' He smiles a lot when he says it. He is like a cross between Sarah Palin and Burl Ives. On the other side of the argument is Rob Corry, a lawyer who made a living out of defending drug dealers, growers and users and who has had his own brushes with the law. He is no stranger or enemy to publicity. There is more than a touch of *Better Call Saul* about him. He is open, engaging and bombastic with a whiff of slidey-eyed desperation. His small office boasts a plastic marijuana plant and on the wall above his desk is a framed magazine feature that proclaims he is one of the most influential people in Denver, which is a bit like being one of the most fashionable people in Swindon. He was an instigator and a fierce champion of the vote to legalise; he's less than euphoric about its outcome. He says it's still fraught with inconsistencies and prejudice and legal uncertainty.

Cannabis-selling and growing for pleasure are still technically illegal, federally. Banks, which have to be indemnified by national government, won't accept funds from the drugs business, which means it all has to be done with cash, and there is a great deal of money in cupboards and under mattresses, making it more open to criminality. Shopkeepers and growers are turning up at City Hall with suitcases of bills to pay their taxes. Colorado is being sued by neighbouring states for exporting drugs and forcing them to have police checks on border roads. There is also a new rule that says only a resident of two years can open a marijuana business in Colorado. He points out that this is implicitly racist. It is the spectre of Latin American gangs coming and taking over drug-dealing. Drug enforcement is unequivocally racist. The state would never insist that someone opening a software company or clothing factory in Colorado has to be local. He points out that the rules that prevent a convicted felon from running a marijuana business pretty much exclude anyone who has any expertise in it. The black market has simply faded away because most customers would rather go to a shop and pay a bit more to get a product that is regulated, that comes with a warm feeling of being modern, debonair but also mainstream and legitimate.

Both Pastor Bob and lawyer Rob are registered Republicans and that is a real political irony, because marijuana law splits the conservatives. Fundamentalists see it as a moral evil, libertarians as free-market deregulation. It's big god versus small government. This may become a testing issue in the race for a Republican contender for the White House. For democrats the legislation is more pragmatic. There are elements of civil rights and the memories of their own youthful experience. Their personal musical soundtracks are smoked in marijuana.

Colorado is called a purple state. It is neither wholly red nor blue. The cities, like Boulder, Denver and Pueblo, are Democrat. The rural communities are made up mostly of old-school Republicans, stockpiling tinned food and ammunition. Smoking a joint is one of the few things they both seem to agree on.

You don't have to buy your grass from a shop; you are now allowed to grow your own, six plants per adult for personal consumption. If you grow them well that works out as quite a lot of dope. David Degraff-Hamill cuts a rather pitiful figure sitting in the neatly dingy

front room of his little apartment in an ugly block that is mostly occupied by pensioners in sheltered accommodation. He shares it with
an absent man who wraps crystals with feathers as spiritual karma.

His card says he is CEO of the Grow School, an educational outfit
giving seminars on how to grow pot. He makes a sparse living giving
online lectures. He used to be a chef. He used to have a girlfriend.
Now he has six pot plants and a cat. The pot shares his bedroom,
segregated in a portable dark room. You need a surprising amount of
kit to grow your own nirvana. Cannabis demands the attention that
cannabis uses. How it ever manages to be a street drug is a mystery.
The Norma Desmond of house plants expects a great deal of light
and then a great deal of darkness, living in a permanent, shy chiaro-
scuro of wilting temperament. They drink a lot and need unfeasibly
gasping extraction fans because their smell is overwhelming. David
explains that the reason skunk is called skunk is that it smells like
skunk.

He talks lugubriously about the nature and history of smoking
dope and interrupts me and says: 'You're confusing being stoned
with getting high.' I'll admit that I've always used the words syn-
onymously. 'That's because you come from the Cheech and Chong
generation. It was weed that you smoked. You got stoned. Felt
heavy, red eyes, munchies, lethargic, giggling, paranoia.' Yes, yes,
that was it. That was what I was thinking about. That and Jaffa
Cakes. 'Well that was the indica plant. That gets you stoned. You
get high from the sativa plant. It's different. It's more alert, relaxed
but euphoric. It's what people want today. It's more bourgeois. They
need more sativa with just a hint of indica.' 'Is that what you smoke
for?' I ask. 'I don't get much of a buzz any more. I smoked for so
long,' he says with a hint of rue and regret, 'it's mostly maintenance
for me now.' He lights up a pipe and the room is filled with the sour,
sweaty compost odour that is the sweet smell of my teens. Even
the smoke curls with a reluctant, sibilant effort. He cracks the dim
grin of the freshly stoned. 'Ah man,' he gasps on the in-breath. 'I'm

getting a hit from this. That's good. Glad you came round.'

Dan Rowland is citywide communications and relations adviser to the mile-high city. He's a flak catcher, sent out to vet people like me before we're allowed to talk to the marijuana tsar. And like most ambitious young men in politics employed to take shrapnel for others, he is a lot brighter than they are and his main problem is to keep that to himself. 'We looked at Amsterdam and wanted to avoid that because of the pot cafés and the disruption of antisocial kids.'

Marijuana-related crime has halved in the city. You'd imagine making it legal would have stopped it being a crime altogether, but then the police are actively writing up more citations for dope in public, and tickets for driving under the influence of cannabis have doubled because the police have gone after people having very, very slow car crashes. Actually, since it was decriminalised, overall crime in Denver has fallen by almost 7 per cent.

Dan's boss, Ashley Kilroy, has the title Executive Director of Marijuana Policy. She is the only Director of Marijuana in America, which must open her up to a relentless ribbing at local-government conventions. She is a dynamic lady who plainly looks into the changing-room mirror hoping to see attractive and assertive, rather than sexy and bossy. She is nervous about talking to the foreign press. She stresses that the decision to legalise marijuana for fun was the public's choice and it is the job of local government to do what the electorate decrees. Well, up to a point: it's their job to do what's in the electorate's best interest. She is keen to let me know that her department is really hot on the regulatory process. She goes on to give a complex and enthusiastic description of how they're monitoring the chemicals and fertilisers used in marijuana growth. Any day now there will be organic dope and GM-free joints. I point out that this is laudable, but didn't she think there ought to be a regulation preventing manufacturers from adding the THC-reactive chemical in marijuana into sweets and chocolate cakes and 'gummy bears'? Potentially a child could eat an entire packet in one go – when a starter dose for an adult is no more than a 'gummy bear's' head. She says she was on the committee that covered edibles and 'perhaps she needs to revisit that'. Quite.

Dan says he can get a large grower to show us round their commercial warehouse. I get a call from an out-of-state PR and lobbyist for Mindful, one of the growers. Their CEO, Meg Saunders, will be happy to show me around their facility. We can take select photographs and she will give a frank and wide-ranging interview, but it will be off the record, if that's all right. 'All of it off the record?' 'If you ask I'm sure she'll give you a quote. She's very good at that.' I must say, I've never been offered a completely unprintable interview before. How could I say no? Mindful's warehouse is opposite the biggest police station in Denver. Still, it's difficult to find and there is no obvious entrance, no signs, no names, no proud declamation, not even a little brass plaque. They don't encourage visitors or advertise their legitimate business. Meg is smart and skinny and multitasking on her iPhone with a furrowed fury. She really doesn't want to talk to me at all. She mutters and shrugs and mumbles her way around the warehouse that is staffed with the sort of young nerds you might expect to find in an iTunes store.

There are a series of hangars that are either bright as interrogation rooms or Stygian-black as depression and, inside, the neurotic pot grows out of bags of coconut husk intravenously fed by drips of water and chemicals. 'Do you smoke marijuana?' I ask her. 'I don't answer that question,' she says icily. I think refusing to answer a question in an off-the-record interview counts as a double negative, so I can print it. How many other CEOs would deny using their own product? Or be embarrassed to admit that they did? The male chairman of a Tampax firm, perhaps? Or the president of a chemical-weapons manufacturer. Politicians and businesses are sulkily evasive about their engagement with grass because this is a social activity in transition. It's changing from being for no-hope losers and a gateway to heroin, crack, dropping out, prostitution and prison, to being a leisure activity for the hip, middle-class and mid-dle-aged. They're waiting for the counterculture to drop in again for coffee and a hash muffin. But cannabis never had much of a palpable footprint in the first place. As David, the dope lecturer, said: 'When you think of a stoned person, it's funny. They are figures of mild ridicule. Slurring, giggly, thick of limb and tongue.' Heroin had a strong and bitter heritage in books and movies, alcohol is a major benefactor of the arts – the list of its creation is too long to write. Acid gave us psychedelia, weird poetry and bad psycho-analysis. Even cocaine has gabbled its way onto movies and TV. But what did dope ever do for us? It gave us Cheech and Chong and T-shirts.

It's been made over as a contestant in America's great leisure-time pageant, with a penchant for self-medication and self-improvement and a palliative for bland, fashionable ailments. It's like carrying a Valium in your purse, a toke for cocktail-party anxiety. It offers a light, natural, herbal buzz, it's mindful, in the moment, a feel-good spritz. What has actually been lost is the nebulous underground fun of the drug. Smoking dope is the cultural satnav of adolescence. It's the smoke of friendship, of a shared secret society, your first important transgression and the self-determination of youth. A passed-around joint is two fingers to the tyranny of uniforms and tests and the predestination of growing up and not running in cor-ridors. It was the magic gift of awkward teenagers. It helped you discard your virginity and say embarrassingly profound things out loud and to laugh at nothing, but together.

But like Facebook and sneakers and Tinder, it's been taken over by the grown-ups. In Denver's one excellent bookshop, Tattered Cover, there is a stunted shelf of marijuana writing, containing nothing you'd want to read straight or stoned. I picked *Ganja Kitchen Revolution: The Bible of Cannabis Cuisine*. This is now the most depress-ing and telling cookbook I own. These aren't instructions for a better way to get high, or for feeding the munchies. This is Indian Shiva skunk chicken curry, French crystal salmon en papillote – give-your-dinner-party-a-lift food.

After more than a year of flinging open the gateway to reefer madness, and in the face of the warnings of moral degradations, social turpitude, organised crime and very, very slow traffic chaos, Denver has discovered that, in truth, nothing much has happened. They estimate the number of cannabis users remains pretty much the same, except now they're not criminals. In 10 years, it's predicted that most American states will have followed suit and then, in time, so will the rest of us. Because that's what we always do. And then a generation will wonder why it was ever illegal or, indeed, terribly popular. And by then someone will have asked, why not decriminalise opiates? Perhaps nothing much would happen then, either. Cannabis may well be the gateway drug to the decriminalisation of addiction.

The rural shopkeeper who voted against 64 said: 'All the states will come round to it in the end, but we'll always be the first. It's what we'll be famous for. Colorado, the mile-high state.'

June 2015

Kangaroo Island

The first thing to love about Kangaroo Island is that there is no mistaking where it is. An island called Kangaroo could only be down under, while the rest of Australia is named with a cringing, doffed-cap infatuation with the old country – Adelaide, Sydney, Melbourne, named after forgotten toffs or for homesickness. Who on earth would want another Perth or a new South Wales? Kangaroo Island is what it says on the label: an island replete with kangaroos.

It was named by Matthew Flinders, who bumped into it off the coast of Adelaide, while making his voyage to discover if Australia was really two islands with a possible inland sea, as it appeared to be far too big to be one place. It still seems to be far too big. Flinders' crew was starving. The kangaroos on the island had never seen humans before, so hopped naively into the pot. There may have been aboriginals here once, but not for a few thousand years. The wildlife is still remarkably sanguine about that human contact; the kangaroos still regard us with a forgiving curiosity.

I've come here on the ferry with a chef and an abalone diver. Jock Zonfrillo is a cook at Orana in Adelaide, by way of Glasgow, and before that of Italian extraction. Paul is a second-generation diver; his father started in the warmer seas off Trieste.

We've come to forage, and before you roll your eyes and sigh, 'Oh no, not another rambling encomium for hippie gardening, for picking twigs and scraping mould and drying moss, as a sort of back-to-Eden alternative to the tyranny of supermarkets and Quavers,' let me tell you that foraging in Australia is really not like blackberrying in Kent. For a start, everything wants to kill you, and most things can.

Jock is the Mad Max of foraging. He has travelled the length and breadth of this continent, searching out the shy, forgotten and neglected edible bits, staying in remote native communities, learning the vanishingly husbanded knowledge; he makes Bear Grylls look like an autograph-hunting boy scout. There is nothing New Age or goopy about his commitment to the raw taste of his adopted country.

At dawn on a chilly spring morning, we go down to the jetty, where a gimpy and worryingly small inflatable boat is being guarded by a posse of beady pelicans. On land they always look cartoonishly ungainly, but with the silent ta-da of prestidigitation, they are transformed into the most elegant, balletic birds when airborne.

'Can you swim?' asks Paul, as he sorts his kit.

'No, I do "briefly postponed drowning".'

'Oh right, well, I've only got one life jacket and it's covered in guts and grease. It'll probably mess up your coat.'

'Well, I'll drown then.'

We chug out into the long, curving bay. Black swans and piebald cormorants bob in the choppy waves. Above, pelicans pirouette and oystercatchers peep plaintively. Paul attaches himself to the airline and puts on his weight belt and picks up a shopping basket and jumps over the side. Abalone-diving is a dangerous job. Overfishing has concentrated the great white sharks into areas where smaller breeds of fish run. Here, tuna come to breed, and there are seal colonies. Two divers have already been killed; others have left the sea in fear. Paul has had 15 close encounters with great whites, but diving is what he does and the Chinese pay a great deal for the greenlip abalone. It's still foraging, even if it's underwater.

Today, he's after king scallops that Jock says are the best he's ever eaten. Paul returns with a bagful of St Jacques shells. He sits

185

on the side of the boat, dripping and panting, takes out a knife and opens one, cleans it and cuts the muscle from its hard bed. He hands it to me. It has that marvellous shy smell of ozone and iodine, a sweetness that is cool and meaty, a taste of the ocean and outdoors that starts as one thing, then subtly changes as it slides down your tongue. It is insistent and utterly memorable.

We sit on the rocking boat while the sun comes up and the shore-line glows lustrous, and stands of gum trees flicker in the sunshine, and the patches of light creep across the hilltops. Altogether it is the most perfectly appointed mouthful of the year.

Paul has also caught us an abalone, a big muscle that moves un-gainly across my hand like a lovelorn, disembodied tongue. Abalone need to be beaten in order to tenderise them. Their flavour is com-plicated and not as richly long as the scallop, but it has an almost embarrassing lascivious taste, an intimate, female eroticism. Some people react with an instant embarrassed exclamation, putting their hands to their mouths.

We chug back to the jetty for a questing walk along the shore. Jock forages as if he were shopping, walking down the dune aisle of a supermarket, fracking and picking and handing me leaves and sprigs and damp shards of stuff with a terse 'taste this', followed by a Latin and then a common garden name: sea blite; neptune's pearls, which are little kelp buds; samphire, more intensely salty and medicinal than the stuff we get in England; sea purslane; graci-laria, saltbush. At the same time, he's teaching my little boy how to throw a boomerang: 'You don't want it to come back,' he says. 'You're trying to break a kangaroo's leg or bring down a bird. If it comes back, you have no dinner.' The stick whirls through the brined air, never to return.

Here's the odd pigface fruit, a grounded succulent that looks more like a livid trotter, and a Moreton Bay fig. Each of these has an intense and surprising flavour, all underlined with the fresh salt-iness of the shore. Jock is very serious, almost messianic about these ingredients. This is not a preprandial stroll to find a trendy garnish for a girl's lunch salad. It's not an accent to a healthy, green, politically correct dinner. Nor is it about edible anthropology, a way back to precolonial campfires. There is no guilty prelapsarian nostalgia here: this is a quest to root Australian cuisine in its native landscape.

The country already has one of the best food cultures in the world. To eat in Sydney or Melbourne is to be offered a range of restaurants that are as good as any place on any continent anywhere, and far better than most. There are specialist producers breeding and growing impeccable ingredients, though very few that originate here. There are exclamatory wines and a cosmopolitan urban middle class disposed to eat well. And while they can eat the world, it's not easy to identify or eat Australian cuisine. They have always looked abroad for inspiration. For years it was mostly old English; then there was the addition of neighbouring Asian ingredients and methods, and with immigration, more regional food from all over. But if you try to think of specifically Australian things to eat, you come up with barbies, Vegemite, meat pies and a lot of odd biscuits. It doesn't come together to make a coherent cuisine. And then there's bush tucker: bet-and-dare reality-TV food, witchetty grubs, which, incidentally, are not at all bad, tasting a bit like veal crème brûlée.

Some Australian chefs see this as a freedom that allows them to cook everything from everywhere, without parochial let or hindrance; but Jock and a growing number of other cooks think that this is part of Australia's long-term cultural cringe, and that there is a need for the country's food to grow from the country.

Kangaroo Island is good farmland. Mild, with fields of grazing sheep and cattle, it's famous for honey, the quality of its meat and a pristine environment. It avoided a lot of the imported plagues of the mainland. There are no rabbits here; pets are guarded and regulated, though there are black pigs of a domesticated variety extinct everywhere else, left here by a French explorer. Other native Australian species have been brought into protected capsule communities.

There are delicate koalas who, close up, are nothing like as charming as they appear. Koalas were once omnivores, but have regressed to eating only certain eucalypts, which have very little protein, so they are forced to sleep for 22 hours a day. And they have managed to develop sexless chlamydia, and due to their delicate digestions they can't be given antibiotics, so they die of it – except in this little community.

The kangaroos, though, are still very good to eat. The island has its own subspecies with a particularly fine fur. The tail meat is best. Apparently, hopping is the most ergonomically economic of all the muscular propulsion methods. You get more distance per calorie if you're a kangaroo than any other runner, slitherer, loper or waddler. There are also thousands of wallabies that come out in the evening. Trapping wallabies was the prime source of meat for the early farmers as they cleared the land for imported animals. The land here was cleared of the spiky grass bushes that they call black-boy, or yakka, whose resin could be used for making fireworks and explosives. 'Hard yakka' is still Australian slang for hard work.

The bush was given to soldiers after the war, on the understanding that they would clear it. Their simple, prefabricated bungalows still dot the landscape. You realise that even this benignly fertile place was tarred and lonely. Australia's relationship with its land has always been an affair of grit and attrition, backbreaking and all too often heartbreaking.

There are a number of edible plants: there's anise myrtle and lemon myrtle and the amazing Dorrigo pepper, a seed that has a hot chilli flavour and numbs your mouth like Szechuan pepper. There are quandongs and ginger limes and little green ants that taste of lemon. And the wild-bee honey, which is thin and dark and has a flavour unlike any other.

We cooked a long barbie lunch for everyone and their kids, roasted a pig and a young kangaroo, and ate the scallops and the abalone and the freshwater crayfish from dams, and made salads and veg and ice cream and pies and damper bread, and there was a lot to drink. Everything was spiked and accompanied and bathed and rubbed with the distinctive flavours of this hard, tough and lucky land.

Early botanists who came out from Kew, avid to collect, press and name the glory of this new continent, unanimously agreed that while some of it was edible, none of it was to be eaten for pleasure, or with manners. A new generation of Australians is looking finally to make peace with this humid place; to admit that culturally, emotionally, you are what you eat.

January 2016

Ravenna

Ravenna is initially memorable for all the things it isn't. It isn't on an international bucket list of places to see before you die. It is in Italy but it isn't in any of the fashionable bits of Italy: not in Tuscany or on an island or on the Mediterranean. It's not got gondolas, and it's not got a Vatican, although it did have popes for a bit. Most notably, it doesn't fit into the collective, comfortable, historical legend of Italy. It is another in my occasional series of brilliant places to visit because everyone else is looking the other way.

Italy has a beautifully written, endlessly memorialised, lavishly illustrated and oft-repeated national story that is its blurb, its brochure, and it comes in two halves: classical, the Roman Empire; and classicism, the Empire reborn, the Renaissance, which slips into the Baroque. You know what you're looking at in Italy because, like the Bible and Shakespeare, you know the gist of the plot. But between the Romans and the Renaissance, there is another slice of history and culture that is quite as dazzling as what came before and after.

In northern Europe, we call the collapse of Rome and the schism of empire the Dark Ages: almost half a millennium of civilisation going into reverse. Fractured, fearful, murderous; rapine, darkness, superstition. In the south, in Italy, it's marked by great movements of people whose names have come to be synonymous with the destruction of civilisations: Vandals, Goths. But it's where Ravenna found its incomparably beautiful moment, in the shards of imperial disorder.

You arrive here and find an immensely agreeable, calm, elegant northern Italian town set in the fertile Po Valley. Ravenna is plainly a city that has money in its past: it's not flashy, but it is bucolically comfortable and generous with itself. The streets meander with a sedate opulence. People move about mostly by bicycle – they're not cyclists, they're pedestrians on bicycles. You'd be hard pushed to find a pair of drop handlebars, but there are lots of grandmothers with white buns and floral dresses, slowly pedalling baskets full of cheese and tortellini. The people move with that wandering, slow saunter that would have you pushed into the gutter in any northern European city. There are squares with cafés and *gelaterie*, small parks with cypress trees and, as this is the edge of Emilia-Romagna, plenty of cheeses and every iteration of pork and stuffed pasta. It's a constantly engaging city to eat in, like one long canapé plate.

Ravenna started out as an Etruscan town. It isn't on any big Roman road, so it quietly got on with trade and farming. Its first moment of celebrity was brought by Julius Caesar, returning with his army from Gaul, when he came to a stream called the Rubicon. The other side was Rome. He paused.

I asked a couple of chaps in a café where the Rubicon was.

'Do you know where the Rubicon is, Paolo?'

'Over there somewhere.'

'Yes, somewhere over there. Why do you want it? It's a little stream – nothing to see.'

'I thought I might cross it.'

'No, no, you don't want to do that. Look what happened to Julius Caesar.'

Ravenna's great moment came in the fifth century. Because of its high walls and its position and its fecundity, it was briefly made the capital of the Western Roman Empire. There were popes here, then there was Theodoric, the Ostrogoth from Hungary.

On our first morning, we walked from the small hotel to the centre of town. There was a sign that pointed to a baptistry, so we took a detour, and there it was – an octagonal brick building with arched windows, plainly of considerable age. It seemed to be squatting in the street. In fact, it had sunk, was sinking, into the earth. We walked in through the low door; there was no one there but a dozing attendant. I looked up and gasped. There, on the ceiling, is Christ, being baptised by John the Baptist, next to the older deity of the River Jordan. There, surrounded by the 12 apostles, like the petals of a giant daisy. It was ravishingly unexpected – certainly not what you'd predict in an Italian church. But this fifth-century baptistry was built by Theodoric, who was a believer in the eminently sensible Arian heresy, which states that Jesus Christ was the son of God and subordinate to the deity, not part of some eternal trinity.

In the early-afternoon heat, I stared up at these immensely vital and confident figures. Back home, this is when Hengist and Horsa were landing with the first Anglo-Saxon invasion of Britain. This is the Dark Ages before the first glimmer of a dawn, and this baptistry is the most modest of Ravenna's splendours. There is the Basilica of San Vitale and the church of Sant'Apollinare in Classe, with a dome containing the saint surrounded by bright flowers and birds, and his marvellous flock of sheep. There are chapels and oratories with starry roofs, and among the saints and biblical scenes there are moments of local life that are prosaic, touching, funny and ribald.

Ravenna has eight UNESCO-listed monuments, seven of which have images in mosaics. The form and the colour remain undimmed; they sing as vividly and as authoritatively as when they were laid. The cumulative effect of these exceptionally moving and limpidly engrossing buildings is like walking through a great song cycle, a brainwashing of gothic orthodoxy. It's dizzying, utterly engrossing and unforgettable. There is nowhere else I know that can present such unusual belief in such a coherent moment, from so far away. And there is barely anyone else here. By the eighth century, Ravenna had had its moment of being in the eye of interesting events and times, and it slid back to a regional somnambulance of cheese and ham and postprandial snoozing. But this Middle Aged gothic image of the tesserae of life and art and God wove its way into our culture – it came to us as romance, as horror, as the craft of William Morris and the aesthetic of John Ruskin. It moved into English cathedrals and the great, mad, architectural Tourette's of the Gothic Revival.

It amazes me that Ravenna isn't as packed as Assisi or Palermo. It remains vividly on my retina: the portraits in San Vitale, the saints and the apostles and the angels looking clearly, unmistakably contemporary – the faces of men and women in the street, collecting their morning focaccia. There could be few nicer cities to spend a long weekend in, strolling around, slipping in and out of the fifth, the sixth century, and back into the slow twenty-first. Mosaic renders the zealous and distant as familiar as neighbours. And then there's Dante. He came here in exile, to the paunchy quiet and bright stones, and finished his epic poem. He is buried here – the small mausoleum a place of pilgrimage for the Divine Comedy of European civilisation. He said: 'There is no greater sorrow than to recall in misery the time when we were happy.' There are also few greater joys than wandering through places that have had their moment of bright, energetic genius, but have now slipped into a long, hot has-been of comfort.

January 2016

Trains

I'm writing this on the train. I don't like writing on trains – the view keeps moving. The one piece of advice I can offer to aspiring writers is never, ever have a desk facing a window. When you look up, you should see only your thoughts. A moving window is not writer's block, but writer's tourniquet. The panorama wraps itself around your imagination, strangling ideas. (Actually, there's one other piece of advice – say everything you write out loud. Not muttering to yourself like a Shakespearean actor rehearsing *Henry V*. Though I don't recommend that on a train, either.)

I particularly like the view from trains. There's something about them that flatters a landscape. Or perhaps they just don't scare it. The country just doesn't look like it's running away or hiding as it does from motorways. The land trusts railway lines; it comes right up to the rails.

I'm travelling from London Euston to Penrith in Cumbria. The train will go on to Glasgow. This is one of the oldest lines in the world, purposefully chugging through towns that were made by the railway – and, in turn, made things that made railways necessary. Trains have been making this journey for over a hundred years; the railway is as much part of the landscape as the trees and the fields that run beside it. It is older than most of the buildings that come to meet it. The railway has both made and been incorporated into the land. So it seems not just part of the natural order, but if you look across a landscape and see a railway, it is the natural order, aesthetically harmonious, a punctuation.

Railways in Europe created the land they serve. In the nineteenth century, the railway was navigated north through rural England. It followed the old Great North Road. The engineers looked for a regional stop and naturally chose Stamford, an ancient market town and coaching stop built on a Roman road. It was the obvious place. Surrounded by the most fertile and prosperous farmland, home to Stilton and Melton Mowbray pies and haslet.

But Stamford was also surrounded, and mostly owned, by a local nob who said, 'You're not driving that damn filthy mechanical thing through my rolling acres, bringing all those unwashed, uninvited, unsavoury, unwanted common people into my town.' So the railway said fine, and they built their station in a small village just outside his fiefdom. No one had ever heard of it. The stop on the east-coast line was built on a place called Peterborough. And today Peterborough is a city, with a population of about 200,000. Stamford, meanwhile, snoozes in an economic decrepitude. It's got a pretty church, and a lot of pubs and about 21,000 souls. There is a small railway there which you can take to Peterborough.

It's an obvious truism that the means of travel change the places you travel to. They can even invent the places you travel to. But there is something particular and peculiar about the railway. It is the herald of the modern age. Before the railway, no one had ever travelled faster than a horse could gallop, if you don't count those who fell off cliffs. Railways were almost immediately romantic. They took ordinary folk from handmade, slow, isolated lives into ones crammed with possibility. The building of railways around the world are heroic stories of nation-forging. The great race to join up America across the prairies and the Rockies, with the creation of Chicago as the queen of plains, encouraging its stockyards that contained the cattle brought up from the south-west by rail and then sent by more rails as beef to New York, where they pretty much invented our idea of steak.

The railway opened up Latin America and Canada and made British investors titanic fortunes. The Indian railway is the second-biggest employer in the world, after the Chinese army. And the European rail network, whose immutable timetable forced the German invasion of Belgium and France and the First World War. Train journeys rattle in smoke, in romance, history and stories. Almost from their conception, they were worked into Victorian novels and from there into films and Country and Western songs. As a travel writer, I'm regularly asked to take rail journeys, which are meant to be moving destinations. They save you from really going anywhere; you're just taking a train. The favourite of these is the Orient Express, where you can dress up like an Agatha Christie character, and the Trans-Siberian Express, a week of mind-numbing boredom with the endless steppe to nowhere, and when you get out you have to get on an aeroplane and fly home.

Railways inspire a particular low form of nerdiness. I know that wonks are now fashionable and occasionally attractive. But there's a long way to go before you feel a twinge of excitement discovering that you're sitting next to a trainspotter. Railways and ships are the two forms of travel where the journey is commensurately as exciting as the destination. But there has to be a destination.

In my case, it's a literary festival on the lakes. There and back to London in a day. I wouldn't have done it if it had been a flight or a car journey. But the idea of six hours on a train has its attractions. I can work and read, but mostly I can watch the landscape slide past.

This is the best of England. The Pennines have a dusting of snow, there are daffodils along the track and the fields are speckled with ewes and new lambs. I've just passed the line where the hedges of the south are replaced by the dry stone walls of the north. Great trees stand alone in undulating fields and occasionally you see a solitary figure going about some silent rural pursuit who stands and stares at the rhythmic clatter of the passing train, still after all this time a thing that forces you to stop and watch, to tell children to make a wish.

The train is a harbinger of effort and endeavour, of adventure and obligation. A loaded jewel box carrying the mind to exceptional stories in rhythm, and businessmen on their phones shouting, 'I'm on the train.'

May 2016

Trump University

I say I never went to university. Well, it's not quite true. I did go once, to an American university, for a day. I say an American university, but that should come with inverted commas. There was some confusion over Trump's bona fides for membership of the academia club.

The date and the exact location are a little hazy. It was in 2009 and somewhere in New Jersey. I was sent on behalf of an American magazine with my American editor, Dana. I asked him if he can remember where Trump University lived. 'It wasn't that close to the city. It was out in the swampy cesspool of central Jersey.' He's a New Yorker: that's how they talk.

There wasn't a campus as such. Trump University didn't waste its students' fees on all that Ivy League collegiate barbershop a cappella singing, Alpha Beta Gamma fraternity campus bonding stuff. It set up in a hotel with convention facilities. Not big, not a grand international medical sort, or a scientific convention facility, but the type where you might get together with the annual Betamax and audio-cassette appreciation society, or a Nazi memorabilia free-trade association.

I remember that even by the standards of anonymous American hotels, it was hang-yourself-from-a-light-fitting depressing, a place that had been conceived from meagre aspirations and possibly as somewhere to pour the concrete onto mafia hits. It was perfect for

198

the assumptions and purposes of Trump University.

We arrived in the morning, got a cup of coffee-scented water from the hopeless school leaver in the humiliating uniform at the door and took a seat. There were a lot of seats in the hall, and it began to fill up with a collection of potential students who had all paid a few dollars to see if Trump's university life was for them. Mostly they were alone; a few had brought a husband or sibling. There was none of the chatter or clannish sitting-together that you'd find on real campuses. None of these people knew each other, or wanted to.

They were mostly late-middle-aged and disaffected. They looked older than their clothes implied. They were mostly overweight and plainly poor. Thinning hair and sallow skin: a lack of care that implied avoiding mirrors was cheaper than getting a facial or a haircut. Most came with bags and rucksacks. They were prepared for a long day: Tupperware boxes of cold pizza, orgies of bologna sandwiches, thermoses of fruit tea and bottles of soda. They trailed collapsible hip-support walking sticks, lumbar cushions and braces to abseil trousers over avalanching stomachs. They suffered from all the conditions of early ageing and bad diet, low maintenance and self-loathing: wobbly gait, thick ankles, bad joints, fat and grunting.

Most carried a demeanour of guarded resentment, rote-learnt disappointment and squandered hope that had been marinated and pickled into a cynical anger. Their battered faces didn't smile a lot. They were weather-proofed for disappointment. They were the Americans we never see in Europe, the ones who don't travel. They are the children and grandchildren of immigrants for whom the American dream reneged and passed over to others.

This was the year of Obama's stimulus package to help Americans out of the banking crisis. The banks had already been bailed out – it was the year they started paying bonuses again. Detroit had collapsed and Warren Buffett had the previous year bought $5bn of Goldman Sachs preferential shares that eventually made him $2bn profit. Michael Jackson died. It was the year of *Fantastic Mr Fox* and the national release of *The Hurt Locker* and when Harry and Pepper, San Francisco's famously gay penguins, split after Harry returned to heterodoxy with a flat-footed beaky widow sadly not called Sally.

In America, last century's industrial and semi-skilled jobs melted away across the border to Latin America and the Far East. Unemployment was 10 per cent. Here, in Jersey, it was closer to 15 per cent. What none of us knew was that seven years later there would be a collective name for all these people: Trump voters.

A man bounced onto a stage at the end of a room and whooped: 'Now, are you ready to make some money? I'm sorry, I didn't hear you. Do you want to make some money?' The crowd grunted and muttered. They weren't selling their enthusiasm cheaply.

He then explained that he was going to teach us how to make some serious real cash. It was easy money – we could all make easy money – but the reason everyone wasn't doing it was that they didn't know how and couldn't be bothered, and we had to be prepared to work at it. In this financial climate there were loads of opportunities to get rich.

My notes indicate he was called Scott. He welcomed us to what would undoubtedly be the most profitable day of our lives and said the great man, Donald Trump, had a message for us: 'If you don't take advantage of real estate in this market, you're an idiot.' The audience warmed.

Scott continued: 'I'm going to teach you why this session is an opportunity for people like you. You don't have to go out to eat, you don't have to go to the cinema,' he spoke like an enthusing mantra. 'You don't have to go on vacation. Do you have to invest in the stock market?' He paused, while the group muttered no. Then he pounced with the punchline: 'But you have to live somewhere.'

That's where we were supposed to make money. Everybody needed a roof. Whatever the fiscal weather, the real weather meant everyone had to have a roof. '$138,000. Would that help your family this year?' He looked expectantly at the audience. They muttered and laughed, without humour, and began shouting back 'Yes. Yes.'

Trump University taught the thing that people who never went to university think universities should teach: how to make money, and how to make money when you have no money. The way rich people make money. Not to be digging holes or banging nails or fetching and carrying, but the magic money way, the secret of whistles and commands that make money come to you.

Scott had an abbreviation. He used it a lot: OPM. He knew we didn't have investment cash, we didn't have good credit ratings, but he could fix that. What we needed was OPM. OPM turned out to be other people's money.

There were ways of buying and selling property that didn't involve money going out; only money coming in. It was all done with the mirrors of timing and research. There was something called the six-figure option system, though I don't think I understood it at the time. It involved things like double escrow closure, which essentially means buying and selling the same property on the same day, so that you register two sales simultaneously. A second buyer pays the first seller and you pocket the difference in the middle. Needless to say, the final owner and the initial owner mustn't know about each other until the deal is done because they might take it amiss and bury you in the New Jersey swamps.

What we were all aiming for was PPCF – Positive Passive Cash Flow. The sound of positive passive cash flow was like the American dream running past, whispering in your ear as it slid by while you sat on the sofa eating doughnuts. The money would just flow upstairs and hide itself under the mattress.

Of course, you couldn't learn all this in one get-together in a horrid hotel. You needed – we needed – to sign up to a series of easy-to-use interactive courses and pamphlets and books that explained everything step by step. And if we signed on the dotted line for the $25,000 enhanced five-star degree, we would get hand-picked mentors who would talk us through the forms and the paperwork, hold our hands through the difficult bits, all the way to the bank.

Scott stoked up all the resentment and fear these people had for forms and clauses and legal documents and men behind desks and being put on hold. This was the recession – unemployment and closed shops and food stamps and welfare. 'A perfect storm of once-in-a-generation opportunity. Foreclosures in your area are booming today. New Jersey is hot right now,' exclaimed Scott in a Trumpish way. 'The recession doesn't affect the rich; it affects the middle class.' (In America, everyone who speaks English as a first language is middle-class.) And he broke off and asked, apropos of nothing: 'What drugs are you on? Do you drink that green stuff?' This was a joke. That's what the middle class over the river drank, with silly money, paying $6 or $7 for a glass of grass juice. He laughed. 'I'm debt-free,' he said, like an ex-junkie proclaiming himself clean. 'Write yourself a cheque for $1m. You can cash it in a year. I guarantee you will be worth it if you sign up and do the hard work.' You don't have to drink stupid grass juice. 'I've got an MBA from Trump University. A massive bank account.' Now the audience was whooping. They liked this mixture of cunning and fundamental religion. They might not be up for the hand-picked mentor, but this was a better way of spending a day than watching QVC and 'I've got an MBA' was good pick-up bar banter.

In the lunchbreak we walked through the lobby and there was a small market of grinning, desperate property brokers, in flashy ties and cheap shoes, trying to interest us in the ground-floor opportunities of investment in potential timeshare golf courses in Colorado or retirement home opportunities – as yet unbuilt – in South Carolina. There was even a shifty and hopeless fat, middle-aged British man trying to sell shares in a proposed brownfield development in south London.

The bright computer-generated posters of sunny bungalows and elegant recreation spaces, with those architecture people tripping past the herbaceous borders, were like the illustrations in bedtime stories, soothing promises of a better tomorrow. We went back for the afternoon session. More turbo-enthused mentors promised a New Jerusalem of magic wealth. Members of the audience asked detailed and confused questions and were answered with clear, head-patting condescension.

Then someone said, with a peculiar intense emphasis that was like a witch's warning: Americans need $1m to retire. Aged 65, 45 per cent of people depend on relatives, 30 per cent depend on charity, 23 per cent are still working, 2 per cent are self-sustained. The starkness of this grim warning fell on this audience like hoar frost. They shifted and sagged in their chairs at the thought of the 98 per cent certainty of begging and insecurity, a handout, coupon-clipping, chilly, lonely old age just round the foreclosed corner.

Maybe this real estate thing was their last chance to be anxiety-free, the comfortable pair in a hundred. Quoting Trump, somebody shouted: 'I challenge you to change your thinking.'

I never wrote the article. The university was a sad shakedown of the detritus of the recession. But the big fairy story at the time was still Obama with the hope and change thing. Trump was just a third-rate furious joke reality-TV presenter who sold mail-order steak and fronted ugly, gilded tower blocks and bankrupt casinos. It wasn't much of a future, and the victims, these willing gulls, were difficult people to sympathise with: angry losers with uncomfortable prejudices and brutal opinions. They weren't part of anyone's solution or future.

But in retrospect it all seems much more prophetic. These marginalised, discarded people turned out to overtake and ransack one of America's two great political parties. What Trump was offering them was a way out; it was riches at the expense of their neighbours. You take advantage of the misfortune of other people just like yourself. There is no community or solidarity; just winners and losers. The more losers there are, the greater the reward for the winners.

Trump talks about the idiots and the fools and the no-hopers.

You're either exploited or you're an exploiter. 'If you watch TV,' said Trump, 'you're a loser. Turn off the TV.' This from a man whose fame and fortune was made by TV. The winners are on the box; the losers are watching.

In a country built on rugged individualism, and with a deep suspicion of collective bargaining and class solidarity, the answer to the recession in the market was for the victims, the poor white middle class, to slug it out among themselves. America promises the opportunity to succeed. There is no guaranteed outcome. Bleakly and bluntly, what Trump University really offered was a course in fiscal cannibalism, where you consumed your next-door neighbour's misfortune so that you would survive. They were treated like rats in a bucket. And, of course, the biggest carrion-eating survivor was Trump himself, who had existed all his life on OPM, starting with his father's fortune.

The millions of Americans who now vote for Trump are an unpalatable, embarrassing and inexplicable mystery to the Americans who wouldn't consider voting for him, as they are to everyone watching from the bleachers of the rest of the world. But they were and are the natural consequence of a society that lauds and mythologises winners. The non-winners don't just go away to be good, acquiescent losers; they get furious and bitter, and they blame the rules and the establishment referee, and they want comeuppance, someone to blame, and they attach themselves to the biggest, flashiest, self-proclaimed carnival-headed winner out there.

In my notes I often draw. And in the Trump University notes there is a sketch of a man holding an umbrella in the rain, but he's not wearing any trousers, just his shirt tails. I don't remember why I drew it. It might have been a reference to the sans-culottes; it might have been something somebody said. But it looks like the thoughtlessness of lending a man a brolly when what he actually needs is pants.

June 2016

Europe

It was the woman on *Question Time* that really did it for me. She was so familiar. There is someone like her in every queue, every coffee shop, outside every school in every parish council in the country. Middle-aged, middle-class, middle-brow, over-made-up, with her National Health face and weatherproof English expression of hurt righteousness, she's Britannia's mother-in-law. The camera closed in on her and she shouted: 'All I want is my country back. Give me my country back.' It was a heartfelt cry of real distress and the rest of the audience erupted in sympathetic applause, but I thought: 'Back from what? Back from where?'

Wanting the country back is the constant mantra of all the outies. Farage slurs it, Gove insinuates it. Of course I know what they mean. We all know what they mean. They mean back from Johnny Foreigner, back from the brink, back from the future, back-to-back, back to bosky hedges and dry stone walls and country lanes and church bells and warm beer and skittles and football rattles and cheery banter and clogs on cobbles. Back to vicars-and-tarts parties and *Carry On* fart jokes, back to Elgar and fudge and proper weather and herbaceous borders and cars called Morris. Back to Victoria sponge and 22 yards to a wicket and 15 hands to a horse and 3 feet to a yard and four fingers in a KitKat, back to gooseberries not avocados, back to deference and respect, to make do and mend and smiling bravely and biting your lip and suffering in silence and patronising foreigners with pity.

We all know what 'getting our country back' means. It's snorting a line of the most pernicious and debilitating Little English drug, nostalgia. The warm, crumbly, honey-coloured, collective 'yesterday' with its fond belief that everything was better back then, that Britain (England, really) is a worse place now than it was at some foggy point in the past where we achieved peak Blighty. It's the knowledge that the best of us have been and gone, that nothing we can build will be as lovely as a National Trust Georgian country house, no art will be as good as a Turner, no poem as wonderful as 'If', no writer a touch on Shakespeare or Dickens, nothing will grow as lovely as a cottage garden, no hero greater than Nelson, no politician better than Churchill, no view more throat-catching than the White Cliffs and that we will never manufacture anything as great as a Rolls-Royce or Flying Scotsman again.

The dream of Brexit isn't that we might be able to make a brighter, new, energetic tomorrow, it's a desire to shuffle back to a regret-curdled, inward-looking yesterday. In the Brexit fantasy, the best we can hope for is to kick out all the work-all-hours foreigners and become caretakers to our own past in this self-congratulatory island of moaning and pomposity.

And if you think that's an exaggeration of the Brexit position, then just listen to the language they use: 'We are a nation of inventors and entrepreneurs, we want to put the great back in Britain, the great engineers, the great manufacturers.' This is all the expression of a sentimental nostalgia. In the Brexiteer's mind's eye is the old Pathe newsreel of Donald Campbell, John Logie Baird with his television, Barnes Wallis and his bouncing bomb, and Robert Baden Powell inventing boy scouts in his shed.

All we need, their argument goes, is to be free of the humourless Germans and spoilsport French and all their collective liberalism and reality. There is a concomitant hope that if we manage to back out of Europe, then we'll get back to the bowler-hatted 1950s and the Commonwealth will hold pageants, firework displays and beg to be back in the Queen Empress' good books again. Then New Zealand will sacrifice a thousand lambs, Ghana will ask if it can go back to being called the Gold Coast and Britain will resume hand-making Land Rovers and top hats and Sheffield-plate teapots.

There is a reason that most of the people who want to leave the EU are old while those who want to remain are young: it's because the young aren't infected with Bisto nostalgia. They don't recognise half the stuff I've mentioned here. They've grown up in the EU and at worst it's been neutral for them.

The under-thirties want to be part of things, not aloof from them. They're about being joined up and counted. I imagine a phrase most outies identify with is 'women's liberation has gone too far'. Everything has gone too far for them, from political correctness – well, that's gone mad, hasn't it? – to health and safety and gender-neutral lavatories. Those oldies, they don't know if they're coming or going, what with those new-fangled mobile phones and kids on Tinder and Grindr. What happened to meeting Miss Joan Hunter Dunn at the tennis club? And don't get them started on electric hand-dryers, or something unrecognised in the bagging area, or Indian call centres, or the impertinent computer asking for a password that has both capitals and little letters and numbers and more than eight digits.

We listen to the Brexit lot talk about the trade deals they're going to make with Europe after we leave, and the blithe insouciance that what they're offering instead of EU membership is a divorce where you can still have sex with your ex. They reckon they can get out of the marriage, keep the house, not pay alimony, take the kids out of school, stop the in-laws going to the doctor, get strict with the visiting rights, but, you know, still get a shag at the weekend and, obviously, see other people on the side.

Really, that's their best offer? That's the plan? To swagger into

Brussels with Union Jack pants on and say: 'Ello luv, you're looking nice today. Would you like some?'

When the rest of us ask how that's really going to work, leavers reply, with Terry Thomas smirks, that 'they're going to still really fancy us, honest, they're gagging for us. Possibly not Merkel, but the bosses of Mercedes and those French vintners and cheesemakers, they can't get enough of old John Bull. Of course they're going to want to go on making the free market with two backs after we've got the *decree nisi*. Makes sense, doesn't it?'

Have no doubt, this is a divorce. It's not just business, it's not going to be all reason and goodwill. Like all divorces, leaving Europe would be ugly and mean and hurtful, and it would lead to a great deal of poisonous xenophobia and racism, all the niggling personal prejudice that dumped, betrayed and thwarted people are prey to. And the racism and prejudice are, of course, weak points for us. The tortuous renegotiation with lawyers and courts will be bitter and vengeful, because divorces always are and, just in passing, this sovereignty thing we're supposed to want so badly, like Frodo's ring, has nothing to do with you or me. We won't notice it coming back, because we didn't notice not having it in the first place.

You won't wake up on 24 June and think: 'Oh my word, my arthritis has gone! My teeth are suddenly whiter! Magically, I seem to know how to make a soufflé and I'm buff with the power of sovereignty.' This is something only politicians care about; it makes not a jot of difference to you or me if the Supreme Court is a bunch of strangely out-of-touch old gits in wigs in Westminster, or a load of strangely out-of-touch old gits without wigs in Luxembourg. What matters is that we have as many judges as possible on the side of personal freedom.

Personally, I see nothing about our legislators in the UK that makes me feel I can confidently give them more power. The more checks and balances politicians have, the better for the rest of us. You can't have too many wise heads and different opinions. If you're really worried about red tape, by the way, it's not just a European problem. We're perfectly capable of coming up with our own rules and regulations and we have no shortage of jobsworths. Red tape may be annoying, but it's also there to protect your and my family from being lied to, poisoned and cheated.

The first 'X' I ever put on a voting slip was to say yes to the EU. The first referendum was when I was 20 years old. This one will be in the week of my 62nd birthday. For nearly all my adult life, there hasn't been a day when I haven't been pleased and proud to be part of this great collective. If you ask me for my nationality, the truth is I feel more European than anything else. I am part of this culture, this European civilisation. I can walk into any gallery on our continent and completely understand the images and the stories on the walls. These people are my people and they have been for thousands of years. I can read books on subjects from Ancient Greece to Dark Ages Scandinavia, from Renaissance Italy to nineteenth-century France, and I don't need the context or the landscape explained to me. The music of Europe, from its scales and its instruments to its rhythms and religion, is my music. The Renaissance, the Rococo, the Romantics, the Impressionists, Gothic, Baroque, Neoclassicism, Realism, Expressionism, Futurism, Fauvism, Cubism, Dada, Surrealism, Postmodernism and Kitsch were all European movements and none of them belongs to a single nation.

There is a reason why the Chinese are making fake Italian handbags and the Italians aren't making fake Chinese ones. This European culture, without question or argument, is the greatest, most inventive, subtle, profound, beautiful and powerful genius that was ever contrived anywhere by anyone and it belongs to us. Just look at my day job – food. The change in food culture and pleasure has been enormous since we joined the EU, and that's no coincidence. What we eat, the ingredients, the recipes, may come from around the world, but it is the collective to and fro of European interests, expertise and imagination that has made it all so very appetising and exciting. The restaurant was a European invention, naturally. The first one in Paris was called The London Bridge.

Culture works and grows through the constant warp and weft of creators, producers, consumers, intellectuals and instinctive lovers. You can't dictate or legislate for it, you can just make a place that encourages it and you can truncate it. You can make it harder and more grudging, you can put up barriers and you can build walls, but why on earth would you? This collective culture, this golden civilisation grown on this continent over thousands of years, has made everything we have and everything we are; why would you not want to be a part of it?

I understand that if we leave we don't have to hand back our library ticket for European civilisation, but why would we even think about it? In fact, the only ones who would are those old, philistine scared gits. Look at them, too frightened to join in.

June 2016

IN HERE

Tweed

———

Do you ever wonder what the rest of the world sees when they imagine us? What is it that is peculiarly, particularly British? Not our history; history is parochial. They're as interested in ours as we are in theirs. The Spitfires are all rust, Rolls-Royces are German, cricket is Indian, nobody wears a bowler hat. Tea or bitter, perhaps? Except we drink more coffee and lager. Poetry, pop songs, taxis in the rain? It might surprise you that it's probably a suit. The suit has colonised more places than our language, has homogenised more culture than Toyota, Hollywood and pizza combined. There is not a city in the world where a tailor won't make you one. If you don't know what to wear, wear a suit. It is the default wardrobe setting; the most successful garment in the history of fashion, and it is wholly, indivisibly, a British invention.

The suit evolved for military and riding kit that awkwardly left it with residual, useless buttons on the cuff, receding lapels, pointless pocket flaps and a lot of weird rules. The suit has been so remarkably successful not because it is particularly well suited to its many careers – it isn't efficient, practical or comfortable – but it does come with pockets full of assumptions that are understood in every language and culture.

A suit says authority, learning, expertise, manners, probity, efficiency, trust and a certain formality: all attributes traditionally thought of as British. As they used to say on Madison Avenue: 'Think

Yiddish, dress Briddish.' You can make suits out of all sorts of stuff: cotton, rayon, linen, silk . . . But the best suits are made from wool. Britain's story, its image, is wrapped and warped in wool. Wool paid for the Hundred Years War, built the industrial mills of Yorkshire and the Borders, as well as the smug manners and boastful churches of the Cotswolds. It was wool that cleared the Highlands, stole the common land and enclosed it with hedges. Britain's stake money to play at the table of greatness and Empire was made from wool, and in recognition of this the Lord Chancellor, in his pomp, sits on a woolsack.

Wool can be woven into a gallimaufry of cloths: calamanco, drap de Berry, shoddy, drugget, duffel, flannel, hodden, linsey, melton, serge, tricot, wadmal, worsted, zephyr . . . But the greatest of all, for which the grandest sheep can aspire to give the coat off its back, is tweed.

I have a bit of a thing for tweed. I love its feel and its smell, I love that it's rough but homely, that it has the ability to deflect the elements with a jaunty nonchalance. Tweed is like a game terrier; always pleased to see you, always wants to go out, always optimistic. In tweed you walk further, breathe deeper. Merely sprightly grows jaunty. Tweed silently hums 'Charlie is My Darling' and 'The Road to the Isles'. It is the perfect balance of utility and panache, and it is my secret vice. Well, not so secret. It's difficult to keep tweed a secret. I have drawers full of bolts that are curled up, nascent suits, coats, chaos and plus fours. So, when a man with a pinstriped, flannel voice called to ask would I perhaps consider designing my own tweed and have it made into, say, a suit by, say, Anderson & Sheppard . . . Well, I said, I'll have to think about it. And then squealed like a big girl.

Tweed is a parable, a stereotype of Britishness. We are tweedy. Tweed is taciturn and hardworking, sturdy, dependable, loyal. Tweed doesn't get soppy or go limp. It fits with the familiarity of first-name terms, and it always has a mint, a penknife and a pebble in its pocket.

The history of tweed begins, like so much history, with a misunderstanding. Though the name plainly comes from the river that rolls darkly along the border between England and Scotland, it is most likely an English mishearing of a Scots weaver saying 'twill', that he'd have pronounced 'tweel'. Tweed is a twill cloth made with a rib; the weft thread goes over two warp threads and then under two, giving a diagonal pattern that can be made into things like houndstooth and herringbone by adding a step. (I'm just passing this on, I don't really understand what it means.)

Unlike ordinary woven fabric, twill has a front and a back with a distinct texture that makes it hang particularly well. It originates from Scotland, with the introduction of the Cheviot sheep, which gave a particularly fine, strong wool. Where Scotland had traditionally grazed skinny cattle, sheep produced more meat, and a double income.

The dark, indigenous Scottish sheep was traditionally used for the old Hebridean Harris tweed, a mix of natural brown or black and white wool, woven to create the original tweed pattern, 'shepherd's check', and was used to wrap newborn lambs. But Scottish tweed is, like so many things, really an English desire, and surprisingly modern.

When the clan system collapsed in the middle of the eighteenth century, and the wearing of tartan was banned, and the chieftains wanted no more of this old, sad song, they sold their clansmen for sheep and their traditional fiefdoms to the English aristocracy with new industrial money, and to a surprising number of brewers, collectively known as the 'beerage', for sporting estates. The most valuable tenants in the Highlands turned out not to be crofters or shepherds, but grouse and deer. Out of the bankruptcy and grieving, a new romantic, sentimental Scottishness was embroidered. The Anglo-lairds wanted to dress up on holiday. They invented estate tweed, using the new wool from the new sheep, from the new mills. It imitated tartan, with checks and patterns that were identified with places, and then families and estates. All your retainers and servants, the stalkers and gillies, were kitted out in your particular tweed. The first, Glen Feshie, was woven in 1841. The patterns and colours grew more expressionistic as bored, aristocratic wives got artistic, like kittens in a knitting shop.

Originally, wool was dyed with the mosses and lichens and peat of the country it grazed over. A particular creamy yellow came from sheep that had been covered in butter and tar to help them make it through the winter. But the accidental discovery of mauveine, and aniline dyeing, arrived in the 1860s, then there was no holding back the hue and dye.

Tweed grew strident and exuberant. Scottish mills and shops offered a bespoke service where a man would come to your estate with his swatches and watercolour box, and, accompanied by the laird and his wife, would mix a tweed that would blend into your craggy acres. A suit that looks like clown's pyjamas in a drawing room may well disappear into the heather at 50 yards. The Lovat mixture, a particularly subtle and beautiful blue-green, contains half a dozen colours that Lord Lovat is said to have noticed on a bosky bank in spring.

The madly dashing Lord Elcho designed a hodden brown-grey tweed that had for years made working men's cloth caps and capes and was worn all over Scotland. Because he was raising the London Scottish Regiment, and didn't want to use a particular clan tartan, he perceptively said that a soldier was a man-hunter and, like a deer-stalker, should blend in with the landscape. This hodden cloth is the origin of khaki and all military camouflage.

The consequence of both the duke and his gillie wearing the same suit meant tweed grew to be a democratic cloth. The colonel and the private, the weekend plutocrat and communist intellectual all wear it. Look at photographs of the football crowds of the 1930s, the Jarrow marchers, the enlistment queues of 1914 . . . They are furrowed fields of tweed caps just like the Royal princes wore.

Tweed is Scottish, occasionally Irish. I had never heard of English tweed until I got the call from Fox Brothers, who weave the stuff in Wellington, Somerset. They are one of the oldest woollen manufacturers in Britain, officially founded in 1772. Along the way they invented flannel, and Douglas Cordeaux is their current Managing Director. Would I, he asked, like to come and see the mill where they would make my tweed?

The factory sits on the quiet, untidy edge of this little triumphalist town. It is vast, like some ancient henge, a brick-built lump of Victorian industrial muscle; beautiful for its steepling, russet self-confidence, a great temple to the warp and weft of Mammon and commerce. And it is completely silent. The mechanical crash of hundreds of looms echoes on the caw of rooks. The windows, through which the sunlight would have caught the falling snow of dancing woollen chaff, are boarded up, the doors padlocked.

Most of the cloth made here was military: 852 miles of Lord Elcho's new khaki were supplied to the Ministry of Defence in the Great War to make puttees. In its day this place must have surged with thousands of workers, hundreds of looms, the air heavy with din and cash. After 20 minutes looking round for a living soul, we found what is left of Fox Brothers: an outbuilding with half a dozen Morris Minor weaving machines worked by a score of dedicated weavers. Still, the rhythmic clatter is like being at a conceptual heavy-metal concert.

Weaving is one of the most ancient human trades, its principles as old as civilisation. The process remains unchanged, but the machines that make the cloth have a fearsome complexity: hundreds and hundreds of threads, the flying shuttle, the myriad hooks that grab the spools that reel the dozens of cogs and levers that know their place. All the moving parts are as temperamental as performing fleas. They shudder and clunk, and slowly the cloth becomes visible a line at a time. This is immensely skilled work, constantly checking tensions, mending broken threads. A moment's inattention can cost a thumb or an arm.

The tweed produced here is as fine and beautiful as any I've seen from Scotland. They use the wool from West Country sheep: hard and durable. But what is really astonishing about this place is its records. The great ledgers of orders and samples go back to before Jane Austen. Teetering piles of swatches line corridors to the ceiling. Dusty, uncollated, uncounted, they are cloth cliffs, a geology of fashion and taste. Pulled out at random, these are culture fossils, hinting of glimpses into the way we once were. Those moments of exuberance and boldness, and the years of dark probity.

The checks run through them like graphs of prosperity and hardship. Dauntingly, you see the possibilities of tweed are endless. The threads of wool are as numerous as notes of music. These mills were great mechanical organs beating out the solid rhythms and folk tunes of British life.

Back in London, I've decided: my tweed is going to be urban. A town tweed. Tweeds are from the country, their colours and purposes are earthy and rural, but I want an estate tweed for housing estates. I'm given a woolly palette of natural colours and told to get on with it, and I begin by having a fatwa on tweed.

I can't look at any more. It's too confusing, too intimidating, so I just go for a walk, and look through my lashes at the city, trying to see it as a landscape of valleys and cliffs, sun-bright vistas and distant, charcoal peaks and escarpments, and to imagine a cloth that will blend into this natural environment.

The town is much lighter than I expected. The dark concrete and the tarmac shine in the flat light, particularly when they're wet. And there is far less brick than you'd imagine. I live in Chelsea, and there's a lot of white stucco, York-stone pavements of lovely shades of fawn and sienna. I'm ignoring the strident dabs of colour, like telephone boxes and buses, and make an early aesthetic decision to veto yellow lines. It's a hellish colour to wear unless you're a

Chinese emperor, and too jokily obvious for a town tweed. And I'm surprised at how much blue there is: road signs, in the smoky blue of exhausts, teal and metallic blue in the shadows. Then I go and do some extemporary drawing on an iPad, which turns out to be rather good for this. I use my children's crayon application to make dozens of impressionistic smudges with my fingers, rub them out, compare them, combine them and email them to the tweed-makers. It is quick and invigorating.

The first series of ideas that come back are a disappointment. I put a line of mauve in some of the drawings, partly as a nod to the original aniline dye and partly as an echo of the absent heather. But the designs all look like the Queen Mother's purple-and-blue picnic rug.

I decide on a type of weave, an unusual diamond pattern, where you might expect a dogtooth. And then comes a blanket, like a quilt, with 20-odd variations on a theme, all fugues on my design. The range and subtlety are wonderful, the choice horrible. But one stands out as being conspicuously what I'd set out to make: a tweed that looks like the city, while still being in harmony with its august country ancestors.

It is sent back to the mill to be woven, and then to Huddersfield to be finished. Finishing is an ancient and ridiculously skilled job to get just the right nap and softness on the cloth. I've chosen a heavy tweed because it drapes much better across the body, particularly in trousers.

A couple of months later, I get a call from Anderson & Sheppard. My finished cloth has arrived, would I like to come in and discuss the suit? I'm out of the door before they hang up.

I unroll the bolt of cloth in the window and can't see it for looking. I'm surrounded by disturbingly suave tailors who each take an expert finger and thumb to my material. Each wears an expression of mild surprise. Tailors train their faces to show no more than mild anything. Extremes of emotion are bad for business.

'Well,' says John Hitchcock, the head cutter. 'I think that's a very nice bit of tweed. Very nice indeed,' he adds for rare emphasis. And I see it. It really is a very nice bit of tweed. A very, very nice bit of tweed. The check of blue, with a cross of faint mauve, a touch of urban green and the York stone, and the warm, dark-grey diamond. I've held first copies of books I've written. None has given me as deep a satisfaction as the thrill of this tweed. I'm hopeless with my hands, at crafty things, but here is a made thing from a great tradition of made things, of beautiful cloth. And I made it, and it isn't an embarrassment, it's fine.

My suit is traditional three-piece, with three buttons. It's comfortable and confident, with the characteristic Anderson & Sheppard cut. It hangs well and moves well, and it elicits glances rather than stares. In the 1930s, Anderson & Sheppard would make 500 suits a week, and a great many of them would be tweed. Now there are fewer, and the percentage of tweed has fallen to very few. We should wear more tweed. In a monochrome-suited world, tweed is individual, and as colourful as you dare to go. It won't let you look like a city drone or an office clone, and it is as close as we will ever come to a national costume, as culturally indigenous as the Masai's red toga, the Buddhist's saffron robe or the cowboy's Stetson. Tweed is who we are.

I walked down Savile Row and Bond Street. It was Valentine's Day. The pavement was full of girls wearing secret smiles. I took the suit to have tea. The next day I was forwarded this tweet by someone called Harriet Evans, who appears to be a lady novelist. 'Saw AA Gill having tea by himself in the Wolseley, in a loud tweed suit with a Tiffany bag next to him, like a villain in an Agatha Christie.' You couldn't get more perfectly, satisfyingly British than that.

March 2011

Fur

—————

It's difficult to tell how big this room is. It echoes like a cathedral, and you could certainly play team games with a ball, if it wasn't gridded with the scaffolding of industrial storage, the vaulting of commerce that creeps up and up, shelf upon shelf, forming perfect perspectives sliding towards vanishing points, each level neatly stacked to uniform capacity with cardboard boxes labelled and bar-coded, all placed just so. There are other hangars like this, with pale, buff cardboard cliffs. The fluorescent light flickers and hums to itself.

Each box hides bodies: 30 or 40, packed snug, smelling faintly of chemicals and decay, like an internet catacomb, a furry Amazon. When the invoices are paid – and not before – they will be shipped out to live again as second skins. Jackets and coats, hats and blankets, and comic codpieces. This serene, bland hall is mink heaven. The number, the sheer repetition of the deceased, is silencing. The industrial scale, the efficiency of this luxury death is astonishing. Who knew that so many people wanted a mink? The thought of just how much speculative, atavistic, grateful and aspirational thank-you sex the shiny pelts in this room represent is exhausting. And who would guess that it would be the Danes of all people – liberal, eco-friendly, concerned, inoffensively decent and caring Danes – who would be supplying all the bodies?

Kopenhagen Fur's auction house, a functionally polite, modern complex in a gently dull bit of the city, isn't a secret or particularly guarded. There are no high walls or barbed wire. The staff are helpful rather than defensive. Behind the Scandy modern desk, smart girls answer phones and hand out brochures. Suited men with briefcases and clipboards have places to be, and technicians in white coats chat professionally. You'd think this was a cosmetics firm or a baby-food manufacturer rather than the world's largest dealer in skin.

Inside, the auction room is frankly disappointing. You want it to be a Viking hall, a furry charnel house, to have Bond-girl models sashaying in full-length fur, or at least a constant squirm of mink being paraded round a ring in malevolent herds. But it's only a screen with numbers, money and lots, and a man with a microphone trying to get through the proceedings speedily and smoothly. This is business, not pleasure or luxury. The excitement is glacial; the tiers of seats are three-quarters full with bidders who pore over the dense, unillustrated catalogue or lounge with a distracted boredom. And here's the surprise: the majority are Chinese. They are buying mink as fast as the little blighters can be skinned, along with everything else in the world that isn't actually nailed down or handcuffed to a radiator. The Chinese, resurgent from a generation of uniform austerity, want fur. In a tsunami of ostentation they are gulping luxury, from claret to gold – a bulimic, bourgeois enthusiasm for riches. These auctions take place five times a year.

Contrary to everything you imagined or heard about the demise of fur, this is a burgeoning, bullish business, and it's not remotely apologetic, shy or retiring. Some 50 million mink skins are produced in the world each year, 14 million of them farmed in Denmark. The Chinese have a particular appetite for Western glamour, so fur has been making a precipitately salacious and suggestive comeback in fashion shows. But it's not just the Chinese: all the other BRIC countries have seen a vast increase in fur sales as economies boom. The Italians and French have always worn lots of fur. In America fur sales are rising. And despite a vociferous campaign here, fur sales in Britain are up 40 per cent on last year. Two-thirds of fur sold around the world is Origin Assured – legally farmed and strictly regulated. The Danes note, with a po-faced pleasure, that in London, Paris, New York and Milan, 80 per cent of catwalks included real fur. Campaigns and protests are also prone to the vagaries of fashion. Bunny-hugging and the ugliness of throwing raccoons at Anna Wintour is now so over. Fashion has moved on. It's a grown-up business, the fourth-largest in the world, and it's really not about to miss out in the glitziest gold-rush, high-end, luxury market in the global shopping village simply for the sake of a little ethical squeamishness, proselytised by people who, frankly, dress like shit anyway. All those sulky, elegant fashionista shops in the smart streets of the old sophisticated capitals of the West are now merely authentication and heritage, billboards for the 'smoking kill' of Shanghai, Singapore and Kuala Lumpur. Fur, and particularly mink, is the wrapping of aspiration and success.

The Chinese fur buyers sit hunched in the auction house's cafeteria, which offers two menus: smorgasbord and noodles. For all the Scandinavian cool liberality and expensive capitalist flash that surrounds them, they still have the heroic, earthy look of the hands-on proletariat. However they dress, however big their watches, they are still a horde, huddled round coffee tables playing unending games of poker with sticky grey cards, and have to be regularly reminded such gambling is illegal in this caring and protective society. The hosts have also provided them with their own lavatories because, I'm told with a particularly Scandinavian, direct delicacy, culturally, Chinese bathroom habits are more extemporarily scatological than we're used to in Europe. The Chinese may want to buy the world and everything in, under and over it, they may yearn for the flower of Western culture, the panache of European taste, but they still want to remain singularly other, and collectively Chinese.

The small in-house shopping arcade displays posters of mercenary girls with too much eyeshadow and carmine leers, wearing hideous, tacky confections of f***-me fur. This year's leitmotif logo, which is everywhere, is a huge tarantula made of mink. I would like to meet the man who imagined that combining an animal that terrifies people with one that disgusts them would be a cute and witty way to rebrand the fur trade.

Next to the auction room are the back halls, where the skins are graded for size on conveyors with spectrometers for colour. The machinery deposits the bodies in bins. They are fed by white-gloved Danes bored to stupefaction. The luxury and value of the product on a conveyor matter not at all. It is still the most deadly, inhuman workplace ever conceived. The skins are strung together in matched swags and hung on racks to make great Narnia forests of silent wildness; fur trees. The white-coated furriers pick and stroke their way through the soft hair, examining pelts on white tables with Anglepoise lights. Their fingers fondle with the practised dexterity of beauticians and lotharios. The pelts are about a yard long, cubes of dense and sybaritic fur. The only thing that identifies them as having once been individual animals is the small currant nose at one end. The males are bigger, the females finer, lighter, more valuable.

Fur comes in a number of qualities and a supranatural range of colours: black, mahogany, brown, glow, pearl-beige, golden pearl, white, sapphire, silver-blue, black cross, var cross, pastel, violet, blue iris, jaguar, palomino and stardust. In the natural world mink arrives as either brown or black. Its fur has two sorts of hair: short, dense, warm, oiled body fur, and longer guard hairs, like cats' whiskers, that let the mink know where it is in its waterside habitat. The length of these hairs helps to denote the quality of the pelt. Mink like swimming, they hunt fish, so the fur has an aquiline dynamic and a mermaid lustre. Even when flayed it possesses a ghostly vitality. Mink is moreish. Stroking it is therapeutic, calming, mildly sensual. It's erotically furtive, a solitary pleasure that's difficult to stop. Each pelt invites a caress, a strumming finger, smooth and soft against the back of your hand. The furriers go about their work with an intense, frotty joy. They have good hands, furriers. Particularly gentle, soft hands, supple and smooth. It's the mink oil.

Denmark is not a dramatic country. It can't boast the fjords and mountains of its Nordic neighbours. Mostly it's a plain of gently undulating agricultural land, hovering above sea level, dotted with modestly functional houses and copses of birch trees and wind farms. It is one of the top 10 greenest countries in the world. It is both privately conservative and communally liberal. Copenhagen has been voted the most liveable city in the world. It takes cleanliness and godliness and civic responsibility very, very seriously. Danes care. So how did they end up as the universe's biggest mink farmers?

First thing, the mink like it here. The commercially farmed mink is not the European variety, but North American. Persecuted in their original habitat, there are millions of them as refugees in Denmark, all behind bars. There is something about the weather they like, and probably the Danes themselves suit the mink: they appreciate their ecological concerns, their humanitarian credentials, their charitable record.

The farm is not what I expected. It's not Mouswitz. It's just a farm with a modest, modern farmhouse, a neat yard, a couple of waggy dogs. There is no security beyond the 'Close the gates' sign, no cameras or panic buttons, just a young farmer: a lady with gamine hair, a warm, open face and a soft voice. She wears denim overalls. Her husband is in the next field, ploughing sugar beet. She takes us to meet the mink.

All our assumptions about fur-farming are of the furtive and violent: that it is a back-street garage business, a hidden, cash-and-carnage trade, a thing of flies and smells and screams in the dark. It should look like Deliverance, or the shaky, hand-held excitement of a sab's home video: the bright eyes picked out in the torchlight, the corpses in corners, the puddles of unspeakable yuck. The reality is, unfortunately, more prosaic. It's farming. Animal husbandry. We walk into a long, low barn streaming with slatted sunlight. The rows of cages stretch away, echoing the shelves of boxes in the warehouse to come. Each compartment is a regulation size. They're small; you wouldn't keep a pet in them, but these aren't pets. By law the cages have to contain a dark area for the mink to sleep and birth, a toy – which means a shelf – clean straw, food and water. They eat a high-protein, turd-brown mulch that is spooned onto the top of their cages, made from by-products of the poultry and dairy industries. They press their noses to the wire, beadily inquisitive. I suck my teeth. They squeak back and squirm through the straw. These females will give birth to about four or five kits in April–May. They will be separated after a few weeks – caged mink have cannibal tendencies – and all the mink not selected for breeding will be harvested – killed – in November. It's a speedy growth and a short life.

The farmer puts on gloves like a nervous wicket-keeper's, and pulls a mink out of its cage. It curls in her big leather hand and regards us as if we all had rabbit ears. She says she would never, ever go near one without the glove. They would take a finger. 'Mink are not,' she says, 'friendly animals. You don't grow fond of them, they don't mellow.' They're not like pigs or cows that evoke empathy, they are murderers, and single-minded.

Occasionally a chicken will get into the barn, fly to the top of the cages to peck at the mulch. The mink will catch its toes and eat it through the steel mesh, one tiny strip at a time. The whole hen.

As a farming rule, we don't husband carnivores, because we don't eat them. The one thing we ask of domesticated animals is that they'll get on with their own species. Mink don't. Won't. They are solitary, and relentlessly aggressive. These are still wild animals in the sense that they could live in the wild if released, but they are no longer the same as their wild cousins. They are much bigger, and glossier. If they were unhappy they wouldn't have value. You can make a miserable animal fat, but its coat is the first thing to suffer from distress or cruelty, and it's the coat that gives the mink value. 'If we don't treat them well, we don't have a business.'

The fur farmers of Denmark work as a collective. If one is found to break the Danish veterinary rules, they all suffer. That's not to say that someone, somewhere in the world, isn't mistreating a mink. Somewhere in the world, someone is mistreating a child; that doesn't make keeping them an immoral business.

Let me show you the killing and skinning process. At the end of the barn is a small tractor, behind it a box on wheels. If animals need to be dispatched because they're sick or injured, they're put in a trapdoor at the top and killed with exhaust fumes in seconds. At the end of the season, when they are killing hundreds of mink a day, there is a purpose-built chamber with canisters of CO_2. The dead mink are stretched over frames and flayed like sausages, without puncturing their stomachs.

One argument against fur-farming is that we don't eat them. The assumption that if something passes through your alimentary canal its death is virtuous, is vain and odd. Here the carcasses are taken away and turned into biofuel. They power municipal vehicles, school buses, street cleaners. It's a very Danish, eco-sensitive solution. Nothing is wasted. The skins are treated with sawdust, dried and graded and sent to auction.

Mink-farming is profitable, but not wildly so. The margins are tight, and, as with most farming, the overheads are high, and the farmers are pessimists. 'This is a boom time for fur,' says the farmer, 'but there are years that are very hard. People go out of business. That's what farming is. When the price is good, you save to pay for when it's not so good.' At this level, fur-farming is no different from any other intensive husbandry. It's ethically inconvenient, but you can't single mink out from any other animal bred for slaughter. Denmark has a huge bacon industry. This farmer also keeps pigs. Morally, it's far harder to justify farming pigs than mink: they're much smarter, more sensitive, perhaps intuitive. They're social and very like us. We can exchange organs. They suffer more distress than mink, and they, too, get used to make expensive clothes.

I looked at the website for PETA, the animal cruelty pressure group. What they've written about fur-farming is much the same as I just have, but they reach different conclusions. I noticed their online shop sells cotton T-shirts that radically yell 'Fuck Fur'. Well, nothing f***s the world like cotton T-shirts. Cotton accounts for 10 per cent of all agricultural chemicals, 25 per cent of all pesticides, and, most damaging for the countries where it's grown, almost 3 per cent of the globe's entire water supply goes to slake the thirst of cotton. One T-shirt will have used 2,700 litres of water. Fur-farming isn't close to being as ethically compromised as that environmental pogrom.

Would you wear something that had been made from an animal that had been boiled alive, simply because it was luxurious and swanky? Probably not. But then again, probably yes: your knickers, your shirt, your dressing gown, your tie, your frock, your hanky. Silk is made from boiling the pupa of a moth. It's not a worm, it's an infant. But maybe you don't mind, because it hasn't got legs or an identifiable face.

When you object to fur, you draw an arbitrary line through evolution. Probably a wobbly line. Yes to a lizard wallet or watchstrap; no to a hamster lining. Fine with peccary gloves (made from a wild-pig-like mammal), but not a fox scarf. You'll eat pork, but not dog; cow, but not horse, although you wouldn't blink at shoes or belts made from cordovan (horse leather). You'll eat food dye made from a thousand squashed bugs, but probably wouldn't wear earrings made from a beetle's jewel-like elytra.

I'm not trying to imply you are a hypocrite or a fool. We have to make decisions about things all the time, but they're personal, and they are not necessarily coherent or consistent. 'I won't kiss someone with a beard or a nose ring.' 'I won't go out with someone who is shorter than me or has a Liverpool accent.' 'I'll eat oysters, but not foie gras.' It's a preference, not a moral philosophy, and it's individual. You wouldn't insist that everyone does the same, never eating onion rings or wearing yellow, because that would be stupid and boring. It should be the same with fur. There is no ethical difference between a fur coat and a leather jacket, crocodile or suede.

I have fur coats made by a friend, a furrier from Reykjavik, Iceland, who is one of the gentlest and kindest men I know. He breeds and rides Icelandic horses, and then he eats them. The fur coats he makes are wholly ethical. He knows where each skin comes from, and everything he makes is completely natural, no man-made material at all. The linings are silk, he uses fish skin for buttonholes and the buttons are horn. He started a business using the skins of stillborn lambs, of which there are quite a few in Iceland – they are normally left for the ravens. I suggested he start a new label, called Born Again.

He gave me a sealskin coat, beautiful and practical, although oddly, and slightly weirdly, sealskin is not waterproof. I've been out seal-hunting with the Inuit of Greenland. It's a traditional subsistence to hunt on ice, by boat, using rifles. The seals are important: as clothing, as income, but also for feeding their huskies. The EU banned the trade in sealskin, and now ethical ecologists are trying to get the ban rescinded. Seals are not endangered. Greenland's way of life is.

It would be laughably impossible to explain to the Kalaallit of Greenland that wearing fur was weird or wrong or cruel. Their entire culture has always been based around seals. I've also been out hunting and trapping with the Bushmen in the Kalahari. Everything is made from antelope skin, and to excuse them, or the Inuit, from the prohibition or the censure of wearing fur would be to say that your morality applies only to modern, urban, First World people. Excluding 'primitives' from higher ethics is pathetically elitist.

I take a last look at the mink standing in their cages, little pink, clawed feet pressed against the bars. I breathe in their musky, feral, fetid smell. The rows of little diamond eyes watch, unblinking, in shafting northern light. Their currant noses twitch the air. They are not lovable. They don't lend themselves to anthropomorphism, there is no Peppa Mink. But that's not their fault, or a fault at all. They are admirable and fascinating, and very strokeable, but only when dead.

I ask the farmer if she has a mink coat. She doesn't look the type. 'Yes,' she says, smiling, 'a jacket in shaved mink.' The truth is, most of our prejudice against mink is not because it's fur, but because it's mink. A mink coat trails a whole, bloody train of naff, ugly associations behind it. A long, brown, floor-length fur makes a girl look like a mahogany wardrobe, like Mrs Ceausescu.

It screams dictators' and plutocrats' wives, with ill-gotten lives. It smells of factory chimneys and tax avoidance and the graft of others. It is the uniform of the old and idle rich. And old and idle and rich are very bad fashion looks. Mink is what men give their mistresses in exchange for sex, and to their wives as their apologies for having mistresses. The traditional mink says a lot about a woman, none of it polite, nice or enviable. And because of the difficulty in cutting and tailoring fur, they tend to be boxy and shapeless; they look engineered rather than designed. But things have changed. Kopenhagen Fur encourages designers to come and play with mink. They're keen that it be treated with irreverence, shorn of its associations. So fur has been de-stuffed, deconstructed and de-coupled from ageing dowagers and divas. In their bright studios, there are mink miniskirts, bomber jackets, cardigans and scatter cushions, keyrings and coffee-mug warmers, sofas and candy-coloured Alice bands. My particular favourite is a mink cycling helmet.

A lot of fur finds itself finally on the racks of vintage and second-hand shops where it gains a born-again life, reclaimed by the young as radical, cheap chic. It becomes ironic, and irony is never out of fashion. Technically there are lots of new, sharper ways to tailor fur; it can be shaved and plucked, plaited, dyed, laser-cut. Much of it still looks hideously naff, but enough of it doesn't. A shaved mink has a lustre and a lightness like the finest velvet, but far better. People are often surprised by the intense feeling it induces: the call of the wild, a sense of wellbeing and comfort. We have a connection, an attraction to the skin of other animals that goes beyond the practical or the merely rational, or even the aesthetic. There is an undeniable frisson when you put on a fur, a feeling that is particular, that is a peculiar pleasure. It is an ancient, tactile memory, possibly our oldest collective memory. We evolved into the naked ape, the hairless upright monkey, because we learnt to steal the coats off other creatures' backs. Stand naked in front of a mirror, if you still dare, and it is as clear as your genitals that you were born to wear someone else's skin.

Clothes are one continuous cultural event. Everyone takes part in fashion – whether you consider it, approve of it or laugh at it, we are all part of it. And the first material from the chilly dawn of our existence is fur. It is the start of all cultural aesthetics, adornment and beauty. The oldest play in the world is merely 2,500 years ago, the oldest story about 5,000, the oldest song (a Bushman chant) perhaps 50,000, but with fur you've got something that has been worn for more than 100,000 years.

It comes with a great blanket of associations and emotions, of being protected and being safe, of power and prestige, of eroticism. It is the fur of kings, of chieftains and warlords and mouldy parkas. But it is also the fur of farmers and hunters and shepherds, the shearling of football managers and estate agents, the mink and sable of courtesans, widows and starlets, and a Guardsman's bearskin. Fur is a menagerie of associations, from back to nature to urban plutocrats and suburban golf clubs. It's male and it's female, it's the swaddling of children and the gift to mistresses. It is old women and Arctic explorers. No material carries with it such a great gallimaufry of contradictory messages: it is beautiful and it is cruel, it is purposeful and it is erotic. It is properly mythical stuff and nobody has a dispassionate or unemotional reaction to it. Try walking past a fur without reaching out your hand to touch it. It is an impulse that is older than language: the feel of fur, the genesis of comfort, the beginning of luxury.

Plainly, nudely, we wouldn't be here, would never have ventured out of Africa, without the borrowed warmth and protection of fur. Our species, the thinking ape, shed its hair, grew naked, because we could wear fur. Our relationship with the mink is older than with any other farm animal. You might say, well, we've grown out of all that. We've evolved. But just wrap a crying baby in a fur, and instantly you'll sense the truth: that we haven't evolved out of mink, but because of it.

June 2011, July 2015

Life Drawing

———

The young man steps through the door gingerly, not nervous exactly, but aware, like he's walking into a doctor's waiting room or
an unfamiliar pub. He's wearing sweat pants; he might have just
got up. He hooks his thumbs into the waistband and pulls them off,
bending at the waist in a practised, fit move. This isn't the first time
he's taken his trousers off in front of strangers.

The room is already half full with people, fiddling with bits of
equipment. They look up and stare at him, men and women looking
without guile, subterfuge or embarrassment. The boy steps up onto
a yard-square box and performs a small, unconsidered transforma-
tion that is one of the most profound in all civilisation: he steps up
from being naked to become nude. Naked is to be without clothes
– Noah was discovered naked by his children; you get naked for a
lover; strippers and corpses are naked. Nude is the reveal of human-
ity, our collective apotheosis.

Nakedness comes with guilt and shame, lust and hilarity; the
nude is a symbol, a metaphor of our highest aspiration. It is innocent and wise: war memorials and Oscars are nude; angels and
muses are nude. David is nude. Nude feels neither hot nor cold,
is ageless, timeless. Adam and Eve were created nude and became
naked with knowledge. This yard-square dirty wooden box becomes
a plinth under the feet of the man who quietly asks how he should
stand. 'However you feel comfortable, with weight evenly spread,' I

say, and to the room: 'Shall we do a five-minute pose to get started?'
A murmur of assent; the boy flexes into his pose. He looks as though
he's been lovingly modelled from toffee and pipe cleaners. The mus-
cles clot and twitch, the room settles to their easels. I'm sitting in a
donkey, a short bench with a drawing board attached that has been
the furniture of artists' studios for 500 years, and listen to the familiar scratch and soft shuffle of charcoal and pencil on paper.

Later on we will be joined by the distinguished *Sunday Times* car-
toonist Gerald Scarfe. Arranged around the nude boy are Michael
Frith, the watercolour portraitist who used to illustrate my column
'Table Talk'; his daughter Frieda, a textiles student; Gary the car-
toonist, who has put off flying to New York to be here; Jon-Paul
McCarthy, a caricaturist who works on Brighton Pier; Charlotte
Mann, who teaches at the Prince's Drawing School; the fashion designer Giles Deacon, who's sketching on an iPad; Cristina Planas,
a first-year student at my old college, the Slade; Polly Morgan, a
marvellous artist who uses taxidermy with a dark, aesthetic élan;
and the portrait artist Emma Sergeant, who was at college with me
and who was something of a star, not just for her very unstudenty
elegance but because she had such a showy facility for drawing,
winning the first BP Portrait Award while still an undergraduate.
And there's me.

I stare at the white paper. I haven't done this for more than 30
years. The unblinking blankness of the pristine surface stares back,
implacable, the old enemy. Artists can get the yips making the
first mark, overwhelmed by the numberless openings: every mark
dictates the next, and the next and the next, all the boundless possibilities for failure.

I remember my first drawing lesson at Central Saint Martins – a
fat, hairy, balding Cypriot with bunions and varicose veins, stubby
fingers and doleful eyes, resting his paunch on his fatty thighs, his
penis straining between them like a mole's nose. Barely the epit-
ome of glory, victory or charity. The teacher, a patrician artist with a

cravat, said: 'First you must overcome the paper, boy.' I didn't hear the comma and thought for a moment it was erotic advice. 'Show it you won't be intimated, defile it.' So, once again, I take the charcoal and with long, slight parabolas, cover the page with grey swags, then look up at the boy on the box, a long, deep look, like the breath before a dive, and start to draw. The forgotten habit: I start where I always started, with an ear.

Life drawing is the oldest of all the plastic art disciplines, but hardly any art schools have life rooms any more. When Emma and I were at the Slade, there were two full-time rooms run by Euan Uglow, with models who would hold cantilevered poses for a term under hanging plumb lines. Lucian Freud would occasionally come to teach or, more often, to take a girl student out to lunch at Wheeler's.

There is a venerable, Grade I-listed drawing room in which Hogarth sketched in the Royal Academy Schools off Piccadilly, where Tracey Emin is the professor of drawing. I went for a meeting to ask if we could use it, but I'm still waiting for the publicist to answer. And there's the Prince's Drawing School, set up by Prince Charles as a sort of nostalgic counter-reformation to all the carbuncular modern art that we find ourselves surrounded by; a place that emphasises craft and skill and all the aesthetic salon of virtues that are old-fashioned but still manage to be timeless. They were hoping to accommodate us until they heard we wanted to draw the Naked Rambler.

The Naked Rambler was a perfect perspective model – he encompasses our very confused views on nakedness. I think he is something of a hero for refusing to wear clothes as he roams the country. I would like to elevate his nakedness to nudity, to draw attention literally and metaphorically to the hypocrisy of a relentless prurience that consumes vast eyefuls of nakedness and takes a salacious fascination in bodies, but will imprison a bloke who wants to be done with kit. That was too much for the Prince's Drawing School.

Apparently, the school had a fit of the vapours and said no, firstly because they had an Islamic centre nearby, then simply because he wasn't the sort of person they wanted to be associated with.

When we asked if they were serious, that a drawing school that extols life drawing wouldn't have a naked man on the premises, they replied that there were models who do this sort of thing professionally. I'm sure it will interest and comfort Prince Charles that there is a very old-fashioned and timeless prejudice about artists' models. In the nineteenth century they were considered socially lower than prostitutes; indeed, many models were prostitutes who had fallen on hard times, or at least on hard artists. The reason was that they offered unveiled visions of themselves indiscriminately to many men at once, whereas your hooker at least got a room and did them one at a time.

Artists regularly married or cohabited with their models. They became not just objects to be recorded and imbued with meaning, but muses, and they were always female. I can't think of one famous male life model, except perhaps for Quentin Crisp, the naked civil servant. Finally, the Royal College of Art came up with a warm room and a warmer welcome. They could accommodate not just artists but the Naked Rambler too. Unfortunately, on the day before he was to pose, he was arrested. As a backup, we'd arranged for a burlesque dancer to stand in, then 10 minutes after she was due to start she flunked and cancelled, a big girl's feather duster, happy to get erotically starkers and flash drunk businessmen, but who couldn't stand still under the unwavering gaze of a dozen artists. Getting the artists wasn't that easy. A handful of Turner prizewinners who had each enthusiastically agreed to join in when I asked them had found they had more pressing engagements when the day drew close. In fairness, most contemporary artists have never been taught life drawing. The art schools have turned their studios into conceptual sculpture workshops or into video suites, and nobody with an auction price to protect wants to be shown wanting in a discipline that the silly philistine public still think of as a defining skill for an artist. And now it's not just the great gawping populace, there is a small but eloquent movement within the self-defining art world that is pointing out that the art emperor is down to his underwear. Contemporary artists have lost contact with art's defining mission, along with an ability to physically make art. It has become a process as opposed to a skill, an obtuse game of words, catalogue notes and jargon-choked articles mediated by gallerists and professional art explainers. It is not just retro-fogeys who are drawing attention to the truth that art marketeers look only to each other for value or validation. Plastic art that was once made to engage the widest public is now made to fit the narrowest of collectors. And the art that is encouraged and produced is becoming ever more ridiculous and anaemic, incapable of standing up on its own without the crutch of curators' footnotes.

Not all difficult art is bad and not all accessible art is innately good. Artists don't have to draw to create, and being able to draw doesn't come close to making you an artist. But there has been a disengagement with the craft of creation that ultimately weakens the image. Art is conceived by people who don't make and made by people who aren't inspired. Twentieth-century art had two dominant paternal family trees: Duchamp and Picasso. Duchamp is the father of Conceptualism and Surrealism, the found object as art, the now clichéd urinal that was exhibited for a day, then lost, but rediscovered as an object of great value. The concept is uncorrupted by craft; it is pure art.

Picasso is the master craftsman, the magician of modern art with his dazzling, astonishing sleight of hand and skill, the dexterity of genius. He is a consummate all-round Jedi of drawing, painting, sculpture, pottery, printmaking and womanising. Picasso is difficult to live up to. Duchamp's is the art of ideas, Picasso's the art of emotion. Duchamp is unquestionably the more motivating movement, even if most artists would rather own or be a Picasso. Conceptual art is about art, it constantly claims to be reinventing, reseeing, reminding, rethinking; it's relentlessly recycling itself. Duchamp himself gave up being an artist to play chess, which he thought was more important. Picasso's legacy didn't wither but it has moved out of the mainstream, as has feeling, replaced by thought; and the human body has been mostly discarded, except as an irony, a cipher, a mannequin to a concept, like the figures on the lavatory door.

Paul Klee believed that the art of drawing was the art of omission. It is a concentrated test of editing. What you choose to leave out is as important as what you put in, every line has an outside and an inside; drawing is a series of problems that need to be overcome in order: a wrong or misplaced mark will ultimately undo all that follows, like the wrong number in a calculation. First there is the problem of scale: how do you fit the figure onto the page? Beside me, Polly draws a small man surrounded by an expanse of empty paper. The space around him makes the figure vulnerable, lonely. Frieda's figures overflow the page, Giles draws simple, beautiful, fluid indications and impressions of a man on his flickering screen. Emma draws over her previous drawings, over and over, turning the page around, burying the image to reveal a reborn image. She ends up with a striking head that has consumed four or five bodies. Gerald comes from composing his political cartoon for the week and watches, to go away and compose later. In China, there is no history of drawing directly from life. An artist would sit and watch a cow for hours, perhaps days, and when he had absorbed as much cow as he could manage, he'd go home and draw essence of cow.

Life drawing is never meant to be art in itself. It is never a finished product, always something stopped at an arbitrary point, always a rehearsal, the best it can hope for is to show promise. It is to painting what singing scales is to opera, it is the rendering of form and volume in two dimensions, the evolution of solidity, which is why sculptors so often make the most beautiful and dramatic life drawings. It is a trick, a sleight of hand and brain and something else, a bat's squeak of inspiration, a breath of the muse that can be love, anger, hunger, boredom, jealousy, sadness, vanity – any of the spectrum of emotions can inspire what it takes to draw.

In this room we all produce very different images, looking at the very same thing. That's not simply the difference in skill or dexterity or a learnt style, it is because the feelings that a nude induces are personal and singular; no two drawings will ever be remotely the same. It is an old truism that in the life room you don't draw the body in front of you, you draw the one inside you. It makes no difference if it's male or female, black or white, old or young; all life drawing is camouflaged, shape-shifting self-portrait: the images of what we search for in life and culture, an empathy with the human condition and the spirit that makes us sparks of the divine.

Staring at a nude provokes profound questions about our humanity, the profound questions that should be at the heart of all art. The concentration in the room is like an exam or a communion. I had forgotten what an intense pleasure just practising life drawing is, the feeling of the charcoal on the paper, the dance of the physical and the mental, the moment when it flows, and the longueurs when you trip over your own fingers, the nonchalance of being able to tear off the paper and start again, the complete attention a body demands. I had forgotten how much I once wanted this to be my whole life and how much I missed it, and the grief when I made the decision to give up because I found something else I did better but loved less. As we packed up, Emma turned from her easel and said: 'Amazing, isn't it? The feeling, the silence a nude body gives to a room.'

December 2012

P.G. Wodehouse

If you write funny, it tends to ruin the reading of funny. We antic scribes look at humorous prose with a professional, competitive eye, nodding with grudging admiration, smirking at old saws dressed up as new hawks. If you have written to amuse for long enough, little comes as a surprise, or with originality. Humour is a series of tricks, assertions, juxtapositions, confusions and puns. And they can be learnt, as I imagine card tricks are learnt, except that on the page there is no sleeve to hide the punchline, no backstage, no CGI wizardry. Writing is exactly what it says it is. It is black and white. There is, though, one exception, one writer who produces humour from out of nowhere, from virtually nothing, the Jedi master of hidden laughter and crouching titter – P.G. Wodehouse.

When I pick up a Wodehouse book, I am like a punchy boxer, ducking at shadows, dodging imagined pratfalls, but I rarely see the amused jabs coming. Even the haymakers are disguised. I have no idea how he does it. It is somewhere in his use of language, colliding vernaculars both antique and modern, with dabs of American film argot and a musical rhythm. Oh, the brilliance of his punctuation, which foxtrots and quicksteps you down the page to fling you into musical chairs.

I was introduced to Wodehouse by my father, who particularly liked his cricketing stories, *Mike and Psmith*. 'Mike nodded. A sombre nod, the nod Napoleon might have given if somebody had met him in 1812, and said, "So you are back from Moscow, eh?"' For my dad's generation, Wodehouse was the salve of pre-TV boredom, the rescue from wet weekends and the measure of humour. Clever but modest, fantastical but homespun and, that most admirable of English virtues, amateurishly effortless. He inspired a generation to write. They all ended up in *Punch*, or compiling books of manners, or churning out English films and farces, and musicals about thwarted love, misplaced letters and mistaken identities. 'Plum' is the master of a peculiarly and specifically English humour, even though he spent much of his life in, and writing about, America. He is, I would claim, a paragon from the top table of English literature.

But who still reads him? I have been asking around. Men of my age and older say yes, they love him, but haven't read any for some time. I have yet to find a younger man with Jeeves on his bedside table. And no women at all. He just doesn't strike any I asked as funny – only mannered and daft, with a lot of class-ridden jokes about idiotic men saying camp and arch things to each other. When there is a woman in one of his books, she is a simpering love interest, a Wagnerianly nagging aunt or a pig. 'She looked as if she had been poured into her clothes and had forgotten to say "when".' Wodehouse, it has been pointed out more than once, seems to have little more than a passing acquaintance with women. They are like front doors: every house needs one, but you don't want to hang around them, polishing the knockers. Then again, he's not got that firm a grasp of men, either. There is barely one that is more than a vague sketch; he doesn't come up with a great deal of what Dostoyevsky might call character.

Wodehouse is not just an Anglophile pleasure, but a manly one. Not really manly, more gentlemanly. I asked my publisher, Alan Samson (a fan – of Wodehouse, not of mine, possibly both of us, but not in the same bracket), if his books sold well. 'Oh, quite well,' he guessed. 'There are a number of good editions in print. I'd have thought it would have been steady. And there was a television adaptation [of *Jeeves and Wooster*]. That always helps. First Dennis Price and Ian Carmichael, then Fry and Laurie. They won't all be in print, mind – he wrote something like 90. Tell you what, I'll find the old figures and call you back. Toodle pip.'

An hour later, he returned to the phone, a chastened man: 'Well, I must say I'm surprised, shocked. In the four weeks over Christmas, the top five Wodehouse titles never made it past triple figures. In fact, none of them managed to sell 500 copies in a month. In the week before Christmas, *Blandings* sold 29 copies, *Thank You, Jeeves* 47. In 14 years, *Leave It to Jeeves* has sold 32,000. That's very disappointing, astonishing.'

Well, maybe it's just humorous writing that's out of sorts. Few things age as sourly as humour. Who's chortling at Pope now? Proper laughter, not academic tee-hees. I'll bet that Evelyn Waugh isn't doing much better. Same sort of thing: class, arch, mannered. 'I'll get back to you,' Alan said. And, a moment later: 'Here's a thing – *Brideshead* sold 142,000 and *Scoop* 69,000.'

I asked my local bookshop if they still sold Wodehouse. They keep a good selection. Some, they said, searching the computer. 'Oh no, not that many . . . I think it's mostly to people visiting hospital. They're good recuperation reads for the elderly.'

Why do so few young readers discover Wodehouse, when Waugh is doing well? Evelyn still finds his way onto school syllabuses, which Plum never has. And Waugh fits far more comfortably into contemporary humour. He is cruel, bigoted, angry and mocking, much closer to the stand-ups on panel shows than Wodehouse would ever be. You see, it's the whimsy: Wodehouse is whimsical. There's no getting round it. He is the Pope of Whimsy (pontiff, not ugly old man of letters). The joke is never barbed or even pointed; it's always gentle and ephemeral, relying on its grace and craft to gain a laugh. Whimsy is just not a current concept. It's too shallow, too light, not loud enough to compete in the bar or on Twitter. It is a word that is rolling over and inverting its meaning. To accuse somebody of whimsy is an insult. Like the word pathos. To say you're pathetic is no longer to mean: 'I care for you.'

Another humorous columnist, a woman, said there has been a change in the nature of books since the war. They have to be about something now; they have to have a point of view, a subject, an opinion, a justification, gravitas. You can't just write divertissements. Samson agrees: 'Books need to tell you things, to inform you. We are in an age that puts a heavy burden on the efficacy of facts and the importance of opinion. We call it "the information age" – everything needs to account for its existence.' 'There are moments, Jeeves, when one asks oneself, "Do trousers matter?" "The mood will pass, sir."' Wodehouse really isn't about anything at all. Nobody ever finished one of his books heavier in the grey-matter department than when they started. They aren't even really about what they appear to be about. You might think they are concerned with class, but they don't have an opinion on the system. You couldn't tell whether Wodehouse was a republican, a communist, an Empire loyalist or an autograph hunter. They are often about love, but there is no examination of love, not even a celebration of it. Again, you wouldn't know if he was cynical about romance or utterly doe-eyed. 'The voice of Love seemed to call me, but it was a wrong number.' And often they are about pigs. But you couldn't make a sausage after reading one.

A constant and engrossing theme is stupidity, an airily happy brainlessness. 'She's got brains enough for two, which is the exact quantity a girl who marries you will need.' Even when he wrote about golf, it wasn't really golf he meant. It was an understudy for his beloved cricket, which he could no longer watch in exile. If you wanted to saddle Wodehouse with an idea, which I don't, it might be that there is a sort of bliss in ignorance, and that innocent loafing is the way to be. Success is not achieved, it's underachieved. His books stand alone like the lilies of the field, neither reaping nor sowing, just being Wodehousian to no discernible purpose, except as an invitation to do the same, to contrarily lean against the march of modern literature and humour. They could almost be seen as subversive. 'Whenever I get that sad, depressed feeling, I go out and kill a policeman.'

January 2013

Rudyard Kipling

Who would have thought, best beloved, that the most conten-
tious and decisive British poet would be Rudyard Kipling? After
all these years when the firebrand Romantics, the sparse moderns,
the concretes and the hedgerow frotters, the deconstructers and
stream-of-conscious free-verse mongers have all slipped comfortably between the limited-edition covers of the lyric establishment,
Rudyard can still beat out the old arguments across saloon bars and
classrooms. He is, of course, that most contrarian of creatures: a popular poet, the most popular poet. 'If', the nation's favourite poem,
is England's national mission statement, the draft of an unwritten
constitution, it is the wish list of personal and parental character, so
naturally it is as despised as it is loved. T.S. Eliot was Kipling's most
unlikely champion, pointing out that 'We expect to have to defend
a poet against the charge of obscurity; we have to defend Kipling
against the charge of lucidity.' Adding that, 'People are exasperated
by poetry they do not understand and contemptuous of poetry they
understand without effort.'

George Orwell was famously contemptuous about Kipling, writing
one of his best essays on the poet, whom he damns with the faintest
sneering Etonian pity and praise for not being educated enough, for
being too middle-class, and for having an opinion. He finishes by
awarding Kipling the honorific that he is a good bad poet, possibly
the best bad poet, the Harriet Beecher Stowe of poetry. Eliot got

round the best-bad-best thing by ruling that Kipling wasn't really a poet at all, he was a balladeer, which was a fine and noble calling, and that good ballads all had a great deal of poetry in them and that Kipling was probably the very best balladeer ever. Ballads have to be immediately understood, their phrases must ring memorably and importantly, they have to mean the same thing every time you hear them, there is none of the mist or nuance, the shape-shifting of poetry; and going back to reread Kipling, what I noticed first was that the lines and the phrases stick to the memory like burrs to a spaniel's ear; they have the potency of cheap music, the tune you can't get out of your head. Kipling is responsible for a lexicon of phrases that have become commonplace truisms: lest we forget, the female of the species is more deadly than the male, east is east and west is west, and never the twain shall meet, the white man's burden, the flannelled fools at the wicket or the muddied oafs at the goals, he travels the fastest who travels alone, dominion over palm and pine, the law of the jungle. He was most probably the person who inserted the pejorative word Hun into the bellicose language before the Great War.

Posthumously, Kipling's life has been edited so he gets his poetic comeuppance with the war: the death of his son Jack at Loos in 1915. The bitter and slight series of epitaphs he wrote for everyone from civil servants to raped women have been seen as evidence of his realisation that his earlier jingoism was culpable – 'If any question why we died/Tell them, because our fathers lied.' 'I have slain none except my mother/She (blessing her slayer) died of grief for me.'

This, it must be said, was not thought in his lifetime. It was assumed that Kipling was a man from a particular moment and that that moment had passed; he looked and sounded as embarrassingly old-fashioned and pompous as our parents' generation invariably does. Kipling wrote and spoke for and to the messianic Britain of the 1890s to the end of the Boer War, a nation that believed itself to be on a crusading moral mission to lead and improve the world. It is a mistake to dismiss him as racist. He firmly believed that Britons were better than the rest, that they had a manifest destiny given to the race by God and blood. But rather than disregarding the other nations, the British had a higher responsibility to them – that is the white man's burden – and racial intolerance and belittling was the currency of the mere Hun. Because the death of his son fits comfortably into a retrospective mawkishness about the Great War, few biographers look further back to a loss that was borne with a pursed silence: the death in 1899 of his adored young daughter from pneumonia that he had also barely survived. She was the best beloved and the *Just So Stories* were written for her. It was Josephine who gave them their title because she wanted them repeated without deviation, just so. He wrote one of his few enigmatic poems, 'The Way Through the Woods', about her death. It had no balladry in it.

As the Empire and the memories of colonialism fade to sepia, Kipling is freed of his political and social context, so the canon becomes Homeric – a little English *Iliad* and *Odyssey*. The marvellous rhythm of his writing, his journalist's ear for a story and a headline, the sternly hugged emotion make a long saga of loss and hope, morality, humour, belonging and bonding, of kin and landscape.

Like soldiers marching in columns, the poems swing their arms and stamp their feet in time. Kipling still speaks to a part of us, trips images and phrases that we understand to be particular to us. His poetry may not be smart or elegant or deft or ironic, it may be full of wincing sentiment and a plodding patronage, but there is not a dishonest or dishonourable line and none of it is doggerel. When nonpoetic, unballaded people reach for verse to record or explain some great moment of triumph or loss – a funeral, a wedding, a birth – mostly what they strive for is to sound like Kipling, and that is quite something. I should leave the last line to Orwell, with his sensitive nose for vulgarity and the tastes of hoi polloi. 'Kipling was,' he wrote, 'a crude and vulgar picture, a patriotic music-hall turn that seems to have got mixed up with one of Zola's gorier passages.' In these days of high/low culture, this begins to sound like great praise.

April 2013

Morrissey: Autobiography

As Noël Coward might have said, nothing incites intemperate cultural hyperbole like cheap music. Who can forget that the Beatles were once authoritatively lauded as the equal of Mozart, or that Bob Dylan was dubbed a contemporary Keats? The Beatles continued to ignore Covent Garden, and Mozart is rarely heard at Glastonbury; Dylan has been silently culled from the latest edition of the *Oxford Companion to Modern Poetry in English*. The publication of *Autobiography* was the second item on Channel 4's news on the day it was released. Krishnan Guru-Murthy excitably told the nation that Morrissey really could write – presumably he was reading from an autocue – and a pop journalist thrilled that he was one of the nation's greatest cultural icons. He isn't even one of Manchester's greatest cultural icons.

This belief in high-low cultural relativity leads to a certain sort of chippy pop-star feeling undervalued and then hoitily producing a rock opera or duet with concert harpsichord. Morrissey, though, didn't have to attain the chip of being needily undervalued; he was born with it. He tells us he ditched 'Steve', his given name, to be known by his portentous unimoniker because – deep reverential breath here – great classical composers only have one name.

Mussorgsky, Mozart, Morrissey. His most pooterishly embarrassing piece of intellectual social climbing is having this autobiography published by Penguin Classics. Not Modern Classics, you understand, where the authors can still do book signings, but the classic Classics, where they're dead and some of them only have one name. Molière, Machiavelli, Morrissey.

He has made up for being alive by having a photograph of himself pretending to be dead on the cover. The book's publication was late and trade gossip has it that Steve insisted on each and every bookshop taking a minimum order of two dozen, misunderstanding how modern publishing works. But this is not unsurprising when you read the book. He is constantly moaning about record producers not pressing enough discs to get him to No. 1. What is surprising is that any publisher would want to publish the book, not because it is any worse than a lot of other pop memoirs, but because Morrissey is plainly the most ornery, cantankerous, entitled, whingeing, self-martyred human being who ever drew breath. And those are just his good qualities.

The book falls into two distinct passages. The first quarter is devoted to growing up in Manchester (where he was born in 1959) and his schooling. This is laughably overwrought and overwritten, a litany of retrospective hurt and score-settling that reads like a cross between Madonna and Catherine Cookson.

No teacher is too insignificant not to be humiliated from the heights of success, no slight is too small not to be rehashed with a final, killing esprit d'escalier. There are pages of lists of television programmes he watched (with plot analysis and character criticism). He could go on *Mastermind* with the specialist subject of *Coronation Street* or the works of Peter Wyngarde. There is the food he ate, the groups that appeared on *Top of the Pops* (with critical comments) and the poetry he liked (with quotes).

All of this takes quite a lot of time due to the amount of curlicues, falderals and bibelots he insists on dragging along as authorial decoration. Instead of adding colour or depth, they simply result in a cacophony of jangling, misheard and misused words. After 100 pages, he's still at the school gate kicking dead teachers.

But then he sets off on the grown-up musical bit and the writing calms down and becomes more diary-like, bloggish, though with an incontinent use of italics that are a sort of stage direction or aside to the audience. He changes tenses in ways that are supposed to be elegant but just sound camp. There is one passage that stands out – this is the first time he sings. 'Against the command of everyone I had ever known, I sing. My mouth meets the microphone and the tremolo quaver eats the room with acceptable pitch and I am removed from the lifelong definition of others and their opinions matter no more. I am singing the truth by myself which will also be the truth of others and give me a whole life. Let the voice speak up for once and for all.' That has the sense of being both revelatory and touching, but it stands out like the reflection of the moon in a sea of Stygian self-justification and stilted, self-conscious prose.

The hurt recrimination is sometimes risible but mostly dull, like listening to neighbours bicker through a partition wall, and occasionally startlingly unpleasant, such as the reference to the Moors murderers and the unfound grave of their victim Keith Bennett. 'Of course, had Keith been a child of privilege or moneyed background, the search would never have been called off. But he was a poor, gawky boy from Manchester's forgotten side streets and minus the blond fantasy fetish of a cutesy Madeleine McCann.'

It's what's left out of this book rather than what's put in that is strangest. There is an absence of music, not just in its tone, but the content. There are emetic pools of limpid prose about the music business, the ingratitude of fellow musicians and band members and the lack of talent in other performers, but there is nothing about the making of music itself, the composing of lyrics, the process of singing or the emotion of creation. He seems to assume we will already know his back catalogue and can hum along to his recorded life. This is 450 pages of what makes Morrissey, but nothing of what Morrissey makes.

There is the peevishness at managers, record labels and bouncers, a list of opaque court cases, all of which he manages to lose unfairly, due to the inherited stupidity of judges. Even his relation with the audience is equivocal. Morrissey likes them when they're worshipping from a distance, but he is not so keen when they're up close. As an adolescent he approaches Marc Bolan for an autograph. Bolan refuses and Morrissey, still awkwardly humiliated after all these years, has the last word. But then later in the book and life, he does exactly the same thing to his own fans without apparent irony.

There is little about his private life. A boyfriend slips in and out with barely a namecheck. This is him on his early sexual awakening: 'Unfathomably I had several cupcake grapples in this year of 1973 . . . Plunge or no plunge, girls remain mysteriously attracted to me.' There is precious little plunging after that.

There are many pop autobiographies that shouldn't be written. Some to protect the unwary reader, and some to protect the author. In Morrissey's case, he has managed both. This is a book that cries out like one of his maudlin ditties to be edited. But were an editor to start, there would be no stopping. It is a heavy tome, utterly devoid of insight, warmth, wisdom or likeability. It is a potential firelighter of vanity, self-pity and logorrhoeic dullness. Putting it in Penguin Classics doesn't diminish Aristotle or Homer or Tolstoy; it just roundly mocks Morrissey, and this is a humiliation constructed by the self-regard of its victim.

October 2013

Childhood

——

The drummer stands straight, stiff and splendid in scarlet and black bearskin. His epaulettes gleam, straps are blancoed, polished boots face ten-to-two. The drum hangs by his side, the sticks hover ready to tap out the rhythm of war. The rest of his regiment lies in tatters: a Life Guard has lost his head, a gun limber is turned on its side, its crew passed into the ranks of the dead.

Opposite him are the lines of blue-coated French, bayonets fixed. Their cavalry, a single Polish lancer, gallops in from the left. Things are not looking good for the drummer. The air echoes with the sounds of volleys – Bang! Bang! The French fire back – Frap! Frap! Suddenly, out of the sky, swoops a pterodactyl. It grips the drummer and lifts him up, across the table, over the carpet to the back of the armchair where the reserves wait: three Zulus, a one-armed crusader and Benito Mussolini.

Beetle, my six-year-old son, says the drummer is his favourite, along with the 25lb field gun and the chap with a pith helmet on a camel, still fresh from defeating the Mahdi's army at Omdurman. And then he embarks – Beetle, not the man on the camel – on a long and circuitous story about the drummer: where he came from, what happened to him, who his parents were, why the other soldiers like him.

The core company of these men were my father's. They came in flat lead sets, representing the sort of small imperial wars Michael

Gove would like all children to remember: the French and Indian wars, the Italo-Abyssinian War, the War of the Spanish Succession. Beetle is the fourth child to command this bent and battered battalion: his grandfather, me, his elder brother all came before him. Lead soldiers, like men, are hard and frail, there is barely one that doesn't bear the injury of play. Most of the bright paint is noticeable by its absence, but this only adds to their glory. The men who can no longer stand are kept in a cotton-wool hospital and are carefully brought out for parades.

My son has a twin sister; she has never shown more than a passing interest in the soldiers, never thought it unfair that he inherited them. 'They are,' she says, 'boys' things.'

Every father who ever was makes the same silent oath at the birth of their children. I will always be there to catch you, for your first step, behind your first bicycle, in the playground, at college, out of love, in work, falling from grace, jumping for joy. We mean it, though the truth of parenthood is an increasing litany of fumbled and missed catches. The promise isn't gender-specific. You don't think a son's grazed knees are less important than a daughter's, or her broken heart any more despairing than his.

When you have twins, people ask 'What are they?' In our case, one of each. And then many ask, 'Are they identical?' And we smile and say, 'No, they're a boy and a girl.' The question is dumb, but dumb for the right reason: babies are infants first and a gender second. The difference is mostly down to whether or not you get peed in the face when you change a nappy. We have continued to treat ours the same: they have always slept in the same room, gone to the same school; they both turned down ballet and took up judo.

The twins are now six and the people they've met, the things they've seen, the stories they've heard, the films they've sat through, are all pretty much gender-neutral – partly by choice and partly because that's just the way they all are. I don't have a single friend who thinks girls belong in the kitchen darning socks, and boys belong in the army, killing people. People like that are almost impossible to find, just as it's difficult to access modern cartoon films or children's books that aren't made with an achingly evangelical blandness.

For a generation, children's sexual equality has far outpaced grown-ups' because it doesn't cost anything to tell a girl she can grow up to be a fireman or an explorer. Yet despite all that, Beetle chose to pick up the sword, Edie to push a pram. Both had soft toys in the crib: hers are still hugged, his are mostly collateral damage. She likes princesses, he likes droids. Beetle is far more physically tentative than Edie is – she loves rollercoasters, he is terrified – but they remain each other's best friend. They play contentedly together, or beside each other. Edie will swordfight if Beetle pleads; he will organise her doll's house. But before anyone said anything, she wanted pink things and he insisted on blue. They come together in a mutual love of animals and nature programmes, but while she will 'Aww' over the puppies and kittens, he is interested only in predators.

The distinction between the two is so marked that it would have taken months of committed prejudice to achieve. Each respects the boyness or the girlness of the other. This is my second family of a boy and a girl, and I notice exactly the same distinctions. A behaviourist might say this is because I am the common ingredient, I manipulate unconsciously, but I feel that's less than likely. Nothing about being a father is unconscious and the pink–blue distinctions only account for a fraction of their lives as children. There is a far larger, shared, genderless landscape: a passion for riding ponies, building camps, telling jokes without punchlines. They are siblings first and last; their destiny and their choices are more likely designed by that relationship than by the one they have with me. I promised to catch, not to push.

The V&A Museum of Childhood is about to put on an exhibition of boys' things. I meet its curators in the bowels of the parent museum, the Victoria and Albert. The toys and the curators sit motionless around a large table in a grown-up, featureless room. There is a collection of soldiers: a troop of kilted Scots, an Indian crawling with a dagger, an armoured car and quite a lot of Nazis parading camply with flags. The curators regard the toys with the nervous concern of zookeepers watching rare frogs. The toys look lost. A museum of childhood is a great institutional oxymoron: who puts childhood into a museum? Museums are dead, defunct, past things. We force children to go to museums to see what they're not: old, dusty and venerable. To take children to a museum of childhood is coals to Newcastle.

Inside the glass cases of the Museum of Childhood's permanent collection, the exhibits jostle together like refugees from happier times. Streets of dolls' houses come with the strict encomiums of their middle-class arriviste heritage. Dolls and teddy bears and tin men and farm animals look discarded and unloved. There is something particularly uncomfortable and childishly sad about toys without children. They bring to mind the end of *Toy Story 2*, where the dolls are sent to the purgatory of a Japanese collector for his museum. There is something peculiarly, spiritually wrong about a toy museum – it's like a zoo for joy. This is the home of grown-up, beardy enthusiasms – men who want to collect and order things, who fuss and tidy up.

After a bit, another truth creeps up on you: the Museum of Childhood, with all its inclusivity, its community spirit and liberal decency, its pushchair-friendly café and gift shop, is hiding something. Half the human race has been left out. The detritus of a lad's bedroom has been brushed aside, put into storage. The swords, the bows and arrows, the guns, the helmets, capes, catapults, the spud guns, the tanks and shields and all the soldiers are absent, just a couple of sorry specimens sectioned in with the dolls for political re-education. It's like the Imperial War Museum without the war or the imperialism.

I asked a minder why the boys' toys are absent. She smiles at me sweetly – this is not the first time she's been asked.

'Do you think there are gender-specific toys? Do you imagine boys don't play with teapots and teddies and dolls?' Well, yes, of course they do, but mostly to tie them up and shoot them for treason. But there is an absence of stabbing, squirting and lassoing and vaporising toys. That's a gender bias, I'm told, that encourages boys to violence. I ask her if she thinks the museum should have a political position, a social point of view. 'Oh yes,' she replies. 'We should celebrate what's good, like the NHS.'

Anyway, we don't need to argue, the evidence is here in an addendum to the permanent display: a whole exhibition devoted to boys' violent make-believe. The soldiers, the bombers, the board games about murdering the Hun. Boys' childhood, men's childhood, is being carted into this ghetto of extinct toys that aren't trusted to play nicely with the girls. Not as nostalgic reminiscence and an interest in empathy, but as a nannying warning, a retrospective rebuke for all the brainwashing and murderous sadism, cruelty and colonialism that has been foisted onto blameless male babies who might have preferred My Little Pony and a skipping rope if they hadn't been taken to the dark side by dads who continue the original sin of men fucking up the world.

And then they brought out the Airfix Spitfire. 'Aah, I made squadrons of these! This is a really early one – look at the cockpit. Can I pick it up?' A nervously apologetic male nanny, who has gone over to the pink side, smiled stiffly and said I'd have to wear rubber gloves. Really? To hold a plastic five-bob Spit? The little thing felt sad, it had been reduced to this girly museum of pity and smiles and cultural realignment – a life of tissue paper and latex, never again to feel the grubby finger of a kid. It yearned to loop the loop one more time. To go down in flames – tacca tacca tacca. I put the plane gently down on the runway of its sorry half-life.

I asked a professor of children's things and education why boys played differently from girls. Well, she said, there's some evidence that it might be due to hormones – increased levels of testosterone. But I think, she continued, it's more likely to be social pressure. We bring up boys and girls differently. I tell her about my twins, and how, much as their mother and I would like to bring them up differently, we don't have the time or the energy. From the earliest moment they've behaved archetypally. Edie has prams and dolls and colours inside the lines, Beetle has swords and Star Wars Lego and can barely be bothered to colour inside the paper.

Yes, she says patiently, in the way that professionals do when they mean no, but you are not the only influence on your children. OK, but is it bad for boys to play violent games? Oh no, she says, the evidence is clear – it's a necessary part of growing up. It's imaginative play. It helps them to socialise. If you leave them alone, boys are very good at making rules. It may look rough, but they very rarely get hurt. Is there any evidence that war games and soldiers lead on to violent behaviour as adults? No. It turns out that boys' play is quite the opposite of learning to be violent: it's a way of managing and understanding the scary bits of life. It is a catharsis.

If war games and conflict narratives are good for boys, that begs the question, should they also be good for girls? Instead of channelling girls into co-operative sitting-down games, shouldn't we be encouraging mini-Amazons and pigtail Boadiceas? Anyone who has sent a child to a nursery school in the last 10 years knows that play-fighting is discouraged. Preschool teachers have ploys to distract the boys' urges into inclusive problem-solving. But children understand very early on the difference between play and reality. They don't mix them up. The children to worry about are the ones who don't socialise, who are solitary, who don't learn the lessons or the benefits of war games.

No one seems to have done a study, or questioned why grownups want to manipulate children. I might suggest it's a projection, a desire to do it again, better, to relive – if only as a pale proxy – the perfect commitment and immersion of childhood games and make-believe. All children know the toys fathers bring home to play themselves: the impossibly complicated models, the kites that don't fly. Why would a grown-up want to curate a museum of toys?

Why do we find it so difficult to leave childhood to children? I watch Beetle kneeling on the carpet, lost in his soldiers: issuing orders, imitating voices, the rapt pleasure of the story unfolding, and I feel a contradictory millefeuille of emotions: the memory of my father and myself, the nostalgia for the gripping make-believe when you could still really believe, and a sad, grey jealousy: I'll never have that again; my pretending is just pretend. And the regret that I didn't understand at the time how wonderful and fleeting this ability to play would be. Grown-ups can collude that play is really practice for adult life. But it isn't. Children don't see it as training for the office or the call centre or the till. In our increasingly rational and over-explained lives, the only things that still have the power of animism are toys. They contain the magic of childhood.

Edie sleeps with a small, soft elephant. If Ellie were lost or left behind I would have to take planes, trains, taxis and rickshaws to bring it home. There would be no point in saying, 'It's only a grubby soft toy.' Ellie is a household totem, it holds the spirit of family, is the recipient of tears and wishes and sleepy legends. Only toys blessed by children have this. And no adult is immune to their fetish power. The lead soldiers will be Beetle's until someday he loses the battle of childhood and moves on. Then they'll lie in their box, waiting for his son. The wounded will grow in number until there is just the drummer left, a final amulet of imagination and play.

All men carry in them a secret, wordless prayer of play. It is a male noise, the noise that guns make, the noise of arrows, of a Spitfire, of a bazooka, of a ray gun, ululations that defy spelling, the sounds that we now rarely make out loud. But they're there inside all of us, all men, ghostly echoes of the good fight of the child.

May 2013

Lord Snowdon

The discreetly elegant Kensington house sits back from the quiet road with its set of dozing speed bumps. It could be the immodest second home of a French hedge-fund manager or the payoff for an oligarch's mistress. The sign on the door says 'Ring the bell in the basement.' It clangs like a retired fire engine. The door opens to reveal a dark little hall with a cheery lady doing the ironing. This is not how the readers of *Majesty* magazine will imagine royalty living. But then Tony Snowdon isn't royalty, he's more important than that. We are let in by his daughter Frances. 'Did he ever take your picture in the studio? Well, come and have a look.'

It's a small suburban conservatory lean-to with a white wall and a lot of natural light. There's a pile of records in the middle with Barbra Streisand smiling up from the top. 'We had a party here,' she says, by way of explanation. At the back there's a desk and a pinboard with photographs of his children and a smattering of homely clutter, *The Book of Common Prayer*, a guide to English table glass. Next door there are the chairs Snowdon designed for the Prince of Wales's investiture: simple, elegant, utilitarian, especially unEnglish, unstuffy, unposh, a brilliant, intense coral-red. 'I think it's called Snowdon red,' says Frances. What, like Matisse blue? Or Barry White? Down the corridor is the darkroom, now unused, the smell of fixative and developer gone, the red light extinguished. There is a flash of sadness in a bright darkroom. On a shelf is a stack of ledgers, the studio day books, a photographer's version of a diary or a sketchbook, Polaroids of subjects, with an assistant's annotation of times, stocks, exposures, addresses, phone numbers, agents. They are an insight into a snapper's technique. You instantly know these are Snowdon's photographs – they have a distinctive look. He is, unusually for his generation, nationality and culture, a sympathetic and subtle photographer of men.

Snowdon sits at a little desk beside the window in a small, cosy, green breakfast room. I remember coming here to pick him up when we first worked together. He has been associated with *The Sunday Times Magazine* since its inception in the early 1960s. Mark Boxer, the *Magazine*'s first editor, made him artistic adviser and he went on to produce incisive reportage features that reflected his own interests. He was always much more than a portrait photographer.

I'd been warned that he could be prickly, mercurial, bloody difficult. I'd begun by asking him what he'd like me to call him.

'Oh, Tony,' he smiled, as if the inquiry were unnecessary.

'And how would you like me to introduce you?'

'Ah, we might fudge that.'

His smile became foxy. He could switch in an instant from Tony to Lord Snowdon, never for self-aggrandising reasons or for a better table, but if Snowdon could get him the access for a better shoot, then he would appear.

If Tony was more congenial and put his subject at ease, then that was who you'd meet. It's trite, but not wholly untrue, to say a great deal of Antony Armstrong-Jones's life came out of the skilful double act of Tony and Snowdon, a mutual ventriloquism where one of them, then the other, plays the dummy.

He looks good, handsome, not just for his age, but any age. His hereditary bone structure and determined follicles have taken him from being a deb's delight to a dowager's delight. He is trim and neat, Turnbull and Asser shirt, striped tie, jacket, accessorised with chunky signet rings and a square watch. He looks up and grins.

'How nice of you to come.' He has that conspiratorial, inclusive, wide-mouth smile that he shares sparingly.

'Drink?' It's 11 a.m. and he's on his first Bloody Mary.

'No, I'm fine, thanks.' The answer doesn't register.

'Drink?'

'I'll have what you're having.'

Frances produces two prearranged Virgin Marys. On the table is the first copy of *Snowdon: A Life in View*, a big, beautifully produced collection of his work, with essays from people he has collaborated with over the years. I expect Rizzoli, the publishers, would call it a coffee-table book, but I doubt Snowdon has anything as gauche as a coffee table. He turns the pages slowly. The first images are all of him in characteristic 1960s ensembles, sitting in the ubiquitous Indian wicker chair in a polo neck with corduroy Chelsea boots – 'I think he's still got those upstairs,' says Frances – and the watch he's wearing today, channelling Simon Templar in emblematic motors, a Morris Minor and an Aston Martin, and rather blissfully sporting lace-up suede boots. 'Do you still have those upstairs?' he sniggers.

There's a priceless snap of Princess Margaret in the bath wearing an elaborate tiara. It's a rather ordinary bath, with a sponge and a non-slip mat. She smiles happily at the camera. 'Nice picture of my foot,' says Tony. There, reflected in the mirror, is his naked foot, missing its lace-up suede boot. The portrait is a nod to the heraldic elephant in the room, but he has done so much more than be merely an accessory to the aristocracy. 'When he married, Cecil Beaton thanked Princess Margaret for removing his primary competitor,' says Frances. Tony waits a beat, then adds: 'But she didn't.' And anyway, Beaton was flattering himself. Tony Armstrong-Jones wasn't competition, he was the future. His early book on London was a collection of amused, observant reportage, views of the capital growing out of the dusty and decrepit city of the war into something new that wasn't quite sure what it would be. Here is a lunchtime stripper in an East End pub, juxtaposed with Crufts dog show. The crowds watching the Trooping the Colour with mirrors on sticks so their backs are to the establishment. Nannies in the park pushing Peter Pan prams and Cartier with its rubbish bins outside, an unambiguous comment on class and cash. 'That's all the waste diamonds in there,' he smiles. The army of portraits includes one of the best ever taken of Laurence Olivier, as the comedian in John Osborne's play *The Entertainer*. Olivier as an actor would become Zelig and disappear in front of cameras, but here his dazzling, mercurial power fizzes from the image. There is a lot of mannered and arched 1960s and early 1970s fashion photography. 'Are you interested in fashion?' I ask. 'No.' Though it didn't stop him coming up with his own line of ski clothes. He looks at the rather impractical but elegant pictures. 'Didn't sell a single one.'

Tony got his interest in design from his uncle Oliver Messel, the flamboyant theatre designer who also designed Princess Margaret's house on Mustique. Messel's style was highly ornate, mixing rococo with fairy-tale fantasy; Snowdon's sensibilities were very different: practical, elegant, functional and modern. There is nothing extraneous or humorous, no toying with fantasy, no extravagance or luxury. Snowdon made things where form rigorously served function.

He contracted polio as a child, when every classroom in the country had a small inmate wearing medieval callipers. Most people would never notice, but today he finds moving about testing. All his life he's been an advocate for the disabled, getting the Royal Hospital and Home for the Incurables in Putney to change its dismal, pessimistic name. Once, finding a woman in a wheelchair strapped into the guard's van of a British Rail train (the only place for wheelchairs was with the livestock and the luggage), he arranged to interview the snobbish Sir Robert Reid, who was in charge. Reid thought he was going to talk about railway design with royalty. It is still a marvellous journalistic trainwreck of the best sort: Sir Robert is left puffing, nursing his injured dignity, Snowdon's anger on behalf of the disabled is cold and implacable. Snowdon turns the page and there is a panorama of the Prince of Wales in his investiture at Caernarfon Castle in 1969. This was a huge national event for a country that had had few celebrations. It was all televised with pomp and circumstance, the equivalent of the Olympics opening ceremony, except that the Queen arrived without a parachute. Snowdon was in charge of it all: he designed the lot, from the red chairs to Charles's new crown, it was all modern, unlike any of the gothic, Victorian, sentimental trumpery that royal occasions usually came with. 'It was marvellous, wasn't it?' Yes it was. It was also an opportunity for the new generation of the royal family to be the first in 200 years to have its own élan and style, and a contemporary relevance to its citizens. But Charles baulked at the opportunity, and reverted to the comforting nostalgia of crafty ruralism. There is the famous picture Snowdon took of the Prince of Wales with Diana with their two boys and the horse in its manqué Georgian set-up. 'I hate this picture,' says Frances. Snowdon touches Diana's face. 'She was wonderful. She had no idea what to do with a horse, of course.'

There is a photograph of Nureyev and Margot Fonteyn, one of the few unequivocally romantic pictures in the book. Tony unbuttons his shirt and pulls out a gold charm on a chain round his neck. It is an elegant bird, an eagle with spread wings. 'This is pre-Columbian,' he says. 'It was given to Princess Margaret by Margot.' Frances gives him a gimlet look and quietly corrects him. 'I think she gave it to you? You've never ever taken it off.'

Snowdon worked as a photojournalist, not least for *The Sunday Times Magazine*. His immensely sympathetic eye was often a surprise to people who knew only his waspish tongue. He observed with a warm detachment the frailty, hope and pity of people. In '66, Snowdon did a piece on loneliness. He photographed an old man who followed the tide on Brighton beach. It turned out he'd been photographed both by Cartier-Bresson and Bill Brandt, a remarkable coincidence. Both of them had snapped him from behind, looking out to sea. Snowdon showed us his face, and actually spoke to him. 'I realised he was a deaf mute. I spoke to him in deaf and dumb language I'd learnt at school. He said he'd lived in a bedsit and no one had spoken to him in 20 years.'

Some years ago, he and I did a story on old age. He caught a moment, an old lady with dementia dancing with one of her carers. I don't think I even noticed, but Snowdon did. During the 1960s and 1970s he made television documentaries that won hatfuls of awards, but they are not what he is remembered for. What he did best was portrait photography.

Pure, strong, uncluttered images were taken like someone gently tickling trout, waiting for the object of his attention to offer something intimate or telling about themselves. You can see that some have been snapped by Tony and some by Snowdon. All have the same defining attachment, the coolness that chooses the shutter moment with an unblinking lizard eye.

We stop at a photograph of Anthony Blunt, the treacherous spy, who was also Surveyor of the King's Pictures and an arch member of the haute establishment. The image has Blunt holding up a slide – the light projects the picture onto his eye. It is a strikingly theatrical photo of a man living a double life. 'It was just luck,' says Snowdon. 'I took it before anyone knew he was a spy.' But there is no luck in photography, it is all timing, observation, experience and cunning.

Snowdon too lived, not a double life, but perhaps parallel lives. The coolness, the manners, the archness that made him such a clever portraitist were also a protection against the establishment, a life he could have been swallowed up by. The detachment allowed Snowdon to be other things, so that now, aged 84, the least interesting thing about him is that he was married into the royal family. We get to the end of the book.

'What am I doing next?' he asks.

'You're having lunch,' says Frances.

'Where?'

'In Maggie Jones's,' a restaurant next to Kensington Palace, where he once lived.

'Oh good. I like it there,' he says, and turns to me. 'You remember why it's called Maggie Jones's, don't you?'

'After your wife.'

'And me!' he adds with faux hurt.

'Is there anything else about your life you'd like to add?' I ask him.

'Fuck all,' he grins.

September 2014

Don McCullin

Cambodia, 1970. A young paratrooper, eyes screwed shut, lips drawn back in the awkward grimace of extreme pain, is trying to sit up. His head is cradled by another soldier. A third looks on. Don McCullin is turning the pages of his new, huge, glossy, retrospective photo book. 'I'd been out there in front of those guys, in the Jeep, but it got frightening and I came back and the mortar exploded just there,' he says. 'That's the guy, the guy they put in the truck with me. That's him dying. He died just in that moment.'

Don had also been hit by shrapnel, but carried on taking pictures two or three feet away from the dying man. He was lying in the blood and the chaos and the terror. His own injury could have been fatal, or worse. 'Actually, I'd got a badly cut dick. I was lying in the hospital. A *Daily Mirror* reporter came to see me and he said, "You'll never get another blow job in this town."'

Now Don's happily married to Catherine, an old friend of mine, and as far from the killing fields as possible, in Somerset. Next month, he turns 80. I wouldn't normally mention a chap's age, but in this case it's astonishing. First, that he's actually made it to 80, and second, how he makes 80 look. He's still movie-star handsome with elegant, dishevelled silver hair, and gimlet pale-blue eyes in a face that is completely unlined. 'I've got a clothes peg round the back.'

He owns one of the most winsome smiles since Paul Newman

handed his in. Skinny, windblown, tanned, he moves with a loping street ease. If you grow into the face you deserve, then Don's got a billion in the karma bank. If your face is a consequence of your experiences, then he must have a really terrifying self-portrait in a darkroom somewhere. He has probably seen more appalling, hellish, pitiful misery and terror than anyone else living. 'It's really cold,' he says. 'I had to stop and buy a vest in M&S. I feel it more now. I've got arthritis. You know, my boy starts secondary school next year? I shouldn't be paying school fees at my age.'

We meet for lunch at the Wolseley in London. As he walks into the room, heads turn. He grins the grin. 'It's nice here,' he says, with a trace of Finsbury Park in his voice. He's constantly aware of his background and the background of others. 'You're quite dyslexic, aren't you? So am I, really bad, but I notice things. I know who everybody is in this room. I pick up on everything.' I know what he means.

He went to art school, but left at 15 when his father died. He did national service in the RAF, was sent to Suez, worked for a photographer, came home, bought a camera, pawned it. His old mum redeemed it and he became, well, he became Don McCullin, the greatest war photographer of his own lifetime. He also helped make the reputation of *The Sunday Times Magazine*.

He started off by taking pictures of a London gang called The Guvnors in a derelict house, and then took himself off to Berlin to photograph the wall being built, and then blagged his way to Congo for a civil war that was being fought by mercenaries who threatened to hand him over to the Congolese police, which would have meant certain death. And then Mad Mike Hoare, a mercurial mercenary major, said that he admired McCullin's pluck, and gave him a gun, and took him off in search of raped and murdered nuns. It's the sort of *Boy's Own* madcap stuff that still inspires kids with Nikons to traipse off to war zones.

He is an interviewer's dream and a nightmare. He talks like he's on a late-night chat show, issuing a stream of brilliantly retold anecdotes that switch from being heroic to utterly parochial – never pompous or self-regarding, always based on the view of that elevating pale eye that misses nothing. The trouble is, half of it is unprintable.

I remember when we worked together years ago, at an agricultural fair in Warwickshire, he'd chat away, usually about the purgatory and infamy of women in general, and ex-wives and girlfriends in particular, and then he'd punctuate the observations by saying: 'Cor, look at the rack on her.' It was very funny. He knows he's funny; he loves conviviality, though he's stopped drinking now. 'I had that heart surgery. Don't do it,' he says, as if it were a cosmetic choice. 'They cut you open, right down here, and peel back your ribs.'

This morning's papers all lead with the photograph of a drowned Syrian three-year-old on a Turkish beach, and on the *Today* programme someone says: 'This is a Don McCullin moment.' A photograph that changes perceptions. Don has become an adjective, the description of a disaster, a universal witness.

The cover of his new book carries one of his most famous and indelible photographs: a shell-shocked soldier from the Vietnam War. It's a simple image. The helmeted man sits white-knuckle-gripping his rifle. He has a thousand-yard stare, an expression of nameless fatigue and sated horror. He looks like a statue, or an illustration for Wilfred Owen's 'Dulce et Decorum Est'. 'His hanging face, like a devil's sick of sin . . .'

Don glances at the image. 'I hate that picture. I'm fed up with it.' It smells of familiarity, the constant repetition. A handful of photographs follow him around like Greatest Hits. I turn the pages to the awful and inerasable image of a starving albino Biafran boy holding an empty can of corned beef like an icon.

'That was the worst one I ever took; I mean it was the most awful to take. I took his picture in one shot and I walked away. I couldn't look at him. I was talking to somebody and I felt this little hand take mine and I turned round and it was him – he'd followed me. I gave him a barley sugar and he went and stood in a corner, licked it and watched me.'

As he goes through the book he remembers everyone. 'The man there, that's his blood, it poured out the back of his head. We both saw the grenade land and I got down faster than he did.'

There's a picture from Chapel Market, Islington, in the 1960s. 'That bloke came at me with a brick. I took it off him and hit him with it and then drove him to hospital so I could watch them put the stitches in. I used to have a temper.'

The war photograph is a genre that grows familiar. It has an accessible formula, like school or wedding photos. You see a picture and you think: 'That looks like Don McCullin.' There is a directness, an intimacy and an engagement to his work, which takes Robert Capa's recommendation to heart that if your pictures aren't good enough, you're not close enough.

Don is always at maximum risk, always black and white, always with a lens that is as close to a human eye as possible. 'I've never really cared about cameras and kits and stuff. It's in my eyes, it's how I see.' He's rarely further than 10 feet from his subject. 'They need to see me, too, to know I'm there, to trust me. I always want to be close, to have a contact.' He doesn't go in for long-lensed sniping. He has helped to invent our vision of what conflict and moments of terrible, violent catharsis look like. No other reportage photographer has imposed such a strong personal vision on the news.

We look through the set of photos he took in the Battle of Huế, during the Vietnam War, one of the most ferocious engagements since the end of the Second World War. 'That man throwing the grenade – immediately after I took that, his left hand was shot off and the next man up to throw grenades was killed. That boy there was Scots; his dad married an American. That officer's been nicked by a bullet in the neck.'

Everyone is still warm, they're just around the corner, just out of sight. 'This one, I call this my Descent from the Cross.' Two American soldiers carry a third who is mortally wounded. 'I carried him out of there.' There are, in many of the images, references to religious art – the compositions, the characters. Don often chooses to push the shutter the moment the participants are caught in an unconscious elegance at odds with their situation. They are moments that transpose tenderness with horror, reflection with chaos; they conjure, perhaps unconsciously, the hell and salvation that is the central dichotomy of votive art.

One of the most profoundly arresting images is of a dead Vietnamese soldier surrounded by his belongings, the photos in his wallet, a girl, school children, spilt bullets. It is – ever the cliché of war fiction – pathetic, in the truest and oldest sense of the word. 'I arranged that,' he says. 'He's dead and American soldiers were going through his pockets looking for souvenirs. I gathered together all the stuff they discarded, the pitiful objects, and arranged them around him as a tribute. It's a memorial to him.'

How do you deal with all this stuff? How do you process it? How do you stop it overwhelming you? If anyone should have post-traumatic stress, it's Don. 'I don't forget anything,' he says, 'I don't deal with any of it. The images are all there in my head, all those people, all the time. I live with all of them.'

He's never watched the internet films of Isis executions. 'Why would I? I've seen enough people executed. Just there,' he points to the next table. 'And I put my camera down.'

He says there were moments when he thought the camera was complicit, or an unjustifiable humiliation and he wouldn't take the picture. 'There was a woman, I took one shot of her in Beirut. She was violently weeping and she came for me, hit me hard. An hour later someone told me she'd been killed by a car bomb.'

Once, McCullin was so incensed by the inactivity, the blindness of politicians and the apathy of the public, that he flyposted an unbearably distressing photograph of a Biafran child trying to suckle from his mother's parched breasts, an image that was agonisingly, simultaneously Madonna nativity and pietà.

'I don't take credit for any of these pictures – the war photography. They belong to the people in them. They are their photographs. I do take credit for the other stuff, the landscapes, the architecture.'

When he returned from the long years of foreign wars, Don produced a book in 1979 called *Homecoming* – landscapes and portraits of England that try to be bucolic and lyrical in a great old English tradition. It's freighted with tension and morbid anticipation. There is the sense of carnage just outside the shot. It is one of the most emotionally tangled and dark photographic essays.

And then he made a classically pure and elegant folio of sights from the Roman Empire, which is mostly bereft of people. Columns stand like bleached bones of an ancient hubris and authority, but even this has a grim premonition of the destruction of Palmyra.

What next, now that he's about to turn 80? With a sly conspiratorial grin, he slides his hand into his inside pocket and shows me the corner of a document, like a love letter or a pirate's map. 'It's a visa application for Iraq. I want to see what the Kurds are up to.'

September 2015

Life at Sixty

Every morning, after taking our twins to school, Nicola and I read the papers over breakfast and I recite the birthday list and she will guess the ages. She's uncannily accurate. Yesterday the *Guardian* will have said: AA Gill, critic and baboon-murdering bastard, 60.

I share a birthday with Henry VIII and the shot that started the Great War. I've always read the anniversary roll and over the years I've watched people my age go from rarely mentioned as sportsmen and pop stars to more commonly as leading actors and television presenters, and now ubiquitously I find myself in the thick of captains of industry, ennobled politicians, retired sportsmen and character actors. You only notice the accumulating years in relation to other people.

Last week an editor breezily mentioned that, as I was coming up to a milestone decade, would I perhaps like to write something about it? You know, is 60 the new 40? Why do you make those little noises when you get out of a chair? Am I considering getting a shed, or a cruise, or Velcro? And what about sex?

The only people who ask about significant birthdays are younger than you. No 70-year-olds are inquiring about my insights on being 60. Age is the great terra incognita. But then, all the people who tell me to do anything are younger than me now.

And please, can we stop this '60 is the new 40' thing? No one is saying 20 is the new 10. And who wants to be 40 anyway? An insipid, insecure age.

My generation, the postwar baby-boomers, are over the meridian of our vital parabolas. We've done our best and our worst, overachieved and underperformed, are either preparing to bask on the sun loungers of our success or suck our bruised fingers in the waiting rooms of failure. So 60 is both a personal summit from which to look back, breathing heavily, hands on my knees, and a generational one.

I was born in 1954 in Edinburgh. Winston Churchill was prime minister, there was still rationing, we were the first generation that would grow up with television, pop music, central heating and a National Health Service. As a child, every old man I knew had fought in the First World War and every young man in the Second.

War still hung like the smell of a damp, grim nostalgia over everything. We played Spitfires and Messerschmitts in the playground and you could, as Kingsley Amis pointed out, walk into any pub in the country and ask with perfect confidence if the major had been in. London was still moth-eaten with bomb sites and black with coal smoke. One of my earliest memories is of the last pea-souper fog.

How do I feel having reached 60? Well, surprised, mostly. And grateful. When I was 30, a doctor told me that I had a dangerously damaged liver and, all things considered, I probably wouldn't see another Christmas. I am an alcoholic and a drug addict but, with a lot of help, I stopped. I haven't had a drink or picked up a drug since. My grandfather died at 59. He was a tooth-puller in Leith. My mother says it was anxiety about the coming of the Health Service that killed him, which is a braw example of Scottish humour.

Globally, I can expect to live to see another two World Cups. But by living in the south of England I should make it for another four. I tell people too quickly that I am 60 and wait, like a needy toddler, to be told I don't look anything like that. One of the surprising

symptoms of getting to be 60 is that I now can't tell how old anyone under the age of 40 is; you all look 16. And don't believe the
beauty-page gush that you are in fact only as old as you feel. It's a
nonsense, based on the assumption that ageing is primarily a physical process. It isn't, it's a maturing one. It's not a feeling, it's an
experience. You are as old as you can remember.

I dictate these articles to clever, overeducated colleagues who
are much, much younger than me. They constantly and consistently don't get references to things that to me seemed to have
happened only a couple of months ago. They've never seen black-
and-white films or known the difference between 78, 45 and 33. So,
if you know who Jan Palach, Gary Powers, Gary Gilmore, Squeaky
Fromme, Adam Adamant, Albert Pierrepoint, the Piranha Brothers,
Harry Worth and Fyfe Robertson are, then you must be 60.

A contemporary of mine, after a number of marriages, found a
girlfriend less than half his age of a transcendent pneumatic beauty
who hung on his every word – and dumped her after a couple of
months. Why, I asked – she was perfect! 'Too many things we didn't
have in common,' he said sadly. Like what? 'Well, the 1980s.'

Which brings us to sex.

Nicola has just exclaimed with unusual force that she has never
slept with a 60-year-old and she's not planning on starting now.
Nobody wants to think about 60-year-olds doing it, least of all
60-year-olds. Another contemporary pointed out that it wasn't finding the first grey pubic hair on yourself that was the doom-laden
shock, it was finding it on the person you were sleeping with.

After a certain age it's best not to have mirrors in your sight line.
And lighting is important: the less the better. But you must have
some, because everything sags and moves about. The pale, flickering
glow of the television is the illumination of choice for most
middle-aged couples.

I've been making a list of the sex that I'm now too old to consider. I will probably never have sex again on a jiggling sofa with her

parents asleep upstairs. Or in a skip. Or in the back of a stationary 2CV or the front of a moving Alfa Romeo.

I won't do bondage, sadomasochism or erotic yoga or miss them. Neither will I partake in role play. I am too old to be a pirate, a policeman, a Viking or the Milk Tray Man (they don't know who the Milk Tray Man was either).

And I realise with a sudden shock that I'm probably too old to sleep with anyone for the first time. The thought of having to go through the whole seduction, will they, won't they, can I, can't I, is far more terrifying than it is exciting.

Sex definitely changes. It is less athletic, more romantic, more intense, more a special event. Not because it's rare, but because it's finite. There is a point in your life when you stop counting up and start counting back. It's not the laps run, it's the laps that are left.

This is one of the biggest changes in ageing. The continuous heart-beat rhythm that tells you your experiences are now rationed. How many more *Ring* cycles will I get to? How many more times will I see Venice emerging out of the lagoon? How many cassoulets, English cherries? How many summits in the Highlands? How many long lunches with old friends? How many old friends are left to me? That sounds maudlin, but it doesn't feel like that. It adds to the pleasure, a sentiment to everything, an extra gypsy violin to life. I linger over things now: flowers, moonlight, Schubert, lunch, bookshops. Also I mind less about standing in queues, sitting in traffic, waiting for a bus or my call to be answered. Everything has a pinch of piquancy, a smudge of melodrama, and I like that.

There are other things to which age adds an imperative. I'm pretty sure that when I'm lying on the gurney and the children are search-ing for the off-switch while telling me sweetly to go towards the light, the thing I regret won't be, as John Betjeman said, not enough sex, and it won't be not enough caviar or cakes. It will be, I think, that I never got to see Timbuktu or South Georgia. Never saw the northern lights. Never travelled up the fjords by boat.

The abiding pleasure of my life so far has been the opportunity to travel. It is also the single greatest gift of my affluent generation. We got to go around the globe relatively easily, cheaply and safely. Postwar children are the best and most widely travelled generation that has yet lived. We were given the world when it was varied, various and mostly welcoming. Whether we took enough goodwill with us and brought back enough insight is debatable. But today the laziest gap-year student has probably seen more and been further than Livingstone, Stanley and Richard Burton.

One of the things that surprises and dismays me is how many of my contemporaries spend their time and money on travelling to sunny beaches. All beach experiences, give or take a cocktail, are the same experience. My advice to travellers and tourists is to avoid coasts and visit people. There is not a view in the world that is as exciting as a new city.

So I regret places and I will also regret not being a better friend. My generation has been profligate with friends. I look at how my parents husbanded theirs, thought about them, wrote to them, talked about them. Because they had lived through the war their friends were innately more precious than ours have been to us. Our friends are not disposable, but they turn out to be forgettable. I regret not making more of an effort to keep up, keep hold and keep close the people I loved. Now their absence and my casual wastefulness upset me.

I noticed in last week's paper that if I were in the army (something, thanks to my father and my grandfather, I've never had to do), being in the 55–59 age bracket I would be expected to do 21 press-ups and 27 sit-ups within two minutes. Now that is down to 17 and 23 as I've reached the end of the tick-box line. I will now be for ever in the 60-and-over category, after which there is just the margin.

Last year, for the first time, a young girl, French, offered me her seat on a crowded bus. I was surprised at how deeply I resented her. Health looms over the elderly like a threatening monsoon. No ache is innocuous. No lump or discoloured, sagging patch of body is ignorable except our toenails, which become the most sordidly repellent things in all nature. We covertly examine ourselves and our effluvia for the premonition of the dark humour that will carry us away. There is no such thing as a routine check-up. They are all life-or-death appointments.

Doctors start all their sentences with 'It's only . . .' But we're not fooled. This generation is also the one that lingers longest over its departure. Death came to our grandparents with a clutched chest and a searing pain. For us it's a slow, humiliating series of it's onlys. What we worry about is dementia, a condition that did not exist in the popular lexicon when I was a child. Mind you, we also thought cancer was as shaming as divorce. Now Alzheimer's is our abiding fear, the thing we can't forget.

My chats with contemporaries are like bridge games where we try to fill in the gaps in each other's sentences to make one coherent conversation. My dad died of Alzheimer's. I once asked him how he was feeling: 'Oh, quite well, except you know I've got this terrible disease, what's its name?' So we go to the gym, we have trainers, I do Pilates. But it's only maintenance. I'm not looking for a beach body, there's no New Me in the cupboard; I just want one that's supple enough to put on my own socks.

After giving up drink and drugs, I continued to smoke about 60 a day until 12 years ago and then I stopped. And people said, 'Well done! How did you manage it? What willpower!' It didn't feel like well done. It felt like a defeat – the capitulation to fear. When I started smoking at 14 I was golden, immortal. I smoked around the world; I took pride in my ability to smoke with elegance, panache and skill. Smoking was my talent and I gave it up because I lost my nerve. I don't miss the cigarettes, but I do miss the me that smoked so beautifully.

Oddly, the one thing that does improve with age is our teeth. Old people get perfect, white, even, marvellous grins. Paradoxically, we simultaneously lose our sense of humour. I've had four children in two batches. It's not for me to say if I've been a good father; that's between the kids and their respective therapists. But I think I've been more benign second time round. With the first two, now 21 and 23, I was a cross between a Butlins Redcoat and Savonarola. I had plans and theories; I thought children were blank and malleable. I was brought up in the 1960s by '60s parents who drank '60s Kool-Aid. Much as I loved them I didn't want to be like them, just as they didn't want to be like their parents.

I had no plan or ambition for my kids and no Tiggerish belief in education. I know all the competitive insecurity that infects parents around schools, exams and universities. I've seen too many desperate kids becoming extensions of adults' vanity, insecurity and desire for a second chance. And I told my children I had no interest in seeing their reports or knowing their exam results. Nothing they achieve will ever make me prouder of them than the day they were born. Nothing they do or don't do will make me love them an iota less.

Through empirical trials I have discovered there is no intergenerational conflict that can't be sorted with a tenner. Just say sorry and I'll give you a tenner. Clean your room – there's a tenner in it. Get your aunt a birthday card; keep the change. It's not money; it's a MacGuffin, a prop that allows everyone to back down without losing face or temper. And oddly, I've managed to produce four of the least miserly and acquisitive children.

How did my generation do? Well, we get blamed for being selfish and self-obsessed and soft and pushing up house prices and saddling the next generation with hideous debts and nowhere to live, and I suppose that's not entirely unfair. We are ridiculously obsessed with food, buy too many things and have too many clothes. But we didn't start a war. Well, not a big one. And we didn't nuke anyone. We defused the Cold War. We believed in the collective good. Although we came to confuse gestures with actions and we think going on a march and writing a letter are the same as doing something, making the world better.

We were the generation that were relentlessly for civil rights, human rights, gay rights, disability rights, equality, fairness. We were implacably against racism and censorship. We defended freedom of speech, religion and expression. We will leave the world better fed and better off than when we arrived in it.

Britain is a far happier, richer and fairer place than it was 60 years ago. And if you think that's wishful self-promotion, you have no idea how grim and threadbare Britain in the 1950s was. You weren't there, you don't remember.

June 2014

The Magpie Café

―――――

I've got cancer. Sorry to drop that onto the breakfast table apropos of nothing at all. Apropos and cancer are rarely found in the same sentence. I wasn't going to mention it, the way you don't. In truth, I've got an embarrassment of cancer, the full English. There is barely a morsel of offal not included. I have a trucker's gut-buster, gimpy, malevolent, meaty malignancy. And I've mentioned it because, as I write in the first person, and occasionally some of you might take me seriously enough to book a table on a recommendation, you ought to know if there are any fundamental, gastro, epicurean, personal changes that would affect my judgment. If I were, for instance, struck down with palaeo-sidereal veganism, which I hope we would all agree would be worse. Or if I had all my teeth kicked out by an Icelandic horse on his way to the butcher's.

Chemotherapy can alter the way things taste. I am being rinsed with commando doses of platinum. My insides are being turned into road-rail, pig-lead, firewood, iron-ware and cheap tin trays. If ever things start tasting like licked battery terminals, I'll tell you. Either that or I'll be eating at Sexy Fish.

I'm forbidden from travelling on trains, boats, buses and planes. Nor can I drive. Jeremy Clarkson says this has nothing to do with getting cancer. I've been banned from riding a bike – even on grass, added the oncologist unkindly. So I'm not going to be plashing through marsh and fen to find outré openings (*no change there — ed*).

281

If there was a good thing to say about cancer, and frankly this is medical bowel-scraping, it's that it gives permission and excuse to friends to say and do generous things that the onset of gout or herpes might not have elicited. So, just after my diagnosis, I got a call from Jimmy Carr, who said, 'Awful news, but I'd like to fulfil a bucket-list wish. I can pretend to be Jimmy Savile for a day. I've always wanted to do Jim'll Fix It.'

'How kind. What were you thinking of?'

'Well,' he said, 'I've got to go up and do ten minutes' filming with Jeremy on his new show, and there's a spare seat in the whirlybird. We can be back in London for tea. What do you say?'

'Where are we going? Paris, Deauville, Barcelona?'

'Whitby.'

'Now you're talking.'

If I didn't have cancer, I would probably have passed on Whitby in October. But the thought that this might be my last chance ever to visit the place again clinched it. Whitby has the best fish and chips in Britain. So, the next morning, I get into the helicopter and there's a manic Jimmy, gurning, 'Now then, now then . . .' and we take off into the chilly Elstree dawn and chug north.

'So,' he asks, 'cancer – what's the silver lining? There must be an upside.' Well, there is: you can stop worrying about Alzheimer's, but even that is a bit tarnished because I'm already an ambassador for the Alzheimer's Society, and getting cancer is like going over to a competing charitable condition. Hey ho.

Whitby appears like a William Blake doodle over the North York Moors. As with most east-facing seaside towns, it both perches and hunches on the grey wet, with its gothic ruin and nudge-nudge naughty postcards.

It's a place that is both eminently dour and practical and utterly, bonkersly up some seaside spectrum. So, everyone on the street has apparently decided to dress at Millets for under £15 and attach themselves to a terrier. Or they're dressing up as role-play therapy

groups: there are goths, vampires and, today, masses of pensioners in Dad's Army costume, platoons of spavined Home Guard and
women going to collect their rations. It's a steampunk version of
Westworld. There are no tourists or trippers. They are just doing it
for their own amusement.

Jimmy and I go in search of the Magpie Café, a fish'n'chip shop
I deemed the best in Britain more than a decade ago. It remains
completely, perfectly true to its calling. At 11.30, the little restaurant
is beginning to fill up with retired couples in cagoules, coming in
for an early lunch. But seaside fish and chips isn't like other meals.
We approach it with a proprietary fondness. This is grade 1 listed
dinner, cultural heritage, a communion of secular us-ness. No one
is eating fish and chips for the first time. Jimmy and I were given
the table in the bay window, looking out at the wandering Private
Godfreys and Van Helsings.

The fish is generous, fresh off the boat, battered with a loving
authority. Beef-dripping twice-fried chips are thick, crunchy and
floury. The curry sauce is authentically indigenous, free from any
Asian aspiration. Mushy peas are marrow-fat bland sog, not blitzed
garden frozen. They dance with a surprising elegance when dabbed
with a douse of malt vinegar. There is bread that has been buttered
as if there was still rationing, and pots of brown, round-vowelled
tea, and jam roly-poly that comes with custard *and* cream.

Jimmy and I are absurdly happy with the whole modest but profound table, each constituent panto part perfectly fitting in with its
neighbour with a warming familiarity. We decided to judge, once
and for all, the ancient north-south question of haddock or cod.
And, as a Scot, I'm happy to say my national preference for haddock
won by a slim, opalescent flake.

This is, all things considered, without pretension but with utter
self-confidence, still the best fish and chips in the world. Naturally,
Clarkson disagrees and has his own Whitby favourite, Mister Chips,
which is run by a messianically enthusiastic team. They have a

board on which they write the name of the particular trawler your fish was landed from and, out of fairness, we took another complete fish dinner back with us on the helicopter.

I have to say it was pretty damn perfect, and no one else in the ether of the world was having superior in-flight catering.

November 2016

My National Health Crisis

———

It seems unlikely, uncharacteristic, so un-'us' to have settled on sickness and bed rest as the votive altar and cornerstone of national politics. But there it is: every election, the National Health Service is the thermometer and the crutch of governments. The NHS represents everything we think is best about us. Everyone standing for whatever political persuasion has to lay a sterilised hand on an A&E revolving door and swear that the collective cradle-to-crematorium health service will be cherished on their watch.

When you look at our awkward, lumpy, inherited short-tempered characters, you'd imagine we might have come up with something more brass-bandy Brit: a bellicose, sentimental military fetishism, perhaps, or sport, or nostalgic history, boastful Anglophone culture, invention, exploration, banking avarice. But no. It turned out that what really sticks in our hard, gimpy, sclerotic hearts is looking after each other. Turning up at a bed with three carnations, a copy of *Racing Post*, a Twix and saying, 'The cat misses you.'

We know it's the best of us. The National Health Service is the best of us. You can't walk into an NHS hospital and be a racist. That condition is cured instantly. But it's almost impossible to walk into a private hospital and not fleetingly feel that you are one: a plush waiting room with entitled and bad-tempered health tourists.

You can't be sexist on the NHS, nor patronising, and the care and the humour, the togetherness ranged against the teetering, chronic system by both the caring and the careworn is the Blitz, 'back against the wall', stern and sentimental best of us – and so we tell lies about it.

We say it's the envy of the world. It isn't. We say there's nothing else like it. There is. We say it's the best in the West. It's not. We think it's the cheapest. It isn't. Either that or we think it's the most expensive – it's not that either. You will live longer in France and Germany, get treated faster and more comfortably in Scandinavia, and everything costs more in America.

I've wanted to write about the National Health Service for a long time, but it's resistant to press inquiries. While the abstract of the NHS is heart-warming, the truth for patients is often heart-stopping. And junior doctor strikes, executive pay, failing departments, slow-motion waiting times and outsourcing tell a different story, and I'm regularly, ritually refused access by PRs and administrators, or they insist on copy approval or preplanned stories.

One of the doctors I approached was Professor Brian Gazzard,who has a reputation mostly for being an exemplary and inspirationally brilliant physician, but also as something of an ocean-going eccentric. He treats, teaches at and runs the Chelsea Aids clinic. I asked him what had changed most about his job.

'When I started, I told every patient that they were going to die. I could make it easier, make them live a little longer, but everyone died. Now I tell every patient they will live. They will need to do what I tell them, they've been silly, but they'll live to die of something else. That's astonishing.' He paused so I would understand the effect it has on a doctor. 'Look, I really don't want to be written about. You won't remember, but we met once before.'

A decade ago, Gazzard diagnosed my foreign correspondent's dodgy tummy as acute pancreatitis, the result of alcoholism. 'Of course I remember. You told me I could never drink alcohol again and I said, 'You haven't read my notes, I've been teetotal for twenty years.' And you gave a sigh and reached into a drawer and lit a cigarette and said you'd been dreading telling a restaurant critic he couldn't have a glass of wine.'

Gazzard laughed. 'You're one of the lucky ones,' he'd said as he walked onto the street clutching an armful of patient files and raised a hand in farewell. He repeated again: 'You're one of the lucky ones. I can always tell.' It was his first misdiagnosis of the day.

What neither of us could know is that my pancreas was already a stuffed wallet of cancer, though not pancreatic – a migrated, refugee, desperate, breathless lung cancer.

I stopped smoking fifteen years ago and as a gift to myself, proof of the clarity of my lungs, I would spend a week stalking on Loch Maree in Wester Ross. Every autumn since, I have climbed the same hills, chasing the deer, and trudging upwards, recited a doxology of mostly extinct snouts I no longer puff: Weights, Guards, Navy Cut, Olivier, Black Cat, Passing Clouds, Number 6, Sovereign, Gitanes, Gauloises (does anyone remember when Paris smelt alternately of Gauloises, pissoirs and Chanel?), Winston, Camel, Sobranie, my father's pipe in the cinema – clouds of sweet latakia smoke in the flickering projection. A Greek cigarette in a red box with a lasciviously smiling girl that called itself Santé, without irony: an untipped fag called Health.

This year, for the first time, I couldn't make it to the top of the hill. I knelt in the heather, weak and gasping. It was the first time all was not well. There was also a pain in my neck that my doctor said was probably a cervical spine thingy and I should get a scan.

He sent me to Harley Street, where another doctor said: 'You haven't got insurance, it's going to be expensive. Why don't you get it done down the road and send me the pictures. A third of the cost.' I said: 'I'm here now, just do it.' And he shrugged. A couple of hours later I went back for the results. He had the bland bad-news face.

'That was the best money you ever spent.' He turned the screen around and there was a beautiful spiral of colour clinging like an abstract expressionist collar to my spine. 'This is cancer.'

That afternoon I was back in my doctor's surgery. He was wearing the antiseptic face, the professional-doctor tragedy mask. I'm getting to see this a lot now. It is as much a protection against the infection of catastrophe for them as a respect for its victim. They glaze the bad news with sweet spittle. They'll say: 'The test results were not quite what we hoped. It might be trapped wind or it might be the thing that hatched from John Hurt's stomach. Realistically, we'll have to assume it's more alien than fart.' My alien was the most common cancer in old men, our biggest single killer: an aggressive, nimble cat-burglar lung cancer that is rarely noticed till it has had kittens.

Guy has been my doctor for thirty years – thirty-two to be precise. He was the doctor who put me into treatment for addiction and he's looked after me and my kids ever since. He's private, so I pay. If I need a test, an X-ray, a consultant, I'll pay. If I need anything more than a couple of antibiotics, I'm going to the NHS.

Within twenty-four hours I have an NHS consultant oncologist and early-morning appointments, for scans, blood tests and X-rays.

You couldn't make up Charing Cross Hospital. Well, not as a hospital you couldn't. It's a monstrous, hideous, crumbling patched-up mess – the Elephant Building. On the way in I notice a couple of posters on the street saying 'Save Charing Cross Hospital'. They're stuck on a municipal noticeboard that's falling over.

It's plainly the result of dozens and dozens of attempts to make things better, and, in fact, it is the physical embodiment of how most of us, trying to make our way through the teetering automatic doors, feel. It has a very good collection of contemporary British art. In some back corridor there is a series of Peter Blake's best silk screens.

I love it: it's how I feel. The lifts take hours to arrive,

emphysemically, wheezingly opening their doors, and when they do, it's without confidence or conviction. A man going up to the cancer ward puts his hand in front of the door and gets out. 'I'm too frightened to take this lift,' he says.

In a waiting room, hundreds of us take numbers to sit like wilted potted plants in an autumn garden-centre sale, to take it in turns to meet the antiseptic face. If this were a set for a film, all the actors and extras would be pulling looks of agony and sadness and fear, but the face of real cancer wipes our expressions to a pale neutral human.

The NHS has one of the worst outcomes for cancer treatment in Europe. It's something to be borne in mind when you're deciding to combine chemotherapy with a safari, or want to embark on a bar-thumping argument about health tourism. It was the first question I asked my oncologist, Dr Conrad Lewanski. 'Why is this such a bad place to get cancer, when we have lots of hospitals, when we teach doctors from all over the world, when we've won more Nobel prizes than the French?'

'It's the nature of the health service,' he says. 'The key to cancer outcomes is the speed of diagnosis and treatment.' The health service was set up with GPs separate from hospitals. The system means you probably have to wait a week or so for an appointment to see first your GP, or a clinic. The average time for that consultation will be seven minutes. Perhaps your cough isn't a priority. And then if your doctor thinks it does need a second opinion, he'll suggest you see a consultant, and that's likely to take a month. If the GP suspects cancer, that referral time is reduced to two weeks. He or she will probably write a letter, often two – all doctors still carry fountain pens.

And then there are all the appointments – for tests, a cancellation, a missed X-ray, a scan – which can put months on a diagnosis. It's not the treatment, it's the scale of the bureaucracy and the Attlee-reverential, immovable-but-crumbling structure of a private-public doctor-consultant arrangement, which was the cornerstone laid down by the 1945 government at the insistence of doctors. That is the chronic tumour in the bowel of the system.

I'm given a talk by a nurse on the consequences of chemotherapy. She uses three pens. Two of them have three coloured barrels each. The scribbling, the underlining, the stars, the acronyms, the exclamation marks become ever more emphatic and decorative. Finally she hands me a notebook that is unintelligibly runic, but says not to worry because it's all on the computer, which she then turns on to show me a heart-warming film about sexual infections and high temperatures.

The hospital flutters with bits of paper like mayflies. They're propped up against screens, wedged up against keyboards, stuffed into teetering files, and then there is the constant Tourette's questions, 'When's your birthday? What's the first line of your address?', all to collide you with the right cancer, to go with all the forms, the signatures, the screens, the machines, the radiation disclaimers and destiny. It makes Kafka look like ee cummings.

I like my oncologist. He doesn't have the morphine face; he looks amused, inquisitive, like a shaved, garrulous otter. All he does is lung cancer. This is his river, tumours his trout. He's been a consultant for fifteen years. Two years in, his father got it and died: 'The worst thing I've ever had to go through. I do know what this is like – so how much do you want to know?'

'Everything, and the truth.'

I've never Googled cancer, but I've discovered that every one of my friends who owns their own house has a preferred cancer specialist and a hospital to go with them. They also have a perfect gardener, an ideal interior decorator and a masseur that they insist – *insist* – I use, because they are all the best and, of course, you only get what you pay for. Lots of them are astonished I'm still in this country of catastrophic cancer statistics.

Those who don't have money for their own homes have magical diets, homeopathy and religious new-age cures, or at least a conspiracy theory about big pharma hiding the efficacy of vitamin C, kale, magnetism and mistletoe. If it doesn't make you better, at least you get snogged a lot.

And everyone, but everyone, will have a mantra story of their secretary's husband or a woman they used to work with who was given three weeks to live and is still stacking shelves or conducting operas ten years later. These little homilies are handed out with the intense insistence of lucky heather, using the language of evangelical religion and locker-room encouragement.

Why is our reaction to cancer so medieval, so wrapped in fortune-cookie runes and votive memory shards, like the teeth and metatarsals of dead saints? Cancer is frightening. One in two of us will get it. It has dark memories, unmentionably euphemised. In the public eye, not all cancers are equal. There is little sympathy for lung cancer. It's mostly men, mostly old men, mostly working-class old men and mostly smokers. There is a lot more money and public sympathy for the cancers that affect women and the young. Why wouldn't there be?

'How do men react when you tell them their cancers are fatal?' I ask Dr Lewanski. 'Always the same way – with stoicism.'

'Bollocks,' I think. 'I thought that was just me.'

Actually it's not being told you've got cancer that is the test of character, it's the retelling. Going home and saying to the missus: 'That thing, the cricked neck. Actually it's a tumour, the size of a cigar.' It ought to come with a roll of thunder and five Jewish violinists, instead of the creaky whisper of fear.

People react differently to different cancers: most women think they'll survive, and statistically they're right. Most men think they'll die – and likewise.

'So, what's the treatment?'

'Chemotherapy. Platinum in your case. It has a very good chance.'

Someone should write a paper on the euphemistic size compar-isons for tumours. There should be an e-site, Euphotumours. The images are very masculine: golf balls, cricket balls, bullets, grenades, ruminant testicles. No one ever says, 'I've got a cancer the size of a fairy cake.'

And what about after the chemo?

'Well, there's a new treatment, immunotherapy. It's the biggest breakthrough in cancer treatment for decades. Cancers camou-flage themselves as chemical markers that tell your body's natural defences that there's nothing to see here, move along. These new drugs strip away the disguise and allow your body's natural system to clean up. It's new and it's still being trialled, but we're a long way along the line and it is the way cancer treatment is bound to go. It's better for some growths than others, but it's particularly success-ful with yours. If you were in Germany or Scandinavia or Japan or America, or with the right insurance here, this is what you would be treated with.'

The doctor looks at Nicola, the missus. His otter face has grown a little sphinxy.

'You remember asking if the treatment Adrian got on the NHS would be any different from being a private patient? And I said a better cup of coffee and more leeway with appointments. Well, this is the difference. If he had insurance, I'd put him on immuno-therapy – specifically, nivolumab. As would every oncologist in the First World. But I can't do it on the National Health.'

The National Institute for Health and Care Excellence (NICE), the quango that acts as the quartermaster for the health service, won't pay. Nivolumab is too expensive – £60,000 to £100,000 a year for a lung-cancer patient; about four times the cost of chemo. And the only way to see if it will work for an individual patient is to give it to them all, and the ones it doesn't work for will weed themselves out. What NICE doesn't say about the odds is that immunotherapy mostly works for old men who are partially responsible for their cancers because they smoked. Thousands of patients could benefit. But old men who think they're going to die anyway aren't very effective activists. They don't get the public or press pressure that young mothers' cancers and kids' diseases get.

As yet, immunotherapy isn't a cure, it's a stretch more life, a considerable bit of life. More life with your kids, more life with your friends, more life holding hands, more life shared, more life spent on earth – but only if you can pay.

I'm early for my first eight-hour stint of platinum chemo. The ward in Charing Cross looks like a cross between a milking shed and an Air Koryo business lounge. I am settled into a hideous but comfortable chair and a tap is jabbed into the back of my hand. A series of plastic bags full of combative and palliative cocktails slowly dribble into my body and every ten minutes I have to shuffle to an invalid's loo to dribble it out again.

I like it here. The nurses are funny and comforting, optimistic, and bear the weight of the sadness, the regret and the pity in the room on their shoulders with an amused elegance and sincerity that comes from their years of experience, or the naivety of inexperience. The other patients shuffle in with their partners to share sandwiches, talk about shopping and the cousins in New Zealand and window boxes. There are children with ageing parents, happy/sad to be able to repay an infant's debt.

I manage to find the one dealer in the ward, or rather she finds me. Her boyfriend's making hash cakes – they've definitely shrunk his tumour, I should definitely have some. I smile, shrug apologetically and say sadly I'm already a junkie. I don't take drugs.

'Really? Even for this?' I'm not giving up thirty-two years of clean time for some poxy lung.

And there are the ones who sit alone, who don't have any friends to play cards with them, to drip the will and the strength and the faith to face this. I don't know how anyone manages to do this on their own.

An old friend sits through the mornings with me, Nicola comes with lunch and Flora and Ali, my grown-up kids, share the afternoon. If it wasn't for the cancer, that would be a really lovely day. If it wasn't for the cancer.

There's a natural break in the article here. It should have been finished two weeks ago, but I had a bad night, a really bad night.

Nicola called Guy, the GP, and he came round and took a look and said: 'He needs to be in A&E now.'

So I'm on a gurney in Charing Cross at nine in the morning. On the other side of the blue plastic curtain, a bloke is being held down by three policemen shouting, 'Don't flick your fucking blood over here, I don't want what you've got.'

A young doctor comes and asks me questions. All doctors in A&E are preternaturally young. One of the questions after 'What's your date of birth and the first line of your address?' is inevitably 'Can I put my finger up your bottom to see if there's any poo or blood?'

The other question is: 'On a scale of 1 to 10 – 1 being a scratch and 10 unspeakable agony – what do you think you're suffering at the moment?' You wouldn't describe this as thin pain. It's 10 out of 10. My stomach is agonised with a terrible wrenching distension. I've lived a middle-class, sheltered, uncombative, anti-violent life, so I don't know how this compares to other more manly men's pain, but this is by miles and miles the worst thing I've ever been through, thank you for asking.

More X-rays and blood tests and the surgeon returns with the complete granite face and says: 'Well, it could be a burst ulcer, but of course it isn't. The tumour in your pancreas has increased in size very fast. It's as big as a fist.' And he shows me a fist in case I'd misplaced the image.

I've decided to call the pancreatic tumour Lucky, as a nod to prophetic Professor Gazzard. So the chemotherapy isn't working. I ask my oncologist what's next.

'It's a bugger,' he says. 'It looked so hopeful, but you're right, it isn't working. The pancreas is a bad place. We can't operate and the side effects of radiation aren't worth the risk.' And there's pancreatic pain, which is famously in a league apart, so at least I can be stoical about that.

'What next?'

'Well, on the NHS we can give you another round of chemo, a bit rougher with slighter outcomes . . . but there is really only one treatment for you: nivolumab.'

From behind the blue curtain, the nurse asks the policeman: 'What do you want to do with him?'

'Oh, let him go,' says the copper.

'I thought you'd arrested him?'

'No. Let him go.'

That evening I'm sitting in bed on the cancer ward trying to get the painkillers stabilised and a young nurse comes in.

'There you are. I've been waiting for you all day. You're supposed to be with me down in chemotherapy. I saw your name. Why are you up here?'

'Well, it turns out the chemo isn't working.' Her shoulders sag and her hand goes to her head. 'Fuck, fuck, that's dreadful.' I think she might be crying.

I look away, so might I.

You don't get that with private healthcare.

December 2016